THE WAR COMPLEX

The War Complex

WORLD WAR II IN OUR TIME

Marianna Torgovnick

The University of Chicago Press   CHICAGO & LONDON

Marianna Torgovnick is professor of English at Duke University and director of Duke's New York Program in Arts and Media. She is author of numerous works, including *Gone Primitive: Savage Intellects, Modern Lives, Primitive Passions: Men, Women, and the Quest for Ecstasy* and the award-winning *Crossing Ocean Parkway,* also published by the University of Chicago Press.

The University of Chicago Press, Chicago 60637
The University of Chicago Press, Ltd., London
© 2005 by Marianna Torgovnick
All rights reserved. Published 2005
Printed in the United States of America

14 13 12 11 10 09 08 07 06 05   1 2 3 4 5

ISBN: 0-226-80855-6 (cloth)

Library of Congress Cataloging-in-Publication Data

Torgovnick, Marianna, 1949–
    The war complex : World War II in our time / Marianna Torgovnick.
        p.   cm.
    Includes bibliographical references and index.
    ISBN 0-226-80855-6 (alk. paper)
        1. World War, 1939–1945—Social aspects. 2. World War, 1939–1945—
    Psychological aspects. 3. Memory—Social aspects. 4. World War, 1939–
    1945—Literature and the war. I. Title.

    D744.6.T67 2005
    940.53′1—dc22   2004024385

♾ The paper used in this publication meets the minimum requirements of the American National Standard for Information Sciences—Permanence of Paper for Printed Library Materials, ANSI Z39.48-1992.

With love and remembrance,
this book is dedicated to two very different
beings who died during Summer, 2004:

Marcel, scholarly, graceful, and very French,
whose life was changed by World War II

Spiral, beautiful, gentle, and wise, who
enriched and changed my life

CONTENTS

AFTER 9/11

I

"After 9/11": the very words have become a cliché that can set the teeth on edge, identifying powerful memories, potent emotions, and a political code. I thought at first that 9/11 would mark an end to the most active life of World War II in our imaginations, that it would move the events of 1939–45 more decisively into the past and that the twenty-first century had *really* begun on September 11, 2001. But the consequences of how we remember World War II, the subject of this book, are in some ways stronger than ever.

The war on terrorism, the Patriot Act, Homeland Security, the doctrine of preemptive strikes, the invasion of Afghanistan and then of Iraq: the Bush administration positioned policies and events within the need for retaliation after 9/11 and the image of Pearl Harbor, with a dollop of apprehension for our safety tossed in, the object of attack being, for some commentators, less important than the revenging act itself.[1] The 2003 State of the Union speech played cannily on evolving memory, listing all the things that *might* happen to us or to our families—suicide bombings, biological or chemical attacks, nuclear explosions in a carefully calibrated politics of fear.[2] Over the following year, we learned with certainty that the speech presented evidence that was erroneous and misleading but nonetheless shaped events. At press conferences and speeches covered by the networks, the president positioned himself as a seer and a father, making hard choices, a leader and a "top-gun" commander in chief.[3]

By spring 2003, despite worldwide protests, the United States had invaded Iraq. The president's words to justify the war were, as the *New York Times* put it on the day the invasion began, "drawn straight from the days of World War II," with "'Munich' invoked at every turn," and D-Day often just around the corner.[4] The administration's expectations were clearly based on Italy or Paris in 1944: girls kissing soldiers, GIs distributing candy to the adoring young, "liberation" rather than "occupation" being the operative word.

As the sixtieth anniversary of D-Day approached, President Bush made a series of speeches reaffirming the doctrine of preemptive strikes, calling his version of the war on terrorism this generation's challenge and comparing it to World War II as "the storm in which we fly."[5] Along with the opening of the World War II Memorial in Washington, D.C., and sixtieth anniversary celebrations of D-Day, the speeches formed a powerful conjunction that showed how the memory of World War II can be used not just to honor veterans and to affirm the desire for peace—unobjectionable goals—but also to support current and future wars. World War II or, more precisely, different versions of World War II, can make things happen.

Yet neither the policies involved in 2003–4 nor the allusions they contained came "straight" from World War II at all. Instead, they had followed several twists and turns, most recently through 9/11, taking shortcuts, cutting some corners, and, in some cases, executing hairpin curves, with Korea, Somalia, and especially Vietnam at the edges of public perceptions. Without a doubt, the strongest supporters of the Iraq war believed the World War II analogy; those who opposed the Iraq war by and large did not.[6] The fact remains that not even June 6, 1944, let alone March 19, 2003, was the D-Day of our imaginations.

It's hard to predict where things will stand when this book appears. As much as anyone, I hope that no further attacks occur in the United States. But, under policies of retaliation and preemption, with continued instability in Afghanistan and Iraq, and with hostility to the United States now common, I also feel less safe than ever.[7] Trust in military action may be (as newspapers claimed was the case for much of 2003) quite strong. But the visible strains on our armed forces and revulsion against continuing deaths may well prove stronger. The preference for diplomacy and negotiation reflected in the large protests that preceded the war with Iraq— important events, though unsuccessful in the short run—may have reconfigured and affected the outcome of events.

Whatever situation prevails, the war on terrorism—a phrase that echoes failed endeavors like the war on poverty and the war on drugs—promises an indefinite prolongation of wartime states of mind. That prolongation suggests one strong reason you should read this book. *The War Complex* probes the costs of sustained wartime consciousness on a society and a culture, which are more than military.

Writing in 1915, as what would come to be called World War I settled in, Sigmund Freud observed that "a multitude of simultaneous deaths appears to us exceedingly terrible,"[8] producing disillusion and disordered, inconsistent attitudes toward death. Part coarsening and celebration with regard to enemy deaths; part mourning and apprehension of losses that come close to home: the altered consciousness produced by total war can persist, as Freud guessed, beyond the formal end of combat. Wartime consciousness heightens complex attitudes toward natural death, which, in its generational unfolding, remains a difficult and somber fact, one generally left veiled in daily life.

Soldiers and civilians have always died in war, sometimes (as in the Thirty Years' War and the Taipei Rebellion) for protracted periods and in huge numbers. But world war multiplies effects, making civilian death commonplace, and even expected, in strategies used by modern, "civilized" nations. What's worse, world war uses the structures of modernity (law, nation-states, technology), the recognizable and necessary structures of our lives, to enforce the brutality of combat.[9] The disabling disillusion or feeling of disjointedness Freud foresaw became a standard theme in the literature of World War I from Eliot thorough Fitzgerald, Hemingway, and Lawrence; it also registered, as Paul Fussell has documented, in multiple ways in modern life: for example in the use of irony and black humor around the subject of war.[10]

Wartime consciousness, I will claim in this book, permeated the twentieth century and persisted into the twenty-first, ready to condition reactions to 9/11. For just as the changed consciousness Freud described did not end in 1918, it did not end in 1945, but was, in some ways, just beginning. In 1945, the world saw death in new and shocking forms: speeded up, multiplied, and dealt by human beings with deliberate and stunning technological speed, often under government auspices and sometimes burning or vaporizing bodies on religious, ethnic, or racial grounds.[11] The combination forms one of the most troubling legacies of the twentieth century. It generates what I call "the war complex": an unresolved and perhaps unresolvable attitude toward mass death caused by human beings wielding technology in shorter and shorter periods of time, death that proceeds under state or political control and sometimes does not just kill human beings, but vanishes bodies. World War I sketched a template; World War II wrote such patterns large; 9/11 echoed in the American imagination because it brought those patterns home.

After an introduction that will say more about "the war complex"— how it begins, how it influences events, how it might end—chapters 1 and 2 turn to important but discrete events of the war and postwar period: D-Day and the Eichmann trial. They are paired chapters because both highlight aspects within each history that have been almost programmatically avoided in popular and scholarly representations. They measure the image of these events against print and video archives in order to challenge existing clichés.

Written in a rather different genre that includes memoir, chapter 3 describes my own and others' attitudes toward Germany and memories of learning about the Holocaust. The chapter tests the common understanding that the Holocaust belongs to Jews as primary victims and to Germans as perpetrators by proposing that the Holocaust may form a kind of citizenship for everyone after 1945, an idea that includes disparate emotions and possibilities: evasion or denial, possessiveness, responsibility, the imperative for action; and, in the absence of moral action (because we were not there, because at the time no action seemed possible), guilt, shame, secrets, hesitations, and blockages.

Chapters 4 and 5, like chapters 1 and 2, are paired chapters. They examine how imaginative literature treats categories of facts that have largely been elided from contemporary memory of war history in the United States and parts of Europe. Chapter 4 uncovers Asian and postcolonial contexts alluded to in literary representations but muted in both scholarly writing and in filmed versions of novels. It brings into focus references to Hiroshima and Nagasaki as well as to a host of other events— Kashmir, Suez, and others—conditioned by World War II but scarcely perceived or registered in American cultural memory. Chapter 5 presents the work of W. G. Sebald as a poet laureate of the sort of missing history about World War II that I interrogate in the book.

All the chapters touch upon and gradually elaborate a process toward what I call an ethics of identification, by which I mean a willingness to sympathize with others, as appropriate. The conclusion refines that idea. It also offers a new way of thinking about representations of sexuality and violence from the early twentieth century through today, grappling with the gap between our culture's fascination with spectacles of death and its avoidance of death as a subject close to home. It then considers possibilities of escape.

Begun as a historical study of the cultural memory of World War II, my book necessarily veered into more contemporary events after 9/11 because the media and the public's responses followed patterns I recognized from my work on the memory of World War II. I had known intellectually for some time that history evolves through technologies of representation but remains to some extent contingent: a tissue of private recollections, public archives, and narrative processes—what individuals, writers, artists, and historians preserve and choose to tell, not necessarily through conspiracy but through a series of choices that form certain patterns and efface others. World War II—let alone more distant events like the Crusades or the bubonic plague—comes to us as a set of established histories with some facts lost or distorted and others hiding in plain sight: available but oddly not part of public consciousness. But we always knew, at some level, what 9/11 showed us on our pulses: that responses then must have been more diverse and more multiple than history has been able to tell.

II

"I was sitting on my terrace in downtown Manhattan on the morning of September 11": I am, perhaps surprisingly in a book about the memory of World War II, about to begin a personal narrative about the events of fall 2001. Such a narrative may seem out of date by the time this book appears, but, if that seems the case, I hope my reader will read on a bit more before deciding, for it uncovers important patterns in how we live and how we experience the news now. Or it may seem self-aggrandizing to use myself as an eyewitness, though I do not aim at self-aggrandizement at all and, in fact, mean to suggest that geographical proximity confers only limited forms of authority. Using a turning point in our lifetimes, I want to demonstrate how memory is constructed even as we are living through events, constructed by the media and by our own selectivity and how the constructions can have real and powerful consequences. So then . . .

I was sitting on my terrace in downtown Manhattan on the morning of September 11, and trying to work. Disturbing sounds entered my consciousness—sounds I could not recognize except as murmurs from a crowd that was clearly gathering on La Guardia Place, one block north of

Houston, *in the street* and not, as would normally be the case, on the sidewalk. Construction workers at a building down the block stopped work and gathered at the edge of the building's shell; periodic shouts erupted that sounded half like cursing, half like prayer. Sirens started up. Lots of sirens.

I thought: whatever it was (a car accident? a fight?) was being taken care of. There were dozens and even hundreds of people in the street and police and ambulances were, clearly, on the way. No one needed me to spread the news or to help. I wanted to work—on this book in fact—which then had the title *World War II and the Modern Imagination*. Disturbed, but still wanting to write, I went inside and received almost immediately a phone call from my younger daughter in Durham, North Carolina, asking in a breathless way: "MOM, are you *all right?*" When I said that I was but that something strange seemed to be happening outside, she said what millions of people said that day: "Turn on the television." When I asked which channel, she dismissed my question, saying, "any channel"—and, indeed, any channel would do. For there, on the screen—less than two miles to the south of my northward-facing terrace—were the facts: two planes, for reasons as yet unexplained at that early hour, had flown into the World Trade Center and the Towers were burning.

Like people everywhere, my daughter and I felt in the presence of history but thought first of family and friends: my younger daughter had called me; I asked her to call my husband (who was at class) and I called my older daughter, who lived in uptown Manhattan and was, I knew, likely still to be asleep. In our own small, instinctive, and, on this occasion, lucky ways, we enacted a concern for a few beloved individuals that forms an archetype within our oldest narratives of war and civil disaster—*The Iliad*, *The Odyssey*, and *The Aeneid*—where characters show concern for loved ones (Achilles for Patroclus, Aeneas for Creusa and Anchises) that history can overwhelm and even trash at will. The pattern repeats in many Holocaust narratives and showed up almost immediately for 9/11 in the missing persons posters that plastered my neighborhood and in the well-known *New York Times* series "Portraits of Grief."[12]

Such positioning of family histories against world-scale history forms a persistent motif in our imagination of disaster, one to which I will want to return several times later in this book. It forms a point of entry into the war complex but, as I hope to show, can also be a point of exit. In New York and all across America, people turned instinctively to family and friends or, in their absence, to random strangers in an overflow of emotions.

But, as one sign that we live in a thoroughly media age, television served as the communal hearth around which we gathered. It became both a companion and a participant, shaping the events of 9/11 even as we lived them. Throughout the day, as at the beginning, I turned on the television, much as people during World War II turned on the radio. I checked in, the world checked in, with CNN.

Wondering, "how could this have happened?" and "had it really happened?" I got dressed immediately. I put on jeans and sneakers in case I would be needed to help with rescue. With the kind of consummate illogic and disbelief that marked the day, I also took a bag of laundry I had packed the night before, just in case the crashes were some fantastic hoax and had not happened after all. As I joined the crowd in the street, I had a direct view down West Broadway of the burning Towers and suddenly understood the murmurs I had heard, because I was uttering them too. Some people were saying "Oh, shit"; some people were saying "Oh, my God." As the flames glowed and the smoke billowed, as people fleeing from the offices began arriving among us, as one Tower collapsed, or immediately before and after, I joined the murmurs involuntarily.

The confusion in that last sentence—as one Tower collapsed, or immediately before and after—reflects some of what I learned about history and cultural memory on 9/11. I was close to the site of the emergency: Houston Street, one block down from my building, was totally sealed off and would be for weeks. My own neighborhood, Greenwich Village, was similarly sealed after the attack—no subways, no buses, no taxis, no entry without passing armed soldiers. I was not in or directly around the World Trade Center, not in the mazelike streets of the financial district, where the smoke and the confusion must have been terrible. I did not have children at school nearby nor a relative in the Towers. I did not know anyone on the NYPD or in the fire department. I was an eyewitness. But I had limited access to facts and relied, like people everywhere, on other people and the media for certain kinds of knowledge (which Tower was hit first; the exact time it collapsed and so forth). In no clear or immediate danger, I even had time to consider various analogies: Germans watching the Reichstag burn was the one that came to mind, though it quickly became taboo once an analogy with Pearl Harbor had surfaced.

My position, then, was in what I will call the middle distance—a feeling of spatial, temporal, or emotional connection, in this case all three, but with my only stakes the stakes available to many others.[13] And yet I went, I must have gone, into a mild form of shock—not "trauma," an overused word that would exaggerate what I felt and its effects—but the jolt of being in the middle distance, which I believe exists alongside trauma and not, as is generally assumed, just within it.[14] Like most New Yorkers, I continued to function calmly, even stoically and at a reasonably high level throughout the day and over the next, though I was very much aware that things were not "normal" and that the conditions we call "normal" might change. Even though I cannot remember, even now, precisely what I saw in person and what I saw on TV.[15]

I do know certain things. I know that, when I got downstairs, the police were already stationed around my building and that, when I asked if I should head downtown to help, they told me that the area was sealed and that I should stay nearby or go back inside. (A policeman was the first to say the words "terrorists" and "attacks"; until then I had been trying to understand how two planes could have flown into the WTC on a clear day.) I know that, as the rumors on the street became more and more fantastic (an assault on D.C., the Pentagon in flames, other hijacked planes en route to California), I went upstairs several times to check on television and the Internet—and that almost all the rumors, on that surreal day, turned out to be true. I know that, on one of my trips downstairs, I brought my laundry—which for some reason I was still holding—to the shop at the corner, wordlessly making the exchange with the owner and later that day losing the receipt in the way that New Yorkers just plain lost things for days and weeks to come. I know that I gave my cell phone to an agitated, thin young man with red hair and freckles who had dashed into the laundry offering the owner extra money to use his phone. I know that he gave it back without getting through, murmuring that New York prayer, "Oh shit. Oh, shit," as he dashed back into the street. I know I spoke to people flowing from downtown who were crying and telling stories of escape. I know I heard upstairs, in my apartment, that once one Tower had collapsed, the other, structurally paired, was also doomed. I know that I stopped looking on the street at that point, because I could not bear to see it happen.

Months later, I developed some film that I had taken on 9/11 but had inexplicably delayed processing. As I write these words (it is November 2001, when I first wrote them), I have before me a photograph I took of what appears to be a cloud of extremely dense dust and smoke and half of one Tower, burning.[16] I do not know exactly why I grabbed my camera that day, nor do I know precisely when I took the picture. I do know that I did not feel exultant or excited at getting the shot. I also know that my feelings had no touch of the voyeuristic or macabre—emotions almost completely absent in New York on 9/11—no desire, even, to show that I was there. As best I can recall, I felt numb except for knowing that I needed to take a picture—to freeze the moment? to establish a connection? A photograph was somehow required, somehow a necessary gesture if one had a camera on hand that day. That's one reason it became so easy to mount a show of photographs so soon after the event, a show that opened two blocks away from where I lived but that I was not, for many weeks, able to bring myself to see.[17]

Barbie Zelizer has identified a photographic template used in 1945, when Allied troops entered Nazi death camps, which recurred for 9/11. The template includes not just the display of horrifying events or evidence of horrifying events but of people "bearing witness."[18] In 1945, alongside stacks of bodies, open oven doors, and portraits of survivors, newspapers and magazines often showed soldiers and officers, government officials, and German townspeople living near the camps witnessing the dead or evidence of the dead. Then they added a layer of "bearing witness" by showing photographs of people looking at the original newspapers and magazines that contained the photographs and (later) viewing public displays of those photographs at memorials like Yad Vashem in Jerusalem or the Holocaust Memorial Museum in Washington, D.C.

Point-by-point comparisons exist for 9/11. Television and newspapers accompanied photographs of the burning towers, bodies falling from buildings, and rubble in the streets with photographs of bystanders looking up at the buildings and reacting strongly. Photographs of people looking at television or at newspapers containing the first two sets of images added an additional layer of "bearing witness." Later, pictures of people at exhibits like "Here Is New York" formed the final layer. Zelizer's template helps explain why I, like so many in New York, instinctively reached for cameras on 9/11. It also helps explain something we will see again and again in *The War Complex:* the extraordinary power of photographic or televised images to fix cultural memory, sometimes deceptively, and to extend it beyond the original witness. But it also helps to explain something Zelizer omits from her analysis that seems quite important: the formation of *trauma-like* (rather than traumatic) reactions to 9/11, which not only encouraged "bearing witness" but also tended to stun public discourse and to allow the Bush administration to do pretty much what it wanted.[19]

Over the next six fragile and volatile weeks, the city danced rapidly to an extraordinary rhythm of expression and repression. One week was a "carpe diem" week, with playgoers drinking and swaggering in the streets. Another was a week of grim jokes or anecdotes about travel. I had read and taught Daniel Defoe's *A Journal of the Plague Year;* now I got to see a real-time enactment. I'd go to see *Norma* at the Met or *The Guys* at a little theater downtown and find myself plunged in thought and part of group reactions. At *Norma,* an opera about war, occupation, love, clashing religions, revenge, and forgiveness, I found myself incredibly moved, even transported, by the heroine's avowal of forgiveness; then, as I left the opera, the smell of Ground Zero hit my nostrils and the talkative crowd fell silent. At *The Guys,* a play about a fire chief and a writer helping him draft eulogies, I was surrounded by random sobs that erupted at different times from different viewers and surprised us all. "A wounded city": the play's first words hit me in the chest. No one outside the city, those inside agreed, could really understand how the city felt. But we did, like some vast collective animal with many limbs. For months, no conversation could begin without a personal account of the disaster and a confused canvassing of politics and opinions. But the city had decided, collectively, to soldier onward. And soldier on it did until, around Thanksgiving, things felt almost normal.

New Yorkers believe that their experience of fall 2001 was more intense than others—and I believe that too. The smell of death and fear in the air; seeing soldiers on the street with machine guns; the sound of refrigerated cars rumbling through the street; the taste of repression and denial; the weird and complicated feeling of release when rumors swirled of new threats, this time 3,000 miles away, in California. Yet I also recognize and accept how intense feelings were elsewhere. My husband, in North Carolina on the 11th and unable to join me in New York the next weekend as planned, briefly felt uncharacteristic support for the president, though he had opposed George W. Bush vehemently in 2000 and would again quite soon. I recognized his emotion as, at least in part, displaced concern for me and for our older daughter, who was also in New York that fall. A friend who teaches in the South but who has lived in Manhattan felt torn by being away when something so terrible was happening to "her city." Such feelings could be multiplied into the millions.

New Yorkers knew they had to take care of one another—and did, at least for a while, when virtually everyone suspended the usual profanity and hurry on the streets. But right from the beginning, New Yorkers disagreed, quite widely and quite loudly, about the meaning of events. Taxi drivers told me, upfront and clearly, that the United States shared the blame because it had backed Osama bin Laden in the past, and armed him. They identified, long before the newspapers did, massive unemployment and a recession in the city. "It took ten years getting the city where it was" (a reference to the Giuliani miracle, although most cabbies retained a deep dislike of the mayor), one taxi driver said as we sailed up Sixth Avenue on a weekday night, without stopping once for traffic, "now it's come apart in just an hour." I heard fears of war and lots of backlash against Attorney General Ashcroft's actions. I saw peace signs pop up within a day alongside flags and the many impromptu shrines to the WTC dead, including large ones I passed daily in Washington Square Park and at Union Square. I also saw and heard, in many places and from many people, on the Left as well as the Right, full support for the war on terrorism and a sense that any demurrals were less than patriotic.[20]

Eventually, a certain rawness in the initial reactions passed into cant and sentimentality. "Go for it Snoopy. You always did fly high," scrawled one man on a poster of his brother that appeared within two days of the collapse. The poster confessed what was already suspected but, during the first week after 9/11, never said: that the rescue operations would produce few survivors. And the words—celebratory of a jump or death in high places—did not seem shocking then, though they do now, when a certain piety has settled in.

I thought at the time that only some of the sentiments I heard, observed, and felt—the unusual cooperation among New Yorkers, the magnificent behavior of the firemen and police, full support for the war in Afghanistan—would make their way into the public record for future historians who relied on the copious information available in newspapers or on TV. And that has, in fact, proved to be the case. Within Congress and the press, a surprising degree of consensus emerged for the administration's version of preventing terrorism, bypassing debate—a combination that may prove more damaging to democracy than the terrorist attack itself. But on the 11th, I wasn't thinking of the official record or of future political consequences. Like almost everyone in New York that day, I was fearful of the present.

I watched a cloud of dust move from downtown and stop just in front of and to the left of my building. I did not know what was in the dust, but knew that asbestos and human remains were more than likely. Within two days, once the wind had shifted, that cloud engulfed my building, fouling the air, as if hundreds of neighbors, on every side, were burning piles of leaves and tossing metal and plastic in by mistake. Like most people, I tried not to think about the smell, and what was in it. The first rain was terrible because it meant that rescue operations had to stop. Later rains were welcome because they meant that smell, that ghastly smell, would be gone for an afternoon, or a day—though it came back, it always came back until around Thanksgiving, filling the lungs with the tragedy, becoming the medium we breathed. For what we smelled was not just rubble and toxic chemicals and not just body parts (though that would have been terrible enough)—but was, rather, the smell of two great buildings and of thousands who had been incinerated and would leave, if anything, only ash and bone.

*   *   *

In the days after 9/11, we experienced an abundance of information on the attack and on how it unfolded, on Afghanistan, on the Taliban, on al-Qaeda, on the war on terrorism, and (soon) everything we wanted to know about anthrax and more. It was followed, in 2002–3, by a relentless drumbeat toward war on Iraq. It became axiomatic that everyone in the WTC that day was a "hero" and that America, united in grief, was somehow stronger and better than ever, even though it was clear that New York and its economy had taken grievous blows. We got a very simple sense of good and evil and of what being patriotic means in the United States. Although the Bush administration's rhetoric wore thin at times and cartoonists savagely satirized vague but cosmic warnings, certain media, like CNN, never seemed to tire of the anthrax scare and of undocumented possibilities like nuclear attack in a suitcase.[21] After 9/11 (those words again), the space for discussion and dissent shrunk, not just in the press and other media but also in the halls of government—a notable contraction of the public sphere.[22]

When I began to write *The War Complex*, some eight years ago, I set out to investigate what our culture remembers or forgets about World War II—where, when, how, why, and to what effect. By "culture," I meant and mean public discourse—newspapers, magazines, books, films, television shows, oral histories: the "context in which explicit statements are made . . . the things that for good or bad draw the people of a particular culture together"—a moving target that includes individual emotions and differing opinions as well as official policies.[23] My plans were large and ambitious, including, as they did, all aspects of the war, and especially the Holocaust, as they exist in cultural memory. But my plans turned out not to be large or ambitious enough.

I always thought that my book was relevant to our times—what writer does not? But after 9/11, events began to resonate in ways I could not have anticipated when I began, giving my attempt to understand how cultural memory works an extra tweak. *The War Complex* can be read in parts—prologue, introduction, and conclusion, the most topical sections of the book—along with selected, more historical, chapters. But it benefits, or so I strongly believe, by being read as a whole. With its extensive endnotes, the book contains two narratives that can be read side by side or sequentially. I've meant for the notes to interact with and enrich what precedes them; my hope is that readers will take the invitation that the notes extend.

A public sphere; public discourse; defamiliarization that pierces through cliché or, better, *clusters of clichés:* can they avoid for the current crisis the kind of repetition, nostalgia, and looking-away that have for so long surrounded World War II? In answering that question, I can only offer words that kept recurring for me during fall 2001: I do not know. These are Socrates' words, I told myself, which seemed right for writing in the middle, as events unroll, and better than the pundit's will to pronounce prematurely or the urge to bury issues yet undead.

HIDING IN
PLAIN SIGHT

In F. Scott Fitzgerald's *The Great Gatsby*, the narrator Nick Carraway tells us that he "participated in that delayed Teutonic migration known as the Great War" where he "enjoyed the counter-raid so thoroughly that [he] came back restless."[1] So restless that he left the Midwest, which had always seemed to him "the warm center of the world," and migrated to the more savage East, where he met Gatsby. It's a peculiar set-up, a peculiar precondition for this story, which critics usually read as a novel about the American dream rather than as a novel about the aftereffects of World War I. Yet if we take the comment seriously—as I think we should—the passage suggests that Nick became afflicted with a blood-lust of retaliation, an enjoyment, to be specific, of killing up-close using bayonets and knives, that made him feel disoriented and out of place in his native Midwest. It took a sojourn in New York and other encounters with death—although smaller in scale, more personal than the war—to restore a sense of normalcy that made him fit to "come back home."

I want to use this passage to introduce some principles of this book about the cultural memory of World War II, which, as the prologue has described, takes selective glances at the evolving memory of 9/11. Picking up on a speculation Freud makes in 1915, I want to claim that the altered state of consciousness produced by large-scale war, what Freud calls *wartime* and I call wartime consciousness, can last beyond the end of hostilities.[2] For World War II, it persisted after 1945 through the Cold War, and (with lapses during periods of Soviet-U.S. détente and especially after the fall of the Berlin Wall) remained ready to be reanimated on

9/11. Like Fitzgerald's Nick, individuals and the collectivities they form feel a restless, disjointed feeling, the feeling of never quite being at home or even worthy of being there, disillusionment or hopeless passivity, and a heightening of our already uneasy attitudes toward death.

Under such conditions, war memory intensifies patterns found in memory-work more generally. It highlights some facts but distorts others and allows still others to exist in limbo—known, but somehow never registered—what I mean by hiding in plain sight. Such adjustments and ellipses are not so much a lapse or a failure of cultural memory, as they are commonly conceived; they are not even, properly speaking, an erasure or a forgetting, two other common conceptions. Instead, they form an integral and crucial part of how individuals and groups construct temporality—the ineffable part of memory itself, necessary for memory's very shape. The adjustment I am proposing in existing models of cultural memory represents a rhetorical shift, to be sure, but, more importantly, it represents a conceptual one.[3]

To be specific for World War II: D-Day, "the greatest generation," citizen soldiers fighting against the forces of totalitarianism, the effectiveness of trials for war crimes and crimes against humanity, the Holocaust as an evil inflicted by Nazis upon Jews, genocide as something that should never happen again. These events and ideas form part of America's image of itself, frequently cited in public discourse and often memorialized.[4] They place Americans in virtuous, heroic roles—how we like to think of ourselves and to present ourselves to the world, even at those times when the United States has been a belligerent and not-much-loved nation. Yet as we shall see, beginning with chapter 1 on D-Day, our narratives about even these uncontroversial events and ideas contain omissions, things misremembered, and more than a few outright distortions.

Narratives of D-Day, for example, tend to fall into the genre I call guy talk: a blend of historicity, retrospective confidence in victory at odds with narrative suspense, casual insouciance, jokes that mask the shock of death but seem too good to be true—the wartime equivalent of big fish stories. Parts of Stephen Ambrose's work exemplify the genre, which begins much earlier, in news reports, posters, and films made during the war inscribing the basic narrative Ambrose and many others follow: a narrative of good versus evil, American multiculturalism (within limits, since racial segregation remained in place) versus the homogeneous racial Übermensch or "Jap," citizen soldiers fighting a necessary war against the forces of totalitarianism, us versus them.[5] The genre encourages hubris and includes a boisterous excitement about war, the sense that life was never quite as rich again in action or comradeship for those who fought, despite pious iterations, which also form part of the genre, that war is hell.

The best military histories—like John Keegan's or Gerhard Weinberg's—raise questions about military decisions and policies. Philosophical books about combat—like J. Glenn Gray's or Craig Hedges's—describe men's immersion in the destructive sublime as a seduction and, for some, an addiction.[6] Guy talk doesn't favor questions or ambiguities in the conduct of war. It favors celebration and the clarity of events like D-Day, the raising of the flag on Iwo Jima (staged, as we learned in 2000), or the liberation of the concentration camps. Such events are typically represented in visual forms like photographs or films that are widely reproduced in the media, factors that help them root in the national imagination. They make us feel good about ourselves and show a face we like to show.[7]

In his classic work on collective memory, Maurice Halbwachs wrote, "the various groups that compose society are capable at every moment of constructing their past . . . [but] they most frequently distort that past in the act of reconstructing it." They distort to "erase from . . . memory all that might separate individuals, or that might distance groups from each other," especially "the group of people with whom we have a relation." Over time, "society tends to erase from its memory all that might separate individuals, or that might distance groups from each other." That is why "society, in each period, rearranges its recollections in such a way as to adjust them to the variable conditions of its equilibrium."[8] If Halbwachs is right, as I believe he is at a basic level, collective memory begins in "relation"; that is, to put the matter concretely, it begins in the family, moves out into the group, neighborhood, town, or city, and then, sifted and refined still further through public discourse and media (newspapers, magazines, books, films and videos, popular clichés, rituals such as holidays, and memorials), becomes national or cultural. As part of a social bargain, individuals and groups agree to look away from unsettling histories, which then form the latent contents of cultural memory—not erased from memory (Halbwachs's concept) so much as a consequential, even active absence: the hole, to put it colloquially, that completes the donut, necessary for the donut's very shape.

What is almost always at the background for groups living in a state of war is an intense form of more general group dynamics: the willingness or felt necessity to suspend or surrender some of our critical faculties and feelings of dissent. The incipient work of memory thus links in multiple, complex ways not just to the creative, and often spontaneous, formation of communities—a factor to which I will want to return—but also to the formation of military or national policies. For the truth is that certain activities and choices (for genocide, for example) might not take place if governments and populations could not count in advance on protective future elisions within the work of memory. We frequently iterate the cliché that memory prevents history from repeating itself, sometimes as the very justification for doing history. But the holes in memory guarantee that the past will have a place to loop back into the present.

Once again, to be specific for World War II: internment camps for Japanese and Japanese Americans; incendiary bombings of cities in Germany and Japan; the atomic bombings at Hiroshima and Nagasaki; and, operating in a different register, the vital Soviet role in defeating the Nazis: while part of the public record, and hence provably "known," such events have never registered in America's image of World War II or in America's image of itself.

In the case of the Soviet losses, a subject to which I will return in chapter 1, fairly straightforward political factors controlled American "looking-away." Allies during the war, the Soviets very quickly became the United States' major postwar opponent, a development foreseen by many. If the claim to Europe after 1945 was staked in blood, as I believe it partly was, the 20 million Soviet dead—a number now expanding, as Soviet archives open, to at least 25 million and as many as 50 million— staked a claim the United States could not match and so could not, politically, acknowledge.[9] Relatively few Americans understand that the Soviets drew the Iron Curtain not just as a power play but also, even primarily, as a buffer against any future possible German aggression. Without ceding Poland, the former Czechoslovakia, Hungary, and the other Eastern European states to the Soviets forever, most Americans could, I believe, have accommodated the complexity of Soviet motivations.

In the case of the internments and bombings, self-image controls the tendency to look-away. For the record has always shown that Americans interned fellow Americans in a history that, since 1973, has become increasingly known. [10] And the record has always shown that British pilots and, to a lesser extent, Americans dropped the bombs that killed as many as 600,000 German civilians and that Americans flew the planes that killed, within hours, as many as 250,000 Japanese in Tokyo, Hiroshima, and Nagasaki.[11] Yet we have still not found a way to talk or even to think about the bombings except in terms of "strategy," "military necessity," and lives potentially "saved" rather than lives lost. Current U.S. policy, designed to prevent other nations from having nuclear weapons even as deterrence, assumes that "we" know how to use nuclear weapons wisely, while "they" do not. Can I say that, without sounding quite glum and dour? Can I further note that the United States remains the only nation to have used nuclear weapons on civilians?[12]

In 1969, Kurt Vonnegut wrote in *Slaughterhouse Five* that "there was almost nothing [in standard histories] about the Dresden raid, even though it had been such a howling success. The extent of the success had been kept a secret for many years after the war."[13] Forty years after Vonnegut wrote, the situation has not changed all that dramatically. W. G. Sebald's "Air War and Literature: Zurich Lectures" initiated sustained public discourse in Germany about the incendiary bombings but may or may not do the same in the United States.[14] In February 2004, Frederick Taylor published *Dresden*—part detailed and grim history, part apologia for the bombing.[15] Most books about the war, even quite good books, omit or move quickly over the topic because, in moral terms and even military ones, they remain quite messy.

Factories, transportation systems, and communication networks were the primary and specified targets. But breaking enemy morale was also seen as likely to contribute to victory. And, though it is less often said out loud, the bombings also served as retaliation. The incendiary and atomic bombings targeted cities, and therefore civilians, not as a genocidal strategy (like the Final Solution) but as a military one to end the war more quickly. The efficacy of the bombings has been challenged and was challenged at the time. Yet even very good histories dwell on the liberation of France and the opening of the concentration camps but move much more quickly over Hamburg and Dresden, Hiroshima and Nagasaki. Why? And to what effect?

The incendiary and atomic bombings targeted, of course, *aggressor* nations: I know that; you know that. And both Japan and Germany had caused, and indeed initiated, many millions of civilian deaths. I do not mean to scant those facts at all nor to set up glib comparisons between German and Japanese civilian deaths and those killed in nonaggressor nations and in the many gratuitous horrors of the Holocaust: the numbers do not match, nor do the contexts, nor do the intentions, nor (for the Holocaust) do the methods. When the Germans used incendiary bombs on London and Coventry, they sealed the fate of their own great cities.[16]

When the Japanese bombed Pearl Harbor and, later, prolonged the war with kamikaze missions, they confirmed the idea—widespread after the fierce battle for Okinawa and the chief justification for the A-bomb—that invasion of Japan would cause massive casualties.[17] By contrast, British and U.S. killing of civilians was understood as a regrettable, but unavoidable, consequence of war, part of war's undeniable ethics of retaliation, which tends, as everyone knows, to escalate out of control.[18]

President Truman's first announcement of Hiroshima and many materials afterward have stressed that the A-bomb eliminated the need for an invasion that would have cost many lives—250,000 in Truman's original statement, 500,000 in his memoirs, 1 million in later statements by U.S. presidents: the numbers have grown in cultural memory and were always hypothetical.[19] The first and major Nuremberg trial, the International Military Tribunal (IMT), carefully structured charges against the defendants to avoid the possibility that using atomic bombs against civilians could be construed as war crimes.[20] Such explanations and actions seem plausible, even now. One understands, though one need not applaud, the needs such decisions served in their historical contexts. Still, that was then and this is now—except that "now" isn't as different as one might think, especially, and surprisingly, on the subject of Hiroshima.

In 1995, for example, an exhibition at the Smithsonian was scheduled to include photographs of the first atomic victims, with brief quotations from their statements. The announcement of the exhibition prompted accusations that the Smithsonian would disrespect the military and be unpatriotic. Under intense pressure, the curators reduced the exhibit to the fuselage of the Enola Gay and a smiling photograph of the pilots, entirely normalizing what had been, after all, a world-historical mission, and omitting the Japanese as victims. In 2003, the Smithsonian permanently installed the Enola Gay in a similarly sanitized exhibition.[21] Then. Now.

After the explosion of the atomic bombs, dissent in the United States was limited and mostly confined to intellectuals, including African Americans and clergymen: it had been a long and difficult war and most Americans were simply happy, indeed overjoyed, to see it ended. John Hersey's *Hiroshima* (1946) was discussed at the time, but that slender, journalistic text, which wears its weaknesses on its sleeve, still remains a major book on the subject almost sixty years later (see chapter 4).[22] In what looks like a case of writers' self censorship or publishers' aversion, a surprisingly small number of major books of nonfiction in English tackle Hiroshima and Nagasaki head-on as historical realities, and they have appeared at widely spaced intervals, some in the 1990s.[23] Richard Rhodes's *The Making of the Atomic Bomb* (1986), Robert Jay Lifton's *Death in Life* (1967); and Lifton and Greg Mitchell's *Hiroshima in America* (1995) are three such books—to a lesser extent, so is Jonathan Schell's *The Fate of the Earth* (1982).[24] An important, though fairly abstract, collection of essays in the journal *Diacritics* (1984) never found book publication, and its energies among literary critics and theorists dissipated. An excellent edition that included many primary materials, *Hiroshima's Shadow,* was not published by a well-known press, a factor that limited its distribution and influence. If one compares the many books on the Holocaust and on aspects of the Holocaust since 1961 and adds, in addition, the many memoirs and testimonies that also exist, one can feel the paucity.

Aside from these major books, what one finds about Hiroshima in the archives is a miscellany—the only word I can use, really: policy reports on matters from bomb shelters to preparations for radiation sickness, to calls for international treaties and debates about nuclear deterrence, to how-to books such as *The Nuclear Survival Handbook: Living through and after a Nuclear Attack* and *The Nuclear Survival Kit.* Sometimes, Hiroshima resides in the imagination as a nameless mushroom cloud, signifying natural or man-made apocalypse, a persistent interest in popular culture.

Anyone who remembers the pre-Vietnam 1960s, as I do, can recall how safety drills at school and popular periodicals like *Life* primed us repeatedly to think about nuclear war in terms of survival, covering with zest the craze for building bomb shelters in suburban backyards. My own private fantasy, in my parent's small two-bedroom apartment in Brooklyn, was outfitting a large armoire as a shelter that would, miraculously, save us all. My private fantasy, I wrote, except that it seems to have been a national fantasy as well.[25] In all these instances, consideration of the past disappears in favor of apprehension for the future. Why? And to what effect?

The War Complex

The holes in the archive, the ellipses constitutive of cultural memory, exemplify the war complex at work, forming patterns that make a certain intuitive sense. Most of us do not dwell upon what enemy civilians experienced: the disappearance of homes, the loss of families, the destruction of the fabric of lives in single days or even moments—events terrible to contemplate.[26] They resemble the Holocaust, with the significant twist that the victims were enemy civilians and that we, rather than Nazis, made them happen. Not so coincidentally, in contrast to the widespread dissemination of photographs after the opening of the concentration camps, we often lack, sometimes as a matter of government policy, photographic records of dead civilians and of events like the mass burning of bodies in Hiroshima.[27] And so we personalize apprehension with regard to civilian bombings, moving it from the definite past to some potential future. Such terrible things *might happen* to us or to our families, but have not yet.

Apprehension for the future, most pointedly for our personal futures, seems or *has come to seem* a natural reaction to catastrophic events. We look to the nation for protection while we cling to those we love. Hannah Arendt and, more recently, Giorgio Agamben have shown that the state serves as the sole enforcer of what we confidently call "universal" or "human" rights, phrases that have no practical force without states willing to guarantee them.[28] Stateless people, or those disowned by the state, are subject to arrest, abuse, and death. The Nazis exploited this fact to kill millions, removing citizenship from German Jews and, in occupied countries, deporting refugees before citizens. The United States exploits it too, most recently to imprison hundreds of suspected terrorists at Guantánamo, Cuba.[29]

Although we have looked away repeatedly, analogous conditions of the state withdrawing its protection from some individuals and even killing its own citizens have pertained in China (Nationalist and Communist), in the former Yugoslavia, in Rwanda, in Sudan, in Israel and the former Palestine, and in other states where human life is subject to nations that do not recognize certain lives as protected. Large-scale war and the events around it open up, as a matter of course, acute instances in which nations knowingly expend their citizens' lives, military and civilian. As a hallmark of modernity, life in the nation-state, *especially though not exclusively totalitarian nation-states,* which remain far more likely to kill their citizens, can be fragile. Using detailed statistics, R. J. Rummel has shown that in *Death by Government.*[30]

How likely, then, even logical, that we have difficulty imagining—steadily and unblinkingly—our nation in oppressive or even murderous roles? How much easier to think of mistakes or misconceptions or temporary aberrations or imperative actions against "barbarians" or "terrorists" rather than national will? How much easier, given the conjunction between our dependence on nations and the priority we give to our safety and that of those we love?

Older than the idea of the state, the idea of the individual within a family or a set of loving relationships, while it can be differently conceived, permeates the models we live by.[31] From our oldest narratives, through recent Holocaust narratives, to narratives of 9/11, we tend to imagine historical catastrophe as it affects loving relationships and families. In this regard, the familial metaphors we adopt toward nations—motherland, fatherland, homeland, Uncle Sam—may point to the hope and faith we place in nations, akin to that we place in families.

Displaced out of the past and into the future, detached from what has actually happened to others, disaster can be contemplated as *potential* spectacle, not yet experienced, and certainly not experienced by us or by our families. Potentially preventable, such disasters form a kind of familial or national Perils of Pauline narrative in which the hero always arrives before the train wreck. The pattern seems like a controlled experiment in simulated loss, a complicated, adult instance of the toddler's game Freud called *Fort/Da*.[32]

By looking away from events such as civilian bombings and the Soviet losses, cultural memory in the United States effected social unity based on processes of othering. The Germans, while like "us" in so many ways (remember Fitzgerald's "reverse Teutonic migration") were evil Nazis; as posters routinely reminded viewers, the Japanese were fanatical, racially different, and even bestial "Japs" who had attacked us at Pearl Harbor; as Ronald Reagan later put it, the Soviets were "an evil empire." Such forms of othering forestall what I will call in this book a more creative—if sometimes problematic and difficult—process toward an ethics of identification.[33]

"Othering" forms the normal and, to some extent, necessary dynamic within war since sane people need to dehumanize enemies to kill and maim them. We can't think about "the enemy" as individuals with faces, interests, and families—and so, by and large, we don't. The enemy becomes a stereotype, a mass, an abstraction. At the furthest extreme, the enemy becomes subhuman or even demonic, linked by some ineradicable trace, often conceived as racial or religious, to pure evil that must be destroyed.[34] Regarding the enemy as pure and irremediable evil is a step beyond the more common "looking-away" from the enemy dead, which is not finally the worst that we can do. For demonizing creates the systematic will to destroy all members of the enemy group; it leads, in fact, to genocide.

Othering forms a link—an important and surprisingly under-explored link—between theories of imperialism, which are abundant, and theories of world war, which scarcely exist as distinct from specific histories.[35] And yet it's easy to see that imperialism and world war occupied the same time and space in the twentieth century. And any number of thinkers from Buber through Levinas and Derrida have written ethical texts after world wars—moved by history, though usually speaking in a universal voice rather than one geared to specific situations.[36]

I am not a philosopher and will not attempt, within the confines of this book, to plumb in detail the large and complex topic of ethical theory. Yet all that a process toward an ethics of identification really requires is awareness of others as beings as important to themselves as we and our friends and families are to us, and a willingness to face realities, even the harsh realities of war, in those terms. All it really requires is an expanded sense of connection and community. "*Of course,*" one says—my reader is likely to say—dismissing the idea in the process. I would point to a different and less knee-jerk kind of process: the process of evaluating and, when appropriate, working toward an ethics of empathy and identification, situation by situation, even in circumstances that take us outside the norms of our culture. While no sure thing, such a process nonetheless can lead to meaningful action and can be, in certain situations, itself a meaningful action.[37]

The war complex—and it is no easy claim to make or, I know, to read—is the difficulty of confronting the fact of mass, sometimes simultaneous, death caused by human volition under state or other political auspices, in shorter and shorter periods of time, and affecting not just the military but also, and even more, civilians: a fact urged on us insistently by World War II, but as insistently deflected. It exposes how life within the nation-state, while necessary and even desirable in modern life, can be quite fragile, especially during times of total war, when the sacrifice expected of the military can, and often does, spill over.[38]

The war complex arises when death comes to too many, too quickly, often through technological means and with rhymes and reasons that remain arbitrary and even meaningless. It undermines our normal tendency to "lay stress on the fortuitous causation of the death" (Freud's words), and to treat those recently dead with "something like admiration for one who has accomplished a very difficult task." It intensifies our natural fear of death, the bracketing off of death that has become routine in many Western cultures—and it ups the ante by not just killing bodies, but sometimes burning or vaporizing them.[39] The war complex shows up as gaps or ellipses in public discourse around histories of quick, technological mass death—which have nonetheless become our familiar.

What about the Holocaust?

I'm roughly two-thirds through my Introduction and the reader may be asking: in a book about the cultural memory of World War II, what about the Holocaust? Acknowledging its special place in American cultural memory and the many excellent articles and books published on the topic, I would say that this book is about the cultural memory of World War II, and especially the Holocaust. But I would also want to put some pressure on the practical effects of the "especially."

In *The Holocaust in American Life,* Peter Novick claims, and the claim has been influential, that modern Jewish identity in the United States coheres around the fact that Jews alive today might have been victims of the Holocaust, but were not.[40] I find the idea intriguing though, among my various disagreements with Novick, I would want to broaden his observation to include many, even most, Americans.[41] Yet even the Holocaust, which has become part of American cultural memory, adopted really as an American theme and the subject of many excellent studies, has been subject to looking-away from certain topics. Specifically, the role of at least some Jewish Council members in the ghettos and the actions of the *Einsatzgruppen* (the German "special task" mobile killing squads) form aspects of the Holocaust that have repeatedly caused intense controversy, the kind of controversy usually possible only for first-time revelations.

Did at least some Jewish Council members, under the press of terrible circumstances, sacrifice others? Did at least some even come to enjoy their temporary power? In 2004, the answer to both these questions is, pretty clearly, Yes. But when Raul Hilberg sought to publish *The Destruction of the European Jews* in 1961, several presses declined to print it although it has since become a standard source of reference.[42] And when Hannah Arendt published *Eichmann in Jerusalem* in 1963, her discussion of these questions, which was admittedly too harsh, uncapped volatile and even toxic debates that persisted for more than a decade, traces of which linger even today: she was accused of being an amateur, of blaming the victims of the Holocaust, and of being an anti-Semite.[43]

Did the *Einsatzgruppen* consist of ordinary Germans who shot and killed thousands of men, women, and children at close quarters? Did the *Wehrmacht* (the regular German army) actively assist the *Einsatzgruppen* and the S.S. to shoot Jews and to transport others to their deaths? In the early 1960s, Raul Hilberg and Hannah Arendt documented both these facts pretty clearly, as did evidence submitted at Adolf Eichmann's trial. After a gap of some thirty years, Christopher Browning revived interest in the subject in *Ordinary Men*, a subtle and intensive study of reactions within a single battalion that ranged from zeal, through the use of alcohol as stimulant or opiate, to minority decisions to evade action or to refuse outright.[44] And yet when Daniel Jonah Goldhagen's *Hitler's Willing Executioners*, which includes graphic narratives of the killing, was published in 1996, the book fell like a thunderbolt.

It's true that Goldhagen's highly narrative methods and thesis were controversial.[45] But the furor generated—which included national and international forums, lavish debates in newspapers and periodicals, books and essays debating his work, historians' reputations made and unmade (see chapter 3)—seems excessive given that the basic facts had long been a part of the public record.[46] Along with a similar controversy over an exhibition of Wehrmacht photographs, the Goldhagen case shows how certain histories from the Holocaust have been articulated and sometimes *pretty fully articulated multiple times* and yet somehow never adequately faced or adequately registered in public memory—a classic instance of hiding in plain sight.[47] Even the publicity surrounding Goldhagen's book may not have finally surfaced the facts, once and for all: when asked, graduate students at my elite institution know nothing about Goldhagen or the *Einsatzgruppen* nor do some otherwise knowledgeable colleagues. Why? And to what effect?

Since the 1970s, Holocaust Studies have evolved alongside and sometimes within trauma theory, which emphasizes repression, dissociation, and silence.[48] As a result, the Holocaust has been surrounded by a rhetoric of silence in excess, I would claim—along with Peter Novick, D. D. Guttenplan, and Andreas Huyssen—of the facts. For, by the end of the twentieth century, substantial amounts of writing and numbers of films about the Holocaust had in fact taken place. As Andreas Huyssen puts it, "The exclusive insistence on the true representation of the Holocaust and its uniqueness, unspeakability, and incommensurability may no longer do in the face of its multiple representations" (256).[49] What's more, as distinguished Holocaust scholars like Raul Hilberg and Alan Mintz have shown, survivor testimony has become the gold standard of evidence since the 1980s, but has also become both abundant and, at times, unreliable.[50] Yet we remain, by and large, unable to evaluate such testimony critically, entranced by a rhetoric of "preciousness," "sanctity," and "silence" linked to the rhetoric of trauma.

By definition, trauma is a shock, a blow (physical or mental) followed by repetitive reenactments that adversely affect daily life; in some theories, including Freud's, trauma involves a "splitting off" or "dissociation" from the original injury, which can then itself produce further, psychological, trauma.[51] Clinicians diagnose traumatic reactions by the presence of some of the following symptoms: "recurrent and distressing recollections [or dreams] of the event"; "acting or feeling as though the traumatic event were recurring"; "efforts to avoid thoughts, feelings, or conversations associated with the trauma"; "markedly diminished interest or participation in significant activities" and a "feeling of detachment or estrangement from others . . . [being] unable to have loving feelings."[52]

These are clinical terms and, as such, cold and chilly. But they usefully distinguish between trauma and relatively mild, short-term reactions by emphasizing extremes of sleep disorder, recurrent distress, and the inability to pursue ordinary life. As Ruth Ley points out, victims of systematic rape in Bosnia or by rebels in Uganda were traumatized; in her lawsuit against Bill Clinton, Paula Jones used the language of trauma, which then had political effects.[53]

In clinical terms, relatively few people, and most of them survivors, display or ever displayed as a result of World War II the full list or even most of the clinically certified symptoms of trauma. It would be more precise and more fruitful, then, to speak of *trauma-like rather than traumatic* reactions in our culture at large to World War II. In fact, although trauma theory may seem to provide an inevitable vocabulary for my book, I found it to be too totalizing and, finally, inappropriate—masking rather than denoting the phenomena I address.[54]

Within literary and cultural criticism, trauma theory favors silence and the idea that, beyond a certain point, discourse about trauma is inappropriate and even (when the trauma is the Holocaust) obscene. It operates on a model of infection, whereby those closest to events (for example, survivors) infect their heirs, those around them, and then the entire culture. Such views date back to Theodor Adorno's famous formulation that there could be "no poetry after Auschwitz," that poetry then would be "barbaric," a speculation embedded in a series of ambiguities in Adorno's prose but usually cited in one of the two ways I have cited it here.[55] Within philosophy and literary theory, a number of subtle variations have arisen: Blanchot's sense, in *Writing the Disaster,* that writing begins "upon losing what we have to say"; Caruth's claim that "trauma is not locatable in the . . . past, but rather in its very unassimilated nature—the way it was precisely *not known* in the first instance"; Felman's congruent sense that trauma's "origins cannot be precisely located."[56] In short, in various complicated ways, Adorno's dictum has merged with contemporary theory and with theories of contemporary life. It has exerted a profound effect on Elie Wiesel, Geoffrey Hartman, Dominic La Capra, and almost every other writer on the Holocaust.

The Holocaust has been a formative event in my own life and psyche, toward which I could feel no disrespect (see chapter 3). But surely the most pertinent questions today are not *can* or *should* we represent the Holocaust but *how* do we represent it? What gets said and what gets omitted? By whom?[57] Why, and to what effect? Given an insistence on "uniqueness" that makes any comparisons an insult to the 6 million, what happens to the memory of other aspects of the war? Why and to what effect? The rhetoric of silence as well, of course, as the facts themselves, may have stifled public discourse by creating trauma-like rather than more demonstrably traumatic reactions to the most distinctive feature of World War II, of which I take the Holocaust to be an apt representative: wholesale, wanton, and capricious civilian mass death caused by "civilized" people living within "civilized" states.

Media

The world entered and left World War II to the sound of radio, spreading in the prewar years what Virginia Woolf called "the voices of Dictators," then the rousing words of Churchill and Roosevelt, among the giants in the earth of that day.[58] Those old enough to remember the war years (children then, most of them) often structure memory around the radio news much as people today focus on television. Reynolds Price recounts how he was reading the "funnies" as they were called (the comic strips) when he heard about Pearl Harbor. It was late morning in the East. His parents were upstairs, in their bedroom, taking a nap, a ritual he was never to disturb—and one loaded with sexual connotations. He chose to slip to the door and ask: "Dad, where is Pearl Harbor?" When his Dad asked,

Why? and received the answer that the Japanese had bombed there, the door flew open and his father roared, "It's started then!"

Life, *Look*, the *Fox Movietonenews*, as well as (from the other side) the photographs of Hans Hoffman, the films of Leni Riefenstahl, and more anonymous work by Axis propagandists displayed events in photographs and film to give radio's voice images where the eye could linger. At most points during the war, government regulations forbade the graphic display of dead Americans; that rule relaxed at times, to stimulate what was felt to be flagging morale.[59] Similar but more stringent rules applied in Japan after Hiroshima and Nagasaki. Americans saw devastated cities, a common enough sight in 1945. But the military occupation suppressed photographs of burn or radiation victims and nixed images that showed funeral pyres for masses of Japanese corpses—most likely because they evoked widely circulated images flowing from the newly liberated Nazi camps.[60] The wide dissemination of images to stimulate or to dampen public perceptions was one of the most striking features of World War II and consequential for cultural memory.[61]

Television technology, already available in 1939, stopped being developed in the early 1940s and looked at first like a casualty of war. But war and technological development go together.[62] Development resumed, and boomed, after 1945 and through the 1950s. By 1960, the percentage of American homes owning at least one television had risen dramatically. Television had become a fact of life in the United States, so much so that the trial of Adolf Eichmann, held in 1961, was widely televised and important to evolving cultural memory.

If World War II was a war of photographs and the *Movietonenews* for people back home, mostly censored, later conflicts, like Vietnam, unfolded not just on the battlefields but also on the nightly news. Media coverage helped shape a persistent contrast: Vietnam was a misguided, unjust, or "bad" war while World War II had been a just and "good" war, especially when evaluated retroactively, with full knowledge of the death camps. We didn't yet have code words, like "symmetrical" and "asymmetrical" wars (wars the United States might lose versus those that were slam-dunks), let alone the recent expectation that war would be relatively free of U.S. casualties.

By the 1980s and 1990s, television had saturated most of the world and fully rivaled, and then surpassed, print media as suppliers of the news. Gradually, the loop between print media and entertainment became stronger, as even venerable organs like the *New York Times* began to emulate (in its magazine, for instance) the more "audience-friendly" visual style of *USA Today*. With the rise of conglomerates—sometimes also called transnationals, a term that underscores one real meaning of "globalization"—journalism and the book business took their place alongside radio, TV, and, increasingly, the Internet, as parts of the same transnational conglomerates. The military-industrial complex has become, in our time, the military-industrial-*media* complex—something new in our world and immensely consequential.[63]

While not all media sources approach the news uncritically—*The New Yorker* and writers like Seymour Hersh, *Vanity Fair*, Bill Moyers's *Now*, op-ed columnists like Paul Krugman and Nicholas Kristof, among others, formed an honor roll in 2004 of media that consistently asked hard questions—some outlets, like Fox News and CNN, the latter available in many airports and other public spaces, often seem to uncritically relay administration sources. As a nexus of institutionalized forces, the military-industrial-media-complex has the potential to steer public perceptions toward specific social and political effects: fear of a foreign nation or of some group more generally; support for the government or for a particular war—and away from dissent or resistance. Our culture remains at a considerable distance from George Orwell's dystopic Doublespeak, in which telescreens tell people what to think and revise memories at will. Individuals in ordinary life and individual instances in the media do speak out and, at least sometimes, prevail. Nonetheless, the more our media speak with one voice, and the more uncritically we receive the news, the closer we come.[64]

The first Persian Gulf War has been described, with some justice, as the first fully televised, live-time war. Like World War II, and in ways we have only gradually been able to see and process, that war dovetailed with long-term U.S. policies in the Middle East in Iran, Iraq, and Israel to water the seeds of events in the news after 2001. It made CNN an institution, the place with the reputation for being first with the news—the network with a certain hold on the public, the network with allure.[65]

Without a doubt, media have altered the way we process and imagine our world. News is everywhere—in airports, in waiting rooms, in elevators, running in ribbons across buildings on city streets. More news is good news, leading to a more informed public . . . or is it? For the omnipresence of the news today can seem invasive and oppressive. And much of the news has become, to a shocking degree, the same news as more and more newspapers, more and more publishing and media, are part of and run by the same conglomerates, with everyone competing for the same market and the same stories.[66] The media introduce a certain rhythm of focusing and of blurring attention that has consequences in public life.[67]

Throughout disasters, life always goes on in quiet corners. Poems like Auden's "Musée des Beaux Arts" put it succinctly: "About suffering they were never wrong, / The Old Masters. . . . how it takes place / While someone else is eating or opening a window or just walking dully along." But by the late twentieth century, the media decided, by and large, what we would be looking at or forgetting as events unfold. We might be looking intensely at Rwanda one month and then have the small African nation drop out of the news in the United States for a decade. We might be gripped by events in Croatia, then forget the Balkans until the news took us into Kosovo. For several weeks after September 11, we saw and re-saw films of the planes crashing into the buildings, the smoke, the devastation. Then, as the economy slowed, somebody or a collection of somebodies acting on their own decided we had seen enough—and the films by and large vanished.[68] In the same way, and perhaps for similar reasons, attention to Iraq has come and gone, though it has, as of this writing, tended to come back.[69]

As early as the 1940s, noting how Hitler used radio to manipulate public perceptions, members of the Frankfurt School saw the dangerous potential of media as propaganda.[70] Although their theories are still read and remain quite influential, they made "the public" seem the passive slave of media, unable to use creatively and variously what the media might give, a process that remains alive and unpredictable.[71] Decades later, Michel Foucault delineated a mechanism that explained the cultural effects more persuasively: most people will embrace, and indeed internalize, discipline and punishment in the guise of greater freedom—sexual freedom or, with a more economic twist that Foucault does not give, the freedom to consume.[72] One sees Foucauldian theory in operation today at some security points around the United States, including my local airport at Raleigh-Durham, North Carolina, where security is oddly tighter than at airports like La Guardia in New York, where I also live for part of the year. Some people seem to embrace the security and submit to the waits almost gladly—even though everyone in line knows that the delays are, almost entirely, meaningless.

It's the "almost" in the "almost entirely" that keeps the game in play: open the pocketbook, remove the shoes, see the suitcase searched, get wanded, get patted down—even though no one, including the searchers, thinks that you are carrying weapons. Policy depends on people's willingness to surrender certain freedoms in exchange for the feeling of security, the right to continue to feel prosperous and "free," even though one's freedoms—to say "no" to the pat-down, to talk back to the inspector—have just contracted, noticeably.[73]

In the mid-1960s, Marshall McLuhan used television to hurtle toward an all-encompassing historical and cultural thesis that "we become what we behold"—a dictum that may seem glib and absolutist at first. But McLuhan's insight makes more sense if we understand that by "media" McLuhan meant anything that changes the pace and tenor of life—patterns of thought and feeling, to use different terms. His use of the term *media* included not just TV and film but also printed materials, spoken language, inventions like the wheel or electric light, institutions like slavery, or though they postdate *Understanding Media* (published in 1964), the personal computer, the Internet, or the war on terrorism. Conceived thus broadly, media are extensions of the self, anything—language, image, means of mass communication, thought patterns instilled into a culture—that comes between us and the world. They create a culture's ambiance and ethos. They necessarily affect perceptions and create what seem like normative responses, even though individuals and groups, whose psychologies remain complex and even deft, still have the potential to react differently and even unpredictably.

The War Complex puts media histories to work in its analysis of cultural memory by adding media analysis to historical, political, and psychological approaches. It traces representations of D-Day, the Eichmann trial, the Holocaust, and civilian bombings across a range of disciplines and media—as well as mapping, to the extent possible, ellipses in memory by tracking changes in cultural representations at different points since 1945.[74] Do we become what we behold? Does something become true if it gets repeated enough? If something is elided, which was once known, how can we recoup its status as a fact? Can we identify instances, even if isolated, when the public resists or rejects clichés?

Seeing things anew through strange eyes so that one can feel the "appliness of the apple" formed one of the most vibrant theories of central European critics before 1939, after which their critical energies were dispersed geographically or, like Walter Benjamin's, ended by death. *Defamiliarization,* they called it: "Art exists that one may recover the sensation of life," Shklovsky wrote, "it exists to make one feel things."[75] In his essay, Shklovsky refers to literature, and especially to the novel, as agents of defamiliarization. During the first half of the twentieth century, critics and artists applied very similar ideas to painting and to other visual arts. And they could certainly be applied today not just to novels but also to film and television, both of which have shown the novel's ability to parody and to defamiliarize their own conventions. They might also be applied, as I suggest in the Conclusion, to instances of spontaneous and peaceful public dissent from official policies. Always relevant, has defamiliarization become crucial once again? Can the electronic media, which have helped to clog perception, help to cleanse it?

The War Complex will move—too freely for some readers' tastes—between specific events and cultural representations, private histories and public controversies, films or videos and statistics, memoir and oral histories, rumination and psychological theories, trying to give just and proportionate weight to all these ways of thinking and all these forms of evidence. My method is cultural criticism, with a characteristic blend of close-readings of printed and visual texts and attention to the public pulse—always difficult to measure. The book does not scorn written history—indeed, it uses it as a constant source. But it believes that the past remains *alive* in the present. And it wants to capture the interplay between the historical record (the archive), the present (cultural memory), and the ellipses always necessary for an archive and for cultural memory to take shape.

In these times of ours, the events of fall 2001 may turn out to be—like Gatsby's death for Nick—a recent disaster that opens up certain possibilities that had remained blocked in the discussion of the past. I felt them play that role in my own relationship to World War II, for I am today far less sentimental and far more skeptical about how my parents' war can be cited and deployed than I was when I began this book. But just as Nick's story is remembered as the story of the American dream rather than as a postwar narrative, numerous factors will intervene between the events of fall 2001 as we experienced them and what history recalls. New myths and memories, new pieties in need of defamiliarization, have been formed and will be formed for many years to come. The historical moment gives a special tweak to my desire to understand how the myths and memories of World War II have come to us.

We begin, in chapter 1, with D-Day, which remains the major American point of entry into the memory of World War II, still potent after all these years, but, as we shall see, subject to distortion.

CHAPTER ONE

D-DAY

On the Beach

On the beaches today, there's not much to see in a material sense: a few rotted and deserted landing craft; intermittent monuments where groups stop to read inscriptions; a small museum and remnants of portable harbors; a few surviving German bunkers, and (at Pointe du Hoc) huge, moonlike craters made by the Allied bombardment. Random picnickers, children at play, a few surfers. Dramatic sky, with roiling clouds against the blue bluster, and intermittent showers, even in July.

But it would be wrong, finally, to say that there is nothing to see on the beaches. The sky testifies to the invasion's risks, since weather in such a climate might quickly change. The small groups include families sharing information with children or teens—a generational chain into the future. Most of all, from Sainte-Mère-Èglise and Utah Beach in the west to Cabourg in the east, the full front of the invasion measures some fifty miles—and the visual impression of distance is impressive in itself.

At Omaha, the bloodiest beach by far, the one the Americans spent all day on, I walked down to the water and then considered the view toward the land. At Colleville-sur-Mer, one would have found a shingle of stones soldiers reached for protection, now a slightly vertical row. One would have seen roads from the beach, which would probably have formed special targets for attack and defense. One would have seen a bluff, now green and peaceful, with other tourists looking down on the beaches while I looked up at them. GIs and Germans would have been in the same visual proximity. Distant. But still discernible as tall or short—much like singers in an opera, seen from the upper balcony.

But what really counts in Normandy is the symbolism of the place, the way that this sand, these beaches, have become a synecdoche for the Allied victory, for the triumph of democracy over totalitarianism, and, once the Nazi camps had been breached and opened, for the defeat of a system of evil that shocked the world. In 1984, President Reagan used the site to invite the Soviets, his former "evil empire," back into the circle of Allies; in 2004, President Bush used the site to shore-up a sagging Atlantic Alliance. When it comes to Normandy, the symbolism is enormous; and, for American presidents, there is truly something about D-Day. [1]

Like its entry into World War I, the U.S. entrance into land combat in Western Europe came very late. Americans had fought for years in the Pacific and had already landed in Italy, capturing Rome at roughly the same time as Operation Overlord; they would fight in Europe for almost a year after D-Day, including the very difficult and costly Battle of the Bulge. Still, D-Day has come to represent the United States' most significant land presence in the Nazi war. After 1945, it came to justify the triumph of American wealth and power and to naturalize the story of American triumphalism, which leads strongly from 1945 to the present.

Some facts, found in almost every history of the war: the Germans expected the invasion at Calais, the shortest distance across the English Channel and a harbor able to receive the supplies and reinforcements any invasion force would need. Because surprise was key to success in Normandy, the Allies surrounded their plans with substantial secrecy. They staged fake build-ups in the south of England to support the idea that the invasion would come at Calais; having broken Nazi codes, they sent false messages intended to be intercepted and to mislead. They built two man-made harbors called mulberries over an extended period of time, breaking them into parts and submerging them underwater so that they wouldn't be seen by German aircraft before they were surfaced, towed after the invasion fleet, and quickly reassembled. Operation Overload had a complicated plan that depended on secrecy and on all components working well. It also depended on tides and weather.

The original date, June 4, 1944, had to be postponed. Continuing bad weather lulled the Germans into thinking no invasion could come in early June when the tides otherwise favored one. Eisenhower cast a roll of the dice when he decided to launch the invasion on June 6 since the next window of opportunity, two weeks later, might have given the Germans time to break the secrecy so important to the Allied plan. He wrote a short, frank letter taking full responsibility if the invasion failed.[2]

With 5,000 ships, the invasion fleet was the largest ever launched and left England slightly after midnight on June 6; landings began around dawn and continued through the day. As anticipated, some of the landings were relatively easy, while others were brutally hard. On Sword and Juno beaches, where the British and Canadians landed, casualties proved light, less than 1 percent of those landed.[3] On Utah beach, successful bombardments also eased resistance, resulting in what John Keegan calls "little loss" there as well (*Second World War*, 386). Cloud cover misled pilots over Omaha Beach, so that the Americans who landed there not only found the fiercest resistance, they also found the least protective cover. Descriptions stress how, at Omaha, the Americans were "visitors to Hell."

Already, the familiar story of the invasion tells only part of the truth. Contemporary sources like the *New York Times* and *Life* covered the story in detail both in advance of the much-anticipated invasion and afterward—how could they not? But the coverage differs from what many today would expect. Pitched in cultural memory as a matter of a single day, of winning or losing the war, the invasion on June 6, 1944, formed only one of a plethora of important military stories albeit, in early June, the newest one and first among equals. The headline of the extra edition of the *New York Times* for that day reads "Allied Armies Land in France in the Havre-Cherbourg Area; Great Invasion Is Under Way." It showed an accurate map, though the full understanding that Normandy was the invasion's site (versus ports like Le Havre or Cherbourg) seems not yet to have been fully digested. Three subheadings cross the front page: "Roosevelt Speaks," about the fall of Rome; "Pursuit on in Italy"; "Eisenhower Acts." Three other front-page stories back up the invasion headline: "Parade of Planes Carries Invaders"; "Allied Warning Flashed to Coast"; and "Eisenhower Instructs Europeans; Gives Battle Orders to his Armies." But the fall of Rome earns two other front-page stories as well. In miniature, the page conveys the sense of Europe at war, the world at war, in which the day's news could be, quite simply, overwhelming.[4]

Because magazines have long lead times, a periodical like *Life* did not run a story about the invasion in its June 12 issue. The coverage arrived in the June 19 issue, with Eisenhower on the cover identified simply by name; his image was one in a series of military cover portraits in 1944, most likely held until the invasion began. The coverage features Robert Capa's photos of the invasion as well as a D-Day diary, which covers most of the standard events.[5]

What's most surprising today is how long it took to declare the invasion a success. When the generals arrive onshore (a few days after June 6, according to the June 26 *Life*), reporters took it as a sign that the invasion will succeed, though success, the magazine reports, cannot be "determined" for about five weeks (21). And, in a tribute to secrecy, both the *Times* and *Life* depend on and quote German sources for some news.

The June 26, 1944, issue of *Life* captures the sense of the invasion dominant at the time. Entirely devoted to America at war, the issue leads off with a story about Normandy, moves to a more extensive story about Rome, and includes stories about the South Pacific and Burma. It prints maps of the war fronts, which show quite graphically that D-Day existed as one among several other fronts. In American cultural memory, D-Day is a singular. In the contemporary record, it formed part of a sequence. The first casualty figures given in *Life*, for example, record those dead in the eleven-day period that began with the invasion (June 26, 1944, 32). As a symbol, D-Day has acquired symbolic importance. But, at the time, it was perceived of and called the opening of a European Second Front.[6]

Although the Allied advance stalled several times, D-Day speeded the liberation of France and shortened the war by taking German troops and supplies away from the Eastern front, a killing field in the summer of 1944 where hundreds of thousands died. Given their diminished air power, it's unlikely that the Nazis could have forced the British, Canadians, and Americans back into the sea, though it would have been possible, had the Germans reacted more quickly to send in better reinforcements (Keegan, *Second World War*, 370–71, 3388–89). Had the Normandy invasion failed, the war would have dragged on, with the Allies continuing the advance from the south and the Soviets continuing the advance from the east until the British and Americans tried again from the west.

But by June 1944, the Reich was done for—and many people, save perhaps Hitler, knew it and had begun to plan, at least provisionally, for what would come after the war. (The famous plot against Hitler's life occurred in July 1944, and was motivated by interest in suing for peace. Although anything but a great humanitarian, Heinrich Himmler issued orders soon afterward stopping the deportation of Jews from Hungary.) The Germans had only a minimal number of fighter planes left in Normandy and precious few to defend German cities, bombed since midsummer 1940 and increasingly so after 1942.[7] After the German retreat from Stalingrad—a major, perhaps the major, turning point of the war—the Soviets roared from the east in a way the Germans rightly feared and the United States, fearing it too, downplayed once the war ended and has downplayed ever since.[8] World War II would almost certainly have been won without success on D-Day. But, had Operation Overlord failed, the war would have lasted longer and the Soviet role in postwar Europe might have been even larger than it was after 1945.

I begin on the beach because, in some ways, American cultural memory of World War II begins there too, albeit somewhat illogically. The United States entered the war after Pearl Harbor; other battles in the Pacific and European wars had been common subjects for newsreels and films made between 1941 and 1944. But D-Day emerged as the chosen symbol of U.S. glory. Britain has its Blitz; the French have the Resistance (the latter, as many scholars have shown, quite equivocal). The United States has Normandy and the D-Day beaches. No wonder, then, that *Saving Private Ryan,* the first major film about World War II combat in some twenty-five years, begins near the beach.

Representing D-Day: Saving Private Ryan, The Longest Day, and Other Movie Cameos

Steven Spielberg's *Saving Private Ryan* (1998)—a film intellectuals love to hate and so often under-rate—opens with a family visiting the Normandy American Cemetery. A patriarch who was, pretty clearly, a soldier in the war visits a grave, accompanied by an older woman likely to be his wife, a younger man likely to be his son, and others one assumes to be his daughter-in-law, three granddaughters, and a grandson. The man is tearful and garrulous, seeking reassurance and even admiration from his wife. For anyone who frequents World War II memorials, as I do, he is a familiar type: aging, but still vigorous and healthy looking; proud of what he did and wanting it acknowledged by those within earshot; saddened by the memory of the men in the graves he has come to visit. The film then switches, for an exceptionally long twenty-five-minute sequence, to June 6, 1944, and the invasion itself, cutting directly from the patriarch's eyes to those of Tom Hanks, later identified as Captain John Miller. For any audience worth its salt, the cut sets up the film's structure of identification and sympathy: with rare exceptions, we see the invasion through the eyes of the character played by Tom Hanks.

The very long invasion sequence, a focal point of reviews, keeps the camera at or below Hanks's eye level, even floating below water at times. It shows us men riddled with bullets before landing craft ever reach the beach. It shows us men drop off boats and, given their heavy war gear, sink like stones. It shows us legs and arms torn off, heads separated from bodies, brains pierced by bullets. Through a cumulative set of horrific images—the sequence's twenty-five minutes are extremely long in cinematic time—Spielberg manages to convey an overwhelming question: how could these men possibly have been deposited on or near these beaches, to face these guns and cliffs, apparently without effective air or tank support or cover?

As the enemy's machine guns begin to rattle and bullets pierce helmets and bodies, one gets the answer: how could these men *not* charge the cliffs at the end of the beach? The invasion included no contingency plans for failure, so that they had, quite literally, nowhere else to go. In a bit of dialogue that deliberately inverts dialogue in movies that had shown the invasion in the past, Tom Hanks delivers one of *Saving Private Ryan*'s memorable lines. In response to a question about what will be his unit's rallying point, he says, "Anywhere but here."

Spielberg exploits the resources of point of view in rendering confusion as the invasion plan collapsed—"collapsed" not being too strong a word at all for the first landing on Omaha Beach. Soldiers in the first wave of the assault would have been aware of soul-shaking exposure; they would have registered men turning all around them from living bodies to detritus. The film's emphasis on carnage rings true on the pulses. But it differs from other films taken on or made about D-Day.

The Army Signal Corps and Coast Guard sent a few cameramen along with the first waves of the D-Day invasion—John Ford, later a famous director, shot color footage, some of it transposed into black and white for movie newsreels. But the government stored the footage for years and years rather than displaying it, and some of the film (including Ford's) was lost, so that we will probably never have a complete, filmed record.[9] Were one to exist, it would probably show much of what Spielberg did. But, with rare exceptions, regulations at the time prohibited magazines, newspapers, or newsreels from showing graphic pictures of the American dead. Ashore with the second wave of the invasion, *Life*'s Robert Capa took several shots of Americans in body bags and one of three dead GIs lying neatly near the shore; the caption describes them romantically as "at the end of their adventure." As Susan Sontag says, "to display the dead, after all, is what the enemy does";[10] so it's not surprising that the only truly graphic photograph in *Life* depicts a rotting German corpse.

The Fox *Movietonenews,* an important source of filmed information in 1944, positioned D-Day much as the *New York Times* and *Life* had: as the next logical step after the fall of Rome.[11] It emphasized the preinvasion bombardment, the invasion plan, and the officers' control over that plan, showing shots of Ike and generals in command on the invasion fleet. It did not show any dead or dying on the beach, nor did it mention any confusion. Indeed, the voice-over assures viewers—some of whom no doubt had family abroad—that the invasion, while difficult, was more difficult in some places than in others.

Reassurance. Control. These two bywords guide one outright falsification in the *Movietonenews* shots. When it displays soldiers exiting the landing craft, they exit the boats neatly, with no sign of panic or even of hurry. Not a single soldier falls dead or wounded. It looks routine and tidy, almost like a barracks inspection; the troops might almost dust and clean the craft before they disembark. But the light in the shot does not match that in the rest of the news footage: it's nighttime, not daylight, with klieg lights discernible just outside the frame. Although no words announce a reenactment, that was in fact the case: *Movietonenews* re-created the unloading to reassure and buoy the folks back home. Since the light doesn't match, and so clearly doesn't match, the falsification might have been an open secret; it's hard to tell at this distance, because such facts tend to remain below the radar screen.

In our own day, cameramen on site by chance at the World Trade Center on 9/11 left their cameras rolling during events but chose not to film dead or dying bodies. On one tape, audible thuds can be heard, but the tape did not show people hurtling through the atrium, some of them aflame. The image of a severed hand circulated in one edition of New York's tabloid *Daily News,* but then disappeared completely (Sontag, 68). After the first few days, newspapers stopped printing and television stopped showing pictures of solo or group jumps from the Towers, perhaps because too many had an uncanny calm and beauty. Given how painful I found it to see shots of people trapped on the upper floors, leaning out of windows and waving for help, these decisions did not register in my mind as censorship, though of course that's what they technically were. Again in our own day, during the war with Iraq, embedded reporters sent home only the shots seeable from the U.S. front lines and even these were preselected for public viewing. Networks almost entirely deleted pictures showing U.S. casualties; indeed, a minor flap erupted when al-Jazeera broadcast films of American prisoners of war and news channels removed two reporters after remarks deemed too critical.

As I write (it is August 2004), newspapers and television (*The News-Hour with Jim Lehrer* on PBS, for example) still print the names and sometimes the pictures of American dead, although the effect has changed since May 2003, when President Bush announced the end of major combat.[12] The much larger number of Iraqi casualties (military and civilian) may never be known, although BBC broadcast an early estimate of around 3,500 civilians (based on hospital figures), noting that the actual totals would likely prove higher and later broadcast estimates from Iraq Body Count suggesting as many as 10,000 killed, with 20,000 wounded.[13] Because fighting has continued, with urban bombardments and siege, the final figures are likely to be higher still. I mention these facts and ellipses for an important reason: when I first wrote about government restrictions and media self-censorship during World War II, I felt smug and superior; regulations and censorship felt archaic—something we had outgrown after Vietnam. Now I understand that both factors remain with us—under conglomerate media, in some ways more than ever.

Prior to *Saving Private Ryan*, the film that most extensively rendered the D-Day invasion was Darryl F. Zanuck's *The Longest Day* (1962), whose distinctive feature was to cover all sides, including the German, in an international panorama. The film shows the French Resistance in action, communications and debates among the Germans, and the British, Canadian, and American landings. Portrayal of the German point of view constituted the film's novelty, with at least some of the Germans seeming sympathetic and no German brutality shown at all: altered conditions in 1962, including the Berlin Wall, made the film's kinder, gentler portrayal of Germans possible. The film aims at historical accuracy and, even more, at a *feeling* of historical accuracy. Shot in black and white at a time when color would have been the usual choice, it resembles, and quite deliberately resembles, *Movietonenews* reports and World War II documentaries, even labeling important characters as they appear in small white letters.[14]

As the film ranges across nationalities, it uses multiple stereotypes. We see a foxy female French Resistance fighter who flirts with the Nazis to trick them; we see a dog-loving punctilious German who feels outraged by his officers' incompetence; we see a middle-aged Frenchman who dashes out of his house to celebrate the invasion; we see casual Canadians; we see fastidious Brits with stiff upper lips. Despite the international cast, the focus remains on the Americans, and especially on Americans of the officer class. Henry Fonda plays Teddy Roosevelt's son, aging and crippled, but still gamely trotting with his cane on the beach as no young and healthy soldier could in Spielberg's film without being chopped into mincemeat. Robert Mitchum plays Brigadier General Norman Cota with macho and swagger. Cigar firmly in mouth, Mitchum strolls the beach as though he had divine assurance that he will survive the war. In one scene, he scolds a soldier who runs for cover, urging the man (addressed as "son") to go back out to retrieve his rifle. The soldier does so, without being shot. Spielberg would render such a moment by killing the soldier for the folly of breaking cover or by having the Hanks character tell him to take a rifle from one of the American dead nearby: the difference marks the change between 1962 and post-Vietnam 1998.

The Longest Day includes many long-shots of the initial assault that show men dying, as the *Movietonenews* prints do not—but the long-shots confer a certain sanitizing distance. When men die at closer camera range, as they sometimes do in the Zanuck film, they take a quick, clean, operatic dive. Critics rightly noted that Spielberg uses shocking close-ups of a kind unavailable or withheld of the first waves of the assault. As shown by Spielberg and as remembered by soldiers who were there, the beaches of Normandy do more than illustrate the cliché that "War is Hell." They are, quite simply, hellish. As one reviewer put it, the sequence conveys a series of images evocative of Hieronymus Bosch's famous rendering of the Inferno. It's hard footage to watch—up close and personal, with very few overviews to set a perspective until the very end. When the perspective-setting shots come, we are once again looking through the eyes of Hanks, now atop the bluff and looking down, who sees fragments of desolation and bodies washed at the shore, dead with the fishes.

Like *Movietonenews,* Zanuck's film stresses the extensive air coverage afforded the first waves of the invasion, showing bombardment of enemy positions both before the soldiers hit the beach and as the landing craft arrive. In most cases, resistance crumples fairly quickly. Omaha Beach— the only invasion beach shown in *Saving Private Ryan*—is an exception. Across the invasion front, and especially at Omaha, *The Longest Day* portrays a difficult but controlled invasion, one that went according to plan. It mentions and shows heavy casualties, but without a sense of absolute and devastating carnage. By focusing exclusively on Omaha Beach, Spielberg gives a different impression.

Immediately, I had to wonder: was Spielberg stacking the deck? Was he making things seem worse than they actually were? The answer, after consulting historical sources, is, No—with an important and surprising exception to which I'll return near the end of this chapter. Soldiers landing on the beach at Omaha had been told to expect a bombed landscape pitted with holes that could be used as protective cover. They found instead an intact beach. Charlie Company and the Second Ranger Division (the soldiers in *Saving Private Ryan* are elite Rangers) had drifted off target for their landing, making their debarkation the deadliest of all. The units took, and had been expected to take, heavy losses. For it is a shocking truth about the invasion that men in the first wave, sent ashore at low tide, carried extra gear that soldiers who arrived at high tide could retrieve from dead bodies on the beach.

In fact, and in Spielberg's film, the D-Day invasion illustrated war at its most impressive, what J. Glenn Gray describes as a kind of destructive sublime.[15] But it also illustrated, extremely well, the ethics of waste and expenditure that are part of any war. As Stephen Ambrose puts it, "war is waste. Men, and equipment, and generals are expendable so long as their destruction contributes to the ultimate goal of victory."[16] When he sent "his boys" off for D-Day, Eisenhower knew, he simply knew, that under worst-case projections many might not come back. The soldiers knew it too. Everyone danced to rhythms not of their own choosing, but chosen by the times, which required actively reversing the Nazi advances of 1940–41. The cacophonous rhythms of war made it hard to hear the names of the dead.

Naming

Like many war films, *Saving Private Ryan* moves between the pitch of battle—when individual losses must be expected and, to that extent, do not and cannot fully count—and interludes in which each loss registers intensely. As old as Achilles' mourning for Patroclus, Troy's for Hector, while hundreds and even thousands of others die anonymously, the contrast seems as old as literature and art about war. War films since Vietnam often enact the theme with a special emphasis.

Post-Vietnam war films often show the needless expenditure of war and the anonymity of large-scale death. But, to preserve narrative drive, they generally focus on at least some developed characters. Frequently, at least one character dies protractedly during a moment of calm or in an unusual way: perhaps killed by a sniper's bullet, perhaps by "friendly fire," perhaps by a self-inflicted wound. Sequences alternate between the pitch of battle, when many die, and relative calm, when individual deaths can matter. *Platoon* performs all these functions well, as does *Full Metal Jacket;* indeed the mix is one signature of the best movies about Vietnam. In *Saving Private Ryan,* Spielberg makes the movement between relative safety and absolute danger, anonymous and sympathetic deaths, into a major structuring principle.

Omaha in the first wave represents absolute danger; the French countryside days later gives the luxury of relative safety. The town of Rammelle before battle signifies relative safety; once the Germans arrive, it becomes maximally dangerous once more. The alternation becomes a theory of war and of the value of individual lives in war. In fact, the film reminded me of a transition in history painting that took place toward the end of the Napoleonic era. Early paintings by Gros, David, and others represent what is sometimes called "the great man theory of history": Napoleon is at the center of the canvas, fully posed with the iconography of the hero. Toward the end or after the Napoleonic wars, individuals, including Napoleon, are barely visible within the flux of events, which register as a force of nature. The apotheosis of this trend is Turner's *Hannibal Crossing the Alps,* in which men and elephants are dwarfed by a raging wave of snow and wind.[17] Nineteenth-century novels explore the same transition. I think of Stendhal's *The Charterhouse of Parma* and more especially of Tolstoy's *War and Peace.*

Except in extraordinary circumstances (like Private Ryan's), war strips individual soldiers—individual men, since the genre is gender-specific—of a particularized identity. It makes sense, then, that particularized identity in war is often conferred by linking characters to their mothers (Achilles with Thetis; Private Ryan with the bereft Mrs. Ryan) or to their erotic partners (Patroclus; Helen; the wives alluded to in *Saving Private Ryan*). When asked to think about Private Ryan's mother, who has lost three sons in one week, Spielberg's "soldier from Brooklyn" puts it trenchantly: "Hey Doc, I've got a mother. You've got a mother. Even the Captain has a mother. Well, maybe not the Captain. But the rest of us got mothers." He half-jokingly pleads for the kind of thinking that cannot exist within active combat. Perhaps that explains why mothers, wives, and daughters usually appear only in flashbacks or in men's conversations in war films, rather than as speaking, fully embodied characters.

The Thin Red Line (directed by Terrence Malick, 1998) shows the soldiers' women in silent cameos, but their images help to unnerve the men, already troubled by the bloody, visceral war in the Pacific. As a whole, the film unnerved audiences too, as evocative (in setting, in race, in military actions, like torching enemy soldiers) of Vietnam. While popular with critics, *The Thin Red Line* sank with popular audiences, perhaps because of its visual echoes of Vietnam. *We Were Soldiers* (directed by Randall Wallace, 2002), the only significant Vietnam movie made after *Saving Private Ryan,* also includes women but opts to suit contemporary tastes. It begins with an extensive sequence showing the men on base with their wives and families and it cuts from time to time from the battlefield to the wives, who are active too, especially in humanely informing each other of a husband's death. The film makes viewers extremely aware of Colonel Moore's (the Mel Gibson character's) name, seen first as a sign on his house and then often on his uniform. While other names are mentioned less insistently in the film, audiences can easily identify the characters by their families: Keegan is the Catholic man with the pretty wife and the new baby, Camille; the tall African American soldier has the feisty wife who makes fun of segregation.

My point is this: the undertow in war films pulls toward conventional narrative—the home the men left and to which they hope to return, with an emphasis on mothers and wives; but the tide flows strongly toward an all-male world, the realm that I call guy-talk, in which identity beyond the chain of command does not matter. It has to be that way. Or else, as in *We Were Soldiers,* the presence of plots involving female characters automatically makes a war film into an antiwar film as well, however many flags wave in the background.[18] Indeed, taken too far, made too literal (as when females fight too), the undertow toward love plot can vitiate a war film. *Enemy at the Gates* (directed by Jean-Jacques Annaud, 2001) begins with a long, bloody scene of carnage at Stalingrad modeled on the D-Day sequence in Spielberg's film. Carnage there was aplenty in Stalingrad, in 1942. But the film devolves into a love triangle with one man ultimately sacrificing himself so that the two other lovers can live. The motif dissipates the film's war energy by making it entirely too personal, as no good war film can afford to be.

Personal. Impersonal. Like most films about World War II, *Saving Private Ryan* relies on stereotypes rather than on fully individualized characters. There is a Jewish soldier who taunts German prisoners, waving his Star of David and saying "Juden. I'm Juden, you know. Juden." There is also a cowardly corporal, a translator, dragged against his will into the mission. Other soldiers in *Saving Private Ryan* are identified almost entirely by place or function. There is the obligatory soldier from Brooklyn. Hanks is a high school English teacher from Pennsylvania, though he withholds that information, teasing his men by remaining simply "the Captain" until the middle of the film.

As in Norman Mailer's early war novel, *The Naked and the Dead*, stereotyping works in *Saving Private Ryan* as a way of suggesting the ethnic diversity of the United States versus the homogenizing racial theories of "the enemy." (*We Were Soldiers* uses this motif too, often showing shots of the men and their wives in a multicultural circle.) *Saving Private Ryan* does not include African Americans in the mix, which jars with recent war films, especially those about Vietnam, where the African American presence was very high. But the absence of African Americans in Miller's unit is historically accurate since on D-Day the army was still officially segregated. In fact, *Life* magazine reported that "Negro military orderlies" had buried the dead on D-Day, performing "steady work" under fire (June 26, 1944, 33).

Like the absence of women save as motivators or as ciphers in conversation (Ryan's mother, Miller's wife), the absence of African Americans *registers* in this 1998 film. It undermines the narrative clichés of the guy-talk genre even as they are being quite massively deployed. So that the film slyly comments on its own genre, the war film, and its guy-ish nature, though it also serves as an example of how the genre works.

In the film, stereotyping underlines the soldiers' overwhelming desire to return home, to resume their stereotypical identities as a guy from Brooklyn, a high school teacher from Pennsylvania, and to cast off the equally confining stereotypes of "private" or "Captain." Working with stereotypes almost with a wink, Spielberg creates a tight thematic modulation between the individual and the mass, identity and its obliteration. Only the loss of identity enables the men to kill and to die under orders. When depersonalization falters, the casual brutalities of war become less thinkable.

The movie makes this point in the not entirely successful incident of the German prisoner who begins speaking English ("Betty Grable. Nice Gams."), undermining the Americans' intention to kill him. When conflict erupts over this prisoner, Miller says, "I just know that every man I kill the farther away from home I feel." The incident, which is already a cliché, should end at this point; the movie errs when it develops the incident further by having the German soldier reappear later to shoot the Captain.[19] But the incident itself articulates the dissonance every soldier must feel between the brutal life he lives in war and the peaceful life he is fighting to protect. As a post-Vietnam Vietnam film, *We Were Soldiers* makes the same point through its repeated contrasts with the homefront and also by humanizing and paying tribute to the courage of the Vietcong—so that their wholesale slaughter registers almost as fully as does the wholesale slaughter of Americans.

At times, *Saving Private Ryan* seems to enact a counter theme in which bravery and honor confer names and future memory on soldiers. But the counter theme always functions quite ambiguously. For example, when the soldier from Brooklyn complains to Private Ryan that his patrol has lost two men to save him, Ryan defuses his hostility by asking, simply, for their names and repeating them back respectfully: Edward Wade and Anthony Caparzo. The scene seems to enact a memorial—but does it? For, on my first viewing, I missed the names completely; on my second, when I was intensely listening, my notes read Erwin Wayne and Adrian Caparzo—names that did not sound right. I had to check the novelization of the film and the very end of the credits to get the correct names of these and the other soldiers (Mellish, the Jewish soldier; Upton, the cowardly translator, etc.). Similarly, although his last name is a given and his first name is mentioned briefly, I had to check to find out Private Ryan's full name: James Francis Ryan. In effect, moments of commemorative naming work symbolically within the narrative of the film but fail to communicate actual names to the viewer. Indeed, one of the film's major narrative effects depends on the withholding of names.[20]

When we see the Captain's full name in writing—John H. Miller (the "H" being entirely new)—we see it on a grave marker at the cemetery in Normandy identical in size and shape to many others. That tombstone shocked first-time viewers at the performances I attended, eliciting outright gasps, since viewers assume (courtesy of the film's first cut) that Captain Miller survived the war and was the grandfather we'd seen at the beginning of the film. Granddad turns out to be the eponymous Private Ryan, who we like well enough but is just not as interesting a guy as the Captain. The audience feels ambivalent, even antiwar, despite the fact that flags wave in the background.[21]

The most important point is this: in *Saving Private Ryan*, war confers identity not on the living, but on the dead. The point dates back to Homer, where Achilles in Hades has become "a name" glorified by war but wishes he could live simply and feel the sun again. On the beach at Normandy, and at many points of the war, individual lives simply do not and cannot count—or at least must count differently within the expectation of high loss. Simple life and the warming sun get put on hold, for some forever. Things are, as the soldiers say, "FUBAR"—fucked up beyond all recognition.

Representing D-Day: Two Cameos of Affect

In the Introduction, I said that cultural memory begins in the family, moves out into the neighborhood, town, or city, and then—sifted still further by scholarly writing and the media—becomes national or cultural. To capture how the memory of D-Day lives today, I need to scroll back from the cultural representations I have discussed so far to smaller units that represent ordinary people on ordinary days. I need to try and capture what registers for individuals—something close to collective memory but impossible to quantify by statistics since it's on the move, on the fly, subjective and emotional, but also tactile: an aura that affects the entire body, like a reflex or a sequence of reflexes.[22]

When collective memory works as Maurice Halbwachs predicts, bonds between strangers become the glue that holds society together, sometimes at the cost of omissions and elisions. In the United States, when the subject is war, Vietnam and now Iraq produce substantial dissonance and disjointedness; the American role in World War II does not.[23] Still, perceptions of these wars run interference with one another continually. Despite its surface of unblinking patriotism, *Saving Private Ryan* has a decided post-Vietnam aura, registered and understood by many people who saw it. I include two brief cameos that capture public remembrance of D-Day as I have experienced it, with others.

* * *

Cameo One: In the Jury Room. When *Saving Private Ryan* was released the summer of 1998, it was a conversation maker and many people initiated discussion. On jury duty, sitting and chatting before trial, a fellow juror asked whether anyone had seen the film. Almost everyone had and approached it via experiences of Vietnam. "I loved it but my husband wouldn't go to see it," one woman, an African American elementary school teacher said. "He was in Vietnam for a tour of duty and thought it would bring back too many memories. He still can't sleep some nights. Drives me crazy hearing him pace around." An older, white retiree talked about how different World War II had been from Vietnam. He said that a friend had told him about shooting Vietnamese children in the war and "there wasn't a one of them that didn't explode, that wasn't carrying a bomb." At this point, my fellow jurors shifted in their seats as I did, uncomfortably, but said nothing in the interest of group solidarity.

When I rented *The Longest Day* and other war films at the video store, similar conversations ensued. Had I seen *Saving Private Ryan?* the clerks would ask. Then they would volunteer, spontaneously, information about whether they had seen it or not and whether they had been in the Army or in Vietnam. *Saving Private Ryan* was about the Normandy invasion. But it tapped into a much more recent American consciousness and was understood to be "about" the military in some larger sense in which World War II and Vietnam form crucial points of reference.

In the conventional wisdom, World War II is the just war, the good war to rid the world of Nazism and the horrors of the Holocaust, a view to some extent retroactively conferred.[24] When cultural memory focuses on Japan, as it has less frequently in the last three decades, in part because of Vietnam, World War II is seen as the war forced upon us by the attack at Pearl Harbor. In contrast, Vietnam is the morally ambiguous war, the one even people who were there and who once supported the war do not think was worth fighting.

For most of 2003, politicians and commentators avoided comparisons between Iraq and Vietnam, although the antiwar movement liked to make them and they crept in by July 2003, once General Abizaid had used the "G" word (guerilla war).[25] Within a year, when no weapons of mass destruction were found, America's strong support for the war had changed; the continued violence in Iraq now makes the war far less popular and the media reported and showed the change.[26] The book remains open on how history will view the Iraq war. But one thing at least is sure: at every point in the build-up, conduct, and aftermath of the war, the Bush administration sanctioned and enacted in photo ops comparisons to World War II. Some examples: echoes of Churchill and of D-Day in speeches; landing on an aircraft carrier to declare the end of major combat; the opening of graves and the display of corpses killed by Saddam's regime, with its visual allusion to the Holocaust; the preposterous expectation that the Iraqis would greet our troops with flowers; suggestions that World War II, the Cold War, and the war on terrorism (the first two won, the last ongoing) line up in a neat and tidy row; the occupation of Iraq and its new constitution as modeled on precedents in Germany and Japan. Among those who opposed war with Iraq, the Bush administration's aggressive use of World War II analogies inspired both resentment and skepticism.

The contrast between World War II and Vietnam was always overly simple, leaving out, for example, Korea and other intervening events. It has become even more tenuous after the first and second Persian Gulf Wars—different in circumstances from each other and from both the earlier conflicts—which edged the country back into a more military mood, at least for a time, albeit not yet in the mood to tolerate many American deaths. But the contrast exists nonetheless in the American imagination. Unlike World War II, Vietnam makes Americans squirm, even though people today typically honor veterans and avoid the animosities the war inspired in the 1960s and 1970s with civility, as they did in my jury room. And Iraq . . . well, dissent on that war ran deep but was, paradoxically, so strongly ignored by the administration in 2003 and much of 2004 that it remains too soon to assess its full and ultimate effects within American culture.

*　*　*

Cameo Two: At the American Cemetery. One enters from the left, and faces a palisade of trees and the bluest of skies, punctuated by the roiling clouds of Normandy. Below the palisade lies Omaha, where the United States sustained its highest losses on D-Day. The Normandy American Cemetery holds almost 10,000 graves, a symbolic number, each marked by a cross, or occasionally by a Jewish star. (I do not recall any Islamic crescents and media accounts do not mention them, but they may be there.) Arranged in mathematically precise rows, the white markers arrest and guide the eye—gleaming against impeccably green grass, as though artifice and nature have healed the wounds of history and time. No inscriptions show on the fronts of the stones, a gesture of simplicity that magnifies the loss. On the backs of the stones, facing the rear of the cemetery, there are inscriptions: these are not, in fact, the graves of unknown soldiers. But the initial anonymity suits the memorial of expenditure and death.

Some visitors comb the rows, looking carefully for one or more particular markers. Indeed, some have come to locate a specific grave. "Do you have the number, Dad?" says one woman to her father, a tall, rangy-looking man, a natural golfer—robust well into his seventies or eighties, his head topped by a beige-colored cap. His body and face seem eager, exuding pride in being a veteran—projecting haste to get to the grave of a relative or, more likely, a "buddy."

People glimpsed at cemeteries are like people glimpsed on trains—it's irresistible sometimes to imagine little stories. The story I tell myself about this man posits a trip to Normandy, long deferred. His wife had never wanted to come: too painful for her as the woman left behind? Fatigue at years of war stories? At her suggestion, he has traveled to Hawaii, Paris, even the Riviera. Now, widowed and with his daughter grown, he comes to Normandy to where he landed long ago—quite possibly as a last trip before he settles with great decency into advanced old age.

Another spot, another story. A group of four—in their twenties or thirties, two men and two women—carefully search a row of graves, video camera in hand. They stop. One of the men begins to speak, resting his hand on the other man's shoulder. The second man drops to his knees while the women wait—two Marys, watchers at the tomb. Grandsons, I suspect, reliving a family legacy.

Some of the graves, a very few, have fresh flowers at their base. Most have nothing at all but the carefully tended, anonymous grass. But as I approach the end of the rows and am about to leave, I pass a single red rose—fresh and erect, stuck into the earth at the foot of a marker. A single red rose, after almost sixty years.

The memorials at the American cemetery are impressive in their way: a rotunda to the rear, with inscriptions; a curved wall of columns, a large statue, fountains, and other inscriptions at the front, a design echoed in the new World War II Memorial in Washington, D.C. But I am not by temperament a visitor of monuments and, for me, the presence of time and nature takes over and I have two, very vivid imaginings.

The first concerns a gathering at the memorial, each night, of the spirits from the graves. Thousands of guys, playing cards, swapping stories, sharing beers—an epic of male bonding. But the spirits feel something missing—as they have for sixty years. They wonder where the wives are. The kids. The girls. The parents. The friends. The reasons why, after all, they thought they were fighting. It's a boisterous but also a melancholy, gray-tinged scene.

The second imagining extends the first. As I leave the cemetery to drive to Utah Beach, I note a house for sale. It sits just outside the cemetery and it's white with green shutters and a screened porch facing east—

more New England, really, than Normandy. I imagine a woman of a certain age, renting the house to be near the graves. I imagine her story: a fiancé or husband lost but a life well lived with children, career; now widowed, children well into middle age, she comes to be near Colleville-sur-Mer and buys this house. The Keeper of the Flame, she calls herself, the Mistress of the Spirits—for the woman is not without a sense of irony. Her female presence leavens the maleness of the scene and creates a further link between it and me.

"The past is never over. It's never even really the past," said William Faulkner. He was alluding to the Civil War in the Southern imagination, but the remark travels well to World War II. The war is over, to be sure—roughly sixty years past. But its effects have lingered in so many ways, subtle and loud. World War II still reaches out with a living hand.

Statistics: Reading Hard Cold Facts

So how, finally, does one tell the story of D-Day? By visiting the site? By viewing documentaries and other films? By reading histories? By collecting oral histories? All the models apply, I would claim: the history of the event consists of contrasting representations, sometimes with the kind of disjunctions that I have tried to capture by allowing this chapter to be one of shifting moods and juxtapositions. But although accounts of D-Day can differ, they overlap in one significant way: almost all convey the sense that D-Day was a day of overwhelming loss for U.S. troops. I'd like to pause and look at that item of consensus. I'd like to check it against some hard cold facts, the kind of facts found in statistics.

But first, I'd like for you, the reader, to participate in an experiment I performed with myself, family, friends, acquaintances, students, and random strangers. I would like for you to estimate Allied and American losses on D-Day and, if you have a piece of paper handy, to write it down.

Everything I have said thus far would prime you to estimate that American losses exceeded other Allied losses and that assumption would prove correct. If you are like the overwhelming number of people I asked, sensing a surprise, you will have modified your initial instincts about American losses (100,000, 50,000, 25,000, 12,000) downward. Most people I asked—and they were people of different ages with different levels of historical background, some quite high—settled at reasonable sounding figures between 10,000 (roughly the number of graves in the Normandy American Cemetery) to 25,000 American dead or, always a vaguer statistic that includes those wounded and missing, 10,000 to 25,000 American casualties.

But the statistics for Allied and American deaths and casualties on June 6, 1944, are far lower than most people think, even when revising downward, in part because they are far lower than media representations and public memorials have led us to expect. In addition, while such statistics can certainly be found, surprisingly often the sources require one to parse, compare, or splice several reliable sources to arrive at accurate figures for those killed. The same statistical difficulties exist, as we shall see, for the Holocaust, for victims of the atomic and incendiary bombings, and for estimates of casualties and those killed in World War II as a whole, which can vary easily by 10, 20, or even 30 million, depending on which events and archives one includes. But such difficulties remain surprising for American losses on D-Day, which have, after all, long been both quantifiable and part of the public record.[27]

According to John Keegan, usually a judicious source, "Most of the 4,649 casualties suffered by the American army occurred" on Omaha, and "Allied casualties at Utah numbered 197," an "insignificant number" given the "23,000 men landed on that beach" (*Second World War,* 383, 387). According to Martin Gilbert, "355 Canadians had been killed" and "the Americans and the British each lost more than a thousand men" out of 155,000 Allied troops landed. According to an appendix in Cornelius Ryan's *The Longest Day,* a book invested in D-Day's importance that is still widely read and almost de rigueur for tourists in Normandy, 10,000 Americans died, "with some estimates" higher. According to the D-Day Museum in New Orleans' Web site, also invested in the importance of D-Day but more scrupulous in avoiding "some estimates," the Allies suffered 4,900 casualties among almost 175,000 ashore by the end of D-Day; according to the same source, 2,403 Americans were killed out of total casualty figures for Americans listed as 3,581.[28] I have consulted additional sources, including official ones; each states and breaks-down casualty and fatality figures somewhat differently.[29] Using an aggregate of reliable sources, the number of Allied casualties (British forces, Canadians and Americans killed and wounded) emerges as 4,900. The number of American casualties (those killed or wounded) on D-Day was 3,581; the number of Americans killed was 2,403.

Three thousand, five hundred eighty-one American casualties, including 2,403 killed: these are large and weighty figures, to be sure, each a son, husband, father, brother, or friend, each a loss to be reckoned with. But without intending any disrespect—for I feel none—we might consider some comparisons. On a single day, at the battle of Antietam, 23,000 died. On the first day of the Somme (July 16, 1916), out of 110,000 attackers, 60,000 were killed or wounded.[30] On many days in World War II, more than 5,000 died. The Battle of the Bulge killed or injured some 70,000 Americans, a figure distinct from, albeit coloring, cultural memory of D-Day.[31] No one wants or needs to win a competition for wartime deaths or casualties. I don't offer these statistics in that spirit at all, but just as a reality check since the actual statistics for D-Day do not match the idea of D-Day in the imagination.[32]

Why, in this instance, has statistical information been hiding in plain sight? Especially since low casualty figures (far lower than the Allies anticipated) might well have been claimed and trumpeted as proof of a great victory in a just cause?

One possible conclusion is that the United States has wanted to stake its claim to victory in World War II and the subsequent influence of the United States in European and world affairs, in American blood. We could not match the Soviet claim in lives lost: 20 million, now expanding, as Soviet archives open, to as many as 50 million.[33] And so, as the Cold War developed, the government and the media downplayed the vital Soviet role in defeating the Nazis until it formed an ellipsis in cultural memory, an ellipsis filled by the image of D-Day. Although I felt hesitant to reach that conclusion at first, recent events confirmed it.

In the months leading up to the invasion of Iraq, when France led international protests against U.S. invasion plans, several commentators in highly visible places ridiculed the French and challenged their right to question a U.S. invasion of Iraq because "we" had rescued "them" on D-Day. Andy Rooney of *Sixty Minutes* (who later seemed to oppose Bush policies in Iraq) claimed to know more about France than the effete Parisians because he had landed on D-Day. A review in the *New York Times Book Review* used the phrase "cheese-eating surrender monkeys" for the French.[34] Towns and cities reportedly changed the names of French fries to Freedom fries—though I have never, in fact, seen Freedom fries on a menu. French restaurants across the country reported a falling off of business; sales of French wine declined. The silliness of it all, and the arrogance, could not have been greater.

As the war began, the political importance attached to the image of D-Day intensified. President Bush's comments, as the *New York Times* put it, were "drawn straight from the days of World War II."[35] Americans would be liberators and saviors, not invaders and occupiers. The taking of Baghdad was supposed to be the liberation of Paris, redux, filled with kisses and flowers.

Despite their opposition to the war, the French, for their part, cooperated in the perpetuation of the myth. For when it seemed time to heal the rift, what did American and French officials choose to do? You might have guessed it: they visited together the Normandy American Cemetery. Sixtieth anniversary celebrations continued the myth, using the visual symbolism of almost 10,000 American graves to suggest that at least that many Americans, and probably more, had died there.[36]

The political explanation I have just given makes sense in Cold War contexts, and now again under the umbrella of America's swagger as the world's sole superpower. But I need to ruminate a little further on the odd but manifest fact that we represent D-Day as both decisive and as a day of signal and bloody sacrifice when the facts suggest that it was not quite so important and that it was not as deadly to Americans as current representations suggest. Why D-Day?

First, I would point to aesthetic factors—not as out of place as one might think in a discussion of war—and to the human liking for tight structure and form. The earliest Greek dramas were set within a twenty-four-hour time period and had a clearly marked, though not necessarily singular, protagonist. These "classical unities" appear in literary works such as *To the Lighthouse* and *Ulysses,* as well as many, many dramas and films. D-Day's action begins at dawn; it unrolls over a day; it culminates that night; although the British and Canadians are there, Americans are, for all practical purposes, the heroes. D-Day fits the classic unities to perfection.

A film like *The Longest Day* stresses temporal unity in its very title; in white superimposed titles like "D-Day plus one," *Saving Private Ryan* does so too. One might go so far as to say that military planning follows the classic unities as well by responding to the pragmatic military need to begin an invasion at dawn and to reach some kind of conclusion, if only a tentative one, by nightfall. Had Operation Overlord taken several days to establish a beachhead, that would have been problematic in the military sense. Had Operation Overlord come to be called D-Week or D-Fifteen-Days or even the Battle for Normandy, those titles would not have had, as almost anyone would admit, quite the same ring.

The aesthetic explanation I have just given is true, I'm sure it's true. But something else pertains historically as well insofar as D-Day functions, and has for some decades now, as a synecdoche for a longer process that included the advance on Caen, the liberation of Paris, the taking of ports like Antwerp, and the Battle of the Bulge. As a totality, these events were far more costly than D-Day itself. The Battle of the Bulge claimed, for instance, some 70,000 American casualties over several months and was America's "sternest test of the European war."[37] But the Battle of the Bulge lacks the appeal of an absolutely clear beginning or end. And the battle's narrative includes mistakes and blunders on both sides, not the strong, sustained forward momentum of the landings at Normandy. D-Day represents an intense burst of military energy, a distilled action able to be represented as a singularity.

But here again, I must press a little further, this time into the statistics themselves—the contrast between our impression of large numbers of losses and the relatively small actual losses on D-Day. Why do we remember D-Day as one of extreme loss and death when the statistics do not support that conclusion? Perhaps because every death on a symbolic day like the landing at Normandy registers as larger than itself, much in the way the World Trade Center dead registered as larger than themselves—as a synecdoche for us, for our nation. But also, perhaps, for more devious reasons that take us right into the heart of the war complex.

D-Day represents to some extent a *simulation* of devastating losses without the accompanying grim realities of massive death. In the Introduction, I used Freud's model of *Fort/Da* to describe the pleasure we seem to feel in the apprehension of catastrophe and in simulations of catastrophe in popular culture, a pleasure impossible to feel when caught up in catastrophe in reality. D-Day may "flash" the possibility of mass military death, without such disturbing accompanying factors as the pragmatic need to dispose of bodies quickly, without burial and due ritual. In this sense, cultural memory may have chosen D-Day *precisely because the statistics do not support the image of massive death.*

Soldiers were lost there—but a countable number, identifiable, buried, and honored. Such basic facts and the satisfaction of such basic needs were not characteristic of the worst days of World War II. Psychologically, it makes sense, then, that we would concentrate on D-Day, making the relatively small losses suffered into an ellipsis within cultural memory and remembering the day, indeed celebrating the day, as one of massive loss.

CHAPTER TWO

EICHMANN'S GHOST

The trial of Adolf Eichmann was the first fully televised trial in history. It unrolled with microphones poised and cameras whirring, leaving taped and filmed records alongside printed transcripts. In Israel, "the proceedings could be heard on the public streets, for the radio voice emerged from every window." In the United States, ABC broadcast weekly summaries; in the New York area, nightly.[1] If one thinks of the trial as a media event—cameras rolling all the time—one comes close to capturing an essential part of its ambiance. Eichmann's trial formed a prototype of the modern "celebrity" trial. But his crime really was the crime of the century: "the slaughter of millions of European Jews."[2]

People who remember 1960 and 1961, as I do, found Eichmann's capture and trial quite riveting, even in an active and exciting year. Amidst the first U.S. manned space flights, against the background of the Cold War and the erection of the Berlin Wall, alongside the beginnings of the Kennedy years, louder than distant rumblings from Vietnam and sharing the news with more transient events like Liz Taylor's Oscar and Sammy Davis Jr.'s interracial marriage, sat Eichmann. An enigma among enigmas, he was called "the man most responsible" for the Nazi murders.

The Eichmann trial and Hannah Arendt's brilliant but controversial *Eichmann in Jerusalem* (1963) formed many people's first encounters with the full, graphic facts about Nazi genocide.[3] But I will want to claim that even readers who have no recollection of 1960, 1961, or 1963 have nonetheless been profoundly shaped by Eichmann's trial. Eichmann's ghost rises whenever facts about the Holocaust become disputed or the world returns to unanswered questions—as it did during the last decade around Daniel Jonah Goldhagen's *Hitler's Willing Executioners* and David Irving's failed libel suit against Deborah Lipstadt. It flits around the edges of the U.S. decision to intervene in Bosnia, triggered in part by images of Bosnian Muslims displaced from their homes and starved behind barbed wire. It tinges reactions to the invasion of Iraq, where the military uncovered mass graves and displayed the corpses at the same time as President Bush visited Auschwitz.[4] It haunts us whenever war crimes are in the news, each time we debate the need for an international court or for a standing tribunal—as we did, in 2000–1, when Slobodan Milosevic was tried at the Hague and the United States withdrew formally from any participation in an international court. As we did, in 2003, when war crimes became issues in Liberia, in the Congo, and for the United States, which not only insisted upon and received another year of exemption from charges against Americans at the World Court, but also bristled at Belgium and NATO for "threatening" to try U.S. citizens.[5] As we did once more, in 2004, when the abuse of Iraqi prisoners at Abu Ghraib hovered at and perhaps crossed the threshold of war crimes.[6] If this past will be dead, it's not dead yet.

The trial's full transcripts—nine dark blue volumes available in English since 1992—provide a thorough written record of the trial.[7] Hannah Arendt's classic *Eichmann in Jerusalem* (1963) provides a juicier, more polemical interpretation, as do the many documentaries and docudramas made before and since.[8] From *Engineer of Death: The Eichmann Story* (CBS, 1961) through *The Trial of Adolf Eichmann* (ABC, 1997), from the landmark historical drama *Holocaust* (NBC, 1978) to Eyal Sivan's *The Specialist* (1999; 2000), from *Sixty Minutes* (1983) through the award winning *The Conspiracy* (HBO, 2002), our culture has shown a repeated, almost continuous, interest in Adolf Eichmann.[9] Why the fascination? And what changes have occurred over time? As for D-Day, some answers can be found by looking further, and more critically, at materials available in the public record, but somehow never fully registered. And, as was true for D-Day, the history of Eichmann's trial contains several surprises, some of them hiding in plain sight.

The Public History of Adolf Eichmann

What Eichmann did in the Holocaust is well known enough and damning.[10] By his own admission, Eichmann worked like a demon between

1938 and 1941 to enroll Jews in the process called "emigration." As a witness at his trial would say: a Jew with a profession, money, a home, and property would enter an office under Eichmann and exit with a permit to leave his nation—but with no profession, no money, no home, no property. Then he worked feverishly to organize deportations into ghettoes and from ghettos into camps. Eichmann was a thug who presided over the looting of millions.

Eichmann secured the necessary trains to send Jews to the death camps; he established schedules, set quotas, reassured Jewish Councils and (sometimes) the governments of occupied Europe so that everything would go as smoothly as planned. It almost always did, except in the few countries that balked at deporting Jews or found ways to elude Nazi plans, like Denmark, Italy, and Bulgaria—three nations that form an honor roll in Arendt's book. The list of Jews deported to the camps from other parts of Europe is long and depressing—except for someone like Eichmann. Eichmann rejoiced at the "elegant" way (his words) it all happened. In Israel, on trial for his life, he could not resist recalling with pleasure the beauty and speed with which the wheels of deportation trains had turned in Holland.

Eichmann never pulled a trigger. So far as we know, he never mauled or brutalized physically a single Jew. It's even possible that, in his own mind at least, he believed, as he claimed, that he not only had nothing against Jews but also admired their long, historical persistence and supported Zionist aspirations. A natural sycophant, he tried to impress his interrogator in Israel with how he could recite Shema Israel (Sh'ma Israel) in Hebrew, the prayer any believing Jew would utter close to death; years later, the interrogator told *Sixty Minutes,* "he must have seen many people die."

In his own words, Eichmann was the one who "transported them to the butcher." He knew that "if [he] had not transported them" so efficiently, far fewer would have died. He admitted what he called "human guilt" for the murder of the Jews—by which I assume he meant private guilt or even, in his own terms, moral guilt. But he saw no legal guilt since he had acted within German law under orders that derived from Hitler. For Eichmann, as for many under Nazism, Hitler's orders seemed rational and even virtuous; *conscience* meant "obeying orders" and the "beauty" and "speed" of his operations trumped everything (*Life,* November 28, 1960).[11]

Eichmann knew—he always knew—how many died as a result of his actions. He understood the pain and suffering the Nazis caused. In 1941, Heydrich ("the Hangman") sent him to Poland to report on the activities of the *Einsatzgruppen,* special task killing squads that shot whole villages. He saw the first mobile gas chambers and reported back that the actions he saw in Poland would drive soldiers mad or make them into sadists. In 1945, he told Rudolf Höss, the commandant of Auschwitz, that bureau IV-B-4 (Eichmann's office) had transported more than 2 million Jews to Auschwitz, so that Auschwitz must have killed over 2 million.[12]

Eichmann clearly understood the magnitude of what he was doing. Although the judges at his trial modified and dismissed certain of the charges made against him because of insufficient evidence, under Israeli law he fully deserved conviction on the rest.[13] While some Israelis— including Martin Buber and Gersholm Scholem—argued that Israel should spare Eichmann's life, his execution was entirely justifiable.

That said, however, honesty demands that other things be said as well. When the war ended, Hitler, Goebbels, and Himmler were dead by their own hand: the major trophy and two potential runners-up had committed suicide and were unavailable for punishment. Yet 30 million Europeans had been killed and Europe lay in ruins. The Allies wanted justice; the Allies wanted punishment; the Allies wanted some sense that they could understand and judge what had happened so that such slaughter could never happen again. They responded with a military tribunal in Nuremberg, the city where Hitler had once held triumphant rallies. The major legacy of the first and major trial—the International Military Tribunal or IMT—would be the idea of crimes against humanity, although the first two charges leveled at the defendants (crimes against peace and conspiracy to wage aggressive war) were designed to prevent any recoil against the British, the United States, or the Soviets from charges three and four (war crimes and crimes against humanity).

The International Military Tribunal (IMT) tried twenty-two defendants as "major war criminals," defined as those whose acts had not been local but had affected all of Europe: Hermann Göring (Deputy of the Reich and Head of the Luftwaffe), Albert Speer (architect and Minister of the Reich), Julius Streicher (Nazi propagandist), Hans Frank (Governor-General of Poland), General Alfred Jodl, and Admiral Karl Donitz were among the defendants. Controversies since elided from cultural memory erupted at the time, especially in the United States, over sharing the bench with the Soviets (themselves guilty of war crimes) and over trying military men for "crimes against peace." Within Germany, the blanket charges leveled against all the men seemed an affront designed to accuse all Germans.[14]

Having organized deportations across Europe, Eichmann might have qualified under the prevailing criteria as a "major war criminal." But, in fact, Eichmann was not indicted or even considered for indictment at the IMT. Ernst Kaltenbrunner, Reinhard Heydrich's successor and the highest living member of Eichmann's branch of the Gestapo (the Reich Central Security Department or RSHA), was indicted instead—and probably would have been, even if Eichmann had been in custody. Eichmann's absence alone did not prevent indictment; Martin Bormann, for example, was indicted in absentia.

Eichmann was fond of saying—and his three older sons, who back him, repeat the idea—that he could no more be held responsible for the Holocaust than the tracks on which the trains ran to Auschwitz or than the engineers who ran the trains. I'm not convinced by the feigned passivity of that image at all—though I do note how it suggests, in the engineers, a host of anonymous, mini-Eichmanns.[15] Still, in the abstract, Eichmann's deeds gave relatively little for the imagination to work on. He negotiated and set schedules, ordered trains, helped set up Jewish governance in the ghettos, and made timetables for deportations to the camps. From time to time, he visited sites outside Berlin, including Theresienstadt (where he had authority) and Auschwitz (where he did not). His first full command away from Berlin came late in the war, in Hungary, where his role in deporting Hungary's Jews was especially damning. Although hideous enough by any measure, Eichmann's deeds were not as graphic as, say, the work of Mengele at Auschwitz, a Nazi doctor who conducted grisly experiments on children, twins, and others. Documents used against Eichmann in Jerusalem show that, in 1960, he was comparatively the third or fourth most notorious Nazi who might have been captured: Martin Bormann, better known and higher in the Nazi hierarchy, would have been a better catch; so would other Nazis who were never found, like Heinrich Müller (Eichmann's superior at the RSHA), or Josef Mengele, who had also fled to Argentina but used his wealth to stay one step ahead of secret agents.

The Israelis found Eichmann after he brought his wife and sons to Argentina and then stayed put, continuing to use the name Ricardo Klement and passing as his boys' uncle while his wife openly called herself Veronica Leibl Eichmann. In fact, Eichmann was what Hannah Arendt called in passing one of the most terrible things under totalitarianism: a family man, most concerned about his private interests.[16] Secret agents tracked him to a suburb of Buenos Aires and snatched him as he got off a bus after work. Once seized, Eichmann readily acknowledged his identity and then proved the most cooperative of prisoners, talking in extraordinarily full ways about his past. He spewed forth a fountain of confession and self-justification to his captors that helped to make the record clearer for the prosecution, even as Eichmann thought that he was helping his case by "setting the record straight."[17]

Eichmann was a war criminal and an accomplice in genocide—he was evil enough, no doubt about that. His deeds in Hungary alone would have been enough to convict him. But he was not the biggest of what was, after all, a big, bad, criminal lot. And he was not, as students and others old enough to know better repeatedly tell me, Hitler's "right hand man," a phrase that most likely confuses Eichmann with Göring, Goebbels, or Himmler. Nor did he devise, initiate, and execute on his own the Final Solution. Can one say that, in 2005, without being misunderstood? I hope so, for the historical record of Eichmann's deeds is quite clear.

Eichmann was guilty under the definition the court employed of the Final Solution as "one comprehensive order" in which "the desire of the main conspirators and perpetrators was identical with the wish of the original initiator" (*Transcripts*, vol. V, 2186). Since he presented himself merely as someone who set the trains in motion, the judges pinpointed the nature of his guilt by measuring it railway car by railway car: "For the despatch [*sic*] of each train by the Accused to Auschwitz, or to any other extermination site, carrying one thousand human beings, meant that the Accused was a direct accomplice in a thousand premeditated acts of murder" (*Transcripts*, vol. V, 2218). Eichmann's own statements—2 million Jews to Auschwitz, 5 million (Eichmann's estimate) killed overall—helped to establish the magnitude of his guilt. But, in all likelihood, Eichmann might have fared better had he been arrested along with Göring and Kaltenbrunner and considered for trial in Nuremberg immediately after the war. He almost certainly would have fared better had he stayed in Germany and not been tried until the 1960s, when a spate of trials produced generally light sentences.[18] In 1960, with no other major Nazi surviving or available for trial in Israel, Eichmann became the symbol for the full complexity of the Holocaust.[19] It was, in a way, his natural fate, the one most consistent with paths he had followed from his boyhood.

Adolf Eichmann was born into the lower middle class in the Rhineland; his family moved to Linz in Austria when he was young. He dropped out of high school and his first steady job was one his uncle got him as a traveling salesman for the Vacuum Oil Company, first in Linz and then in Salzburg. He rose in life mostly by joining the S.S. in 1932. Later, when Eichmann described himself as a "traveling salesman for the Gestapo," he was thinking of his Linz experience, which he had loved (*Life*, Part 1, 102). Vacuum Oil or S.S. deportations: selling was selling for Eichmann.

Adolf Hitler shared an awful lot of Eichmann's background. Hitler was Austrian too, and, like Eichmann, he loved Linz, where he planned someday to retire.[20] Like Eichmann, Hitler didn't match stereotypes of Aryan good looks—in fact, once again like Eichmann, he looked (and was accused of being) partly Jewish, an idea that persists in the popular imagination. Like Eichmann, Hitler had been unemployed. So far as we can tell, during his lean years, Hitler lived amiably in a men's hostel with many Jewish tenants,[21] just as Eichmann claims to have gotten along in his youth with Jews.

It remains one of life's mysteries that Adolf Hitler rose to be the German Führer—and Eichmann loved that story. Even in 1957, long years after the fall of the Reich and Hitler's suicide, Eichmann remembered most of all how, "I recognized him joyfully, and I still defend him."[22]

One cannot write about Nazis or Nazi war crimes without coming up against Adolf Hitler either as a presence or as a silent, protected absence. In Eichmann's case, he's both, for although Eichmann honors Hitler, neither the defense nor the prosecution mentioned Hitler much at Eichmann's trial. After its opening statement—an overview of the war and of "the Final Solution" in which Hitler's name could hardly be omitted—the prosecution avoided Hitler. It didn't want to raise the larger demon when the lesser demon was at hand. The defense didn't stress him either except under the general rubric of "orders," since Hitler was the ultimate source of all orders in the Reich. The defense had enough to do just defending Eichmann; it didn't want to tackle the missing Adolf as well.

Still, the more I thought about Hitler's relative absence at Eichmann's trial, the more it seemed a key to understanding Eichmann and his place in the world. When one thinks of Eichmann, one thinks he must have been a Nazi bigwig. He must have danced at lavish parties in Berlin—his wife clad in white silk, the champagne flowing. He must have talked with the

Führer all the time. Popular dramas like *Holocaust* show Eichmann at the parties, drinking the champagne. Was he not, after all, in charge of Jewish affairs—affairs close to Hitler's heart? Why wouldn't Eichmann have talked with Hitler?

But, so far as I can tell, Eichmann didn't talk with Hitler. He got letters from Himmler and talked regularly with Heydrich, Kaltenbrunner, and Müller—all very high in the S.S. hierarchy, to be sure, but not the very top. It's even likely that Eichmann never met Hitler, although as a matter of course they would have been in the same place at times. Eichmann didn't mention any meeting in interviews or during his interrogation, and, if one had happened, Eichmann would have treasured it and bragged about it as he bragged about so many other things. When he spoke about Wannsee, for instance—the conference he helped to organize, which set the contours of the Final Solution—he stressed relaxing and having a drink with Heydrich ("the Hangman")—something that might not have been known without his information.

Surviving members of Hitler's inner circle, like Albert Speer—who wrote about the Reich and gave many interviews until his death in 1981—don't mention Eichmann. In Speer's biography, he mentions Ernst Kaltenbrunner, Eichmann's boss, only once, in terms of contempt, as the man who visited him after the 1944 plot against Hitler's life and asked questions with "that menacing look of his." For someone like Speer, Kaltenbrunner was a thug. He was not a daily associate.

We know that Eichmann's name first began to surface at Nuremberg in private interviews conducted by Michael Musmanno, later an American Supreme Court justice and a witness at Eichmann's trial, who had been sent to the IMT to investigate whether Hitler had truly committed suicide. Out of court, Göring, Kaltenbrunner, and others listed Eichmann as the one most responsible for the murder of the Jews after Hitler, Bormann, Goebbels, Himmler, and Heydrich. [23] Court records include a statement from Rudolf Höss, commandant at Auschwitz, documenting conversations with Eichmann about the number dead. But the most popular book about Nuremberg, American psychologist G. M. Gilbert's *Nuremberg Diary*, mentions Eichmann just once—and even then only when indexing testimony by Dieter Wisliceny (Eichmann's subordinate). Several other books about Nuremberg give Eichmann just a perfunctory mention, even with a retrospective sense of his importance. What are we to make of Eichmann's relative obscurity at Nuremberg? That Eichmann was indeed less visible and less important in the Reich than those named as "major war criminals"? Or (as the prosecution at Eichmann's trial suggests) that Eichmann's very obscurity was a ploy to make him look less important than he was—a suitable smokescreen to hide secret activities? Yes, to both—perhaps. But it's also clear that Eichmann's infamy grew enormous only gradually and snowballed after 1960.

My own belief, one consistent with Arendt, is that one need not exaggerate Eichmann's role in order to justify his trial and conviction. For in the Gestapo unit charged with Jewish affairs (the RSHA), Eichmann stood just below and just above men tried and executed after the war. His superior Kaltenbrunner and his subordinate Wisliceny both implicated Eichmann for the murder of the Jews. His position in the Reich and the evidence at his trial more than justifies a guilty verdict. Still, and we really should admit it, for the Nazi bigwigs, Eichmann was a nobody. He was like Richard III's henchmen when they kill the young princes: useful, but not valued, and certainly not someone you would want to have around. And he was far more like those henchmen than he was like Richard.

In his biography, Albert Speer describes a moment shortly after the war when he opened a red velvet case holding a portrait of Hitler that the Führer had given him. Having begun in his mind and his actions to betray Hitler, the moment was cathartic: Speer cried himself uncontrollably to sleep and felt it was a turning point in his life, one that "liberated him."[24] Eichmann had no such red velvet case, no such portrait, no such moment either of betrayal or release. Eichmann never got that close. Instead, he was a lowly member of the audience looking longingly at Hitler from afar.

I know it's dangerous to think of Eichmann this way. It collapses back, or seems to, into the "little man" theory—Eichmann's own image of himself as "a cog in the machine." It runs the risk of being misunderstood as believing in Eichmann's self-presentation and hence, perhaps, as excusing Adolf Eichmann. But, as I have said more than once now, I believe that Eichmann was guilty of mass murder. Still, I want to understand why we react to Eichmann as we do—with fascination, laced with contempt, far more than with fear or with horrified awe. It is, I believe, a class reaction, based on Eichmann's lack of elegance and of the proper social class.

I have mentioned Albert Speer several times now, for a reason. Speer remains in many ways Eichmann's double in the ranks of Nazi criminals. The two most famous Nazis alive and in prison in 1960, the two men nonetheless presented themselves quite differently, were covered differently by the press, and produced very different kinds of reactions in the public mind. If you doubt that, just ask yourself: would *Playboy* have photographed and interviewed Adolf Eichmann the way it interviewed Albert Speer?[25]

Speer, architect of the Reich's impressive rallies and its industrial manager, was an educated man from a wealthy, indeed an "immensely rich" family. His parents owned an estate where Speer would live years later. Handsome, charming, and charismatic, Speer was immediately attractive to Hitler and to almost everyone else who met him. At the end of his life, at seventy-five, he died in the arms of his blond, much-younger lover—and Gitta Sereny, his eminent biographer, seems both embarrassed and impressed. She repeats several times that the woman was tall, blond, and somewhere between thirty and forty years old. She tells us that, in a photo, the woman wears a flimsy white negligee. Sereny apparently cannot help but feel happy (as her informants do) that Speer found "erotic love" at the very end of his life. She also, and understandably, cannot help but feel that Speer's late fling was tough on his wife, who had chastely waited and brought up the children during her husband's twenty years in prison.[26]

People who knew Speer and Hitler say that the two men fell under each other's spell very quickly. It was a kind of love—not sexual, but erotically charged: intensely friendly in a way that made both men think in terms of devotion, betrayal, and forgiveness. Speer became an intimate in Hitler's circle and Hitler liked to commission Reich photographer Heinrich Hoffmann to show the two together. In one image from 1934, Hitler and Speer examine architectural plans, leaning toward each other with a casual, masculine intimacy. Light flows in from windows to the rear, bathing the two figures in a romantic glow. It's a staged photograph, on the kind of stage where no one would place Adolf Eichmann.

Speer lived near Hitler at Berchtesgaden (his home in the Bavarian Alps) and was asked to bring his family to live there too. In Hitler's social circle, Speer's special favorites were Magda Goebbels, wife of Joseph Goebbels (Hitler's Propaganda Minister and chief henchman), and Eva Braun, Hitler's mistress. That seems right and typical of Speer—to befriend and like the women of the chief Nazis as much, or even more, than the men themselves. The bonds with the women cemented his bonds with the men but also complicated things. Speer's first feelings of dislike for Hitler came when the Führer insulted Eva and made Magda break off an affair, a real love match (Sereny, 192-93). He always sided with Magda Goebbels over her womanizing brute of a husband. And Speer hated

Goebbels's decision to have his wife and six young children take poison along with him in the final days of Hitler's rule. In the same way, near the end of the Reich, when Hitler's bunker was a shambles, Speer was frightened that Eva Braun would tell Hitler that he had spirited away his family to a safer part of Germany, one destined for the British (505). Hitler would have considered the action treasonous—so that Speer had to lie to Eva, whom he had always thought of as a "darling girl" who retained her "simple" tastes despite Hitler's grossly "bourgeois" ones. Like all classy men, Speer judged easily the classiness of others.[27]

Even from this brief description, one can feel right away the differences between Speer's career and Eichmann's. Both of them made the Third Reich function. The factories run by slave labor and the camps "processing" Jews might never have worked so well without Speer and Eichmann. But Speer was always recognized as charming and brilliant— the kind of man who wears a smoking jacket and ascot quite easily. His fellow Nazis found Eichmann loyal and efficient but, at best, a buttoned-up kind of guy in a uniform or a stiff dark suit.

Interrogating Speer around the time of the IMT at Nuremberg, John Kenneth Galbraith described him as exuding "personality, authority and . . . humor. By any standards, he was quite exceptionally intelligent, with a phenomenal memory and breadth of technical knowledge."[28] Yet in *Nuremberg Diary*, G. M. Gilbert, the court psychologist, notes that Speer scored 128 on IQ tests, in the lower fiftieth percentile of the defendants, below Göring and ten others.[29] Still, to most observers, Speer was, as George Ball put it, "the one interesting person on the Nazi side."[30] Gitta Sereny shares that sense and quotes Galbraith and Ball approvingly; in her excellent biography, she remains able to like Speer despite his flaws, which were considerable, including coldness and the ability to exploit others, even those he loved. But just below the surface lies a persistent feeling that whatever else one might say about Speer—and that was a lot—the man had class. He was indisputably a rich man's son and someone who handled himself gracefully.

Speer was "elegant" as a prisoner at Nuremberg and his elegance formed part of his defense strategy, which saved him. To American psychologists and then later, on the stand, he repeatedly acknowledged a generalized feeling of guilt about what the Reich had done and a willingness, as a leader, to take responsibility for actions he had not performed or, he claimed, even known were happening. He looked for explanations of how a civilized nation had performed uncivilized deeds. Knowing that the Soviets, whose troops had been impressed into slave labor in his factories, would hang him if they could, Speer played to the Americans by treating the Soviets with contempt.[31] But he never admitted—even decades later—that he had known what was happening to Jews or to the slave laborers in his factories. He said he knew that his workers had been slaves. He said that he could have known about their horrible working conditions and that he should have known. He even said that he would have known—except that he had never really wanted to know.

In fact, as Sereny concludes, Speer must have known—just from random conversations taking place around Hitler (409). By 1943, Speer had seen a hideous underground factory called Dora and had been warned by a friend never, ever, under any circumstances, to visit a concentration camp. Speer "sensed" but never thought about the horror behind that warning because, in his heart, he did not want to know. And so he existed in a state that was "a twilight between knowing and not knowing": that was Speer's explanation—simple, yet complex, and extremely elegant.[32] Like many charming men, he compartmentalized.

As a man of taste, Speer did not bad-mouth Hitler, admitting that, "If he [Hitler] had been capable of [friendship] I would indubitably have been one of his closest friends."[33] Indeed, at the end of the Reich, Hitler designated Speer, rather than Göring, as his successor. But unlike Göring—or Eichmann—Speer didn't defend Hitler. Indeed, he tried to counteract Göring's influence on the Nuremberg defendants and to bring them around to his own way of thinking.

In the end, Speer got twenty years at Nuremberg—not a short sentence, but not death by hanging, either. He was released from Spandau prison at the age of sixty-one and wrote books that became best sellers.[34] Oddly enough, Eichmann's own ambition was to write a book—a memoir, though (as Judge Halevi warned him at the trial might happen) it did not see the light of day.[35] Speer's books caused the architect some grief; old friends considered him a traitor. But the books also made a fortune— despite hefty taxes and very large donations to charity, including Jewish ones (Sereny, 678, 680–82). Even that gesture, Speer's donations to charity, had class.

Eichmann may have studied Speer's defense at Nuremberg and understood what he had pulled off—the evidence suggests it. In his own trial, Eichmann imitates Speer's posture. He admits "human guilt," though not legal guilt for what had been done to Jews. It's similar to what Speer had done in accepting a generalized sentiment of blame. Given his office in the Gestapo, Eichmann could hardly have hoped to credibly maintain that he did not know what Nazis did to Jews—though, if one thinks about it, neither could Speer given *his* position. So perhaps it's not surprising that Eichmann would have tried Speer's strategy. He admits he ran the trains that transported the Jews to camps, and with maximum efficiency (*Life*, Part I, 21,109). Then he claims that he simply and deliberately did not think about what happened to the Jews once they had alighted. In short, he too, but less charmingly, compartmentalized.

It's typical of Eichmann and his lack of class that he went too far in making his professions of ignorance. Eichmann claimed, for instance, that for all he knew, many Jews counted among the dead had really left the camps and were now safe and "happily alive"—maybe even living in Israel. He refers to Jews thought dead as "sprouting like mushrooms" in the forests of Poland. He calls the death march he organized in Hungary "elegant," "hygienic," and "safe"—as it demonstrably was not (*Life*, Part I, 109; Part II,148).[36] Such remarks show the kind of bravado, the kind of bad taste, of which Speer would never have been guilty.

Speer's strategy didn't work for Eichmann as it had for Speer for at least three reasons. First, Eichmann made too many slips—like the indiscretions above, and more. He revealed, for instance, his drink with Heydrich at Wannsee, which no one need have known; he shared with men like Rudolf Höss careful records of transporting Jews and indicated knowing quite well what transportation meant. At his trial, where Höss's written statement was introduced as evidence, he felt shocked that Höss, whom he had always liked, had betrayed him. By contrast, after Speer's friend warned him not to visit a concentration camp, neither the friend nor Speer repeated the conversation while it mattered.[37]

Second, Eichmann was tried in an Israeli court—not in a German court or in a tribunal dominated by the Americans, both of which might have been manipulated as Speer had manipulated the IMT. It's entirely likely that an Israeli court would have hung Speer too. Still, Eichmann's strategy failed for an interesting third reason: he was tempted by a different model from Nuremberg other than Speer and, when tempted, succumbed.

That model was the substantial figure of Reichsmarschall Hermann Göring, the chief defendant at Nuremberg and Speer's rival for leadership of the defendants. Göring had been a mess during the war but had redeemed himself at Nuremberg in German eyes. Fat and sloppy, he had previously been a figure of fun—a known drug addict, a greedy glutton who snatched up wine and art, a screw-up whose power came from years before the war, when he'd been an early, stalwart Nazi. Toward the end of the war, Hitler didn't want Göring in power when he was not around to oversee him and so he asked for (and received) Göring's resignation. But Göring lost weight and was de-toxed during his imprisonment. He debated with the judges and with Justice Jackson—and, on some days, he seemed to win. He rallied the defendants and became accepted as their leader by everyone but Speer. Göring cheered the hearts of Germans who resented the trial at Nuremberg. He sealed his legend when he managed to kill himself with poison and evade the dishonorable hanging to which he had been sentenced. Göring predicted that, in fifty years, Germany would erect statues in his honor because he had stood by Hitler. Speer, who had not stood by Hitler, feared Göring might be right.[38]

At his trial, Eichmann wanted to be a little like Göring. In fact, Eichmann's plea in court—which some people found confusing—was neither guilty nor innocent but Göring's plea at the IMT: "In the sense of the indictment not guilty." It was the classic mistake of trying to be just a little bit pregnant. He said that a bad S.S. officer would have spared some Jews—but that he was a "good" S.S. officer.[39] A more sensible man might have pointed to one time he did save Jews in Hungary, albeit in return for loot.[40] Eichmann saw himself as frank and forthright in his statements. In his mind, he probably compared himself favorably to Göring, Speer, and to the other major Nazis at Nuremberg who never admitted knowing about the murder of the Jews. Eichmann never seemed to realize how appalling his "frank," matter-of-fact admissions sounded nor did he seem to realize how they damned him. In fact, he seemed to need approval so strongly as to be tone-deaf.

In an interview, Eichmann recalled how, toward the end of the war, when his superior Müller gave out false papers to anyone who wanted to hide, Eichmann made the gesture of refusing. It's typical of Eichmann that he felt proud of the incident because of how it must have affected his boss, Müller: at that moment, Eichmann says, "Müller must have known I was a regular guy" (*Life*, Part II, 152). It's also typical of Eichmann that, despite his boast, he later sought, and used, several sets of false papers. Eichmann doesn't seem to understand that Muller himself used false papers and was never found. So that, if Müller thought at all about Eichmann's refusal, he probably thought it was foolish.

When all is said and done, Speer got off without a death sentence. Göring committed suicide rather than hang and became a hero among some Germans. Eichmann, who had done a bum's job during the war, got to be a bum. No one ever thought he was a "regular guy"—not even his fellow Nazis. No one ever thought he had an ounce of class—though he tried, he really tried, in Jerusalem.

Life *on the Master of Death*

When Prime Minister Ben-Gurion announced in the Knesset that Israel had Adolf Eichmann and would try him, the *New York Times* reported that members of the parliament sat "startled by the news" and then, according to eyewitness accounts, burst into applause (May 24, 1960, 1). But the international press had to introduce Eichmann, quite literally, to an unknowing world. Within days, it began to seem entirely natural that Eichmann (and not Bormann or Mengele) should be on trial as a major war criminal. Newspaper accounts identified him incorrectly as a "General," not a Lieutenant Colonel, in the Gestapo. The *New York Times* ran a story that described Eichmann as "baby faced, with a slightly twisted lower lip, effeminate features, high forehead, and receding hair," effectively putting him into the category of the effeminate other. It claimed, as no additional source did, that Eichmann had had plastic surgery after the war, perhaps as a way of explaining why no one, including the Israelis, had previously gone after Eichmann.[41]

Stories about the Eichmann case appeared regularly from his capture to the time of trial but most were placed inside the paper or, when they made front-page news, below the fold. Before the trial began, Eichmann formed headline news only sporadically—most notably during a dramatic United Nations debate about the legality of his capture, at Israel's formal indictment, and at the appointment of the judges for the trial who, in accordance with Israeli law, served as jury.[42] But by the time the trial began, in April 1961, Eichmann formed headline news, indeed banner headline news, backed by a substantial number of tributary stories. What had intervened? The U.N. debate about his capture and other public controversies about holding his trial in Israel, to be sure. But also, and I suspect most, truly shocking revelations by Eichmann himself.

In November and December of 1960, four months before the trial began, *Life* magazine ran an extensive interview, from which I have already quoted several times but about which I now need to say more, for, read now, the interview raises many questions. Eichmann had given the interview in Buenos Aires to Wilhelm Sassen, a Dutch-German journalist, several years before his capture. Did Sassen know from the start that he was speaking to Eichmann, or did he discover it, as he later claimed, only gradually? Why did Eichmann give the interview, which was quite damning? How did *Life* get it and who was paid? Did Eichmann realize that the interview might figure in a future trial or did he expect it to appear only after his imprisonment and death—two events he probably believed would follow quickly upon each other? How much of the interview came straight from Eichmann and how much did the interviewer enhance Eichmann's words?

Such questions were raised during Eichmann's trial from April to August of 1961, in which *Life* magazine and its interviews proved active players. The prosecution at the trial wanted the entire interview to count as evidence. Two of the three judges disagreed, allowing only portions annotated in Eichmann's own hand to enter as evidence. But Eichmann admitted under questioning that other portions of the interview were true in substance, so that these portions also entered into court. What's more, virtually everyone at the trial had read Eichmann in *Life*. The transcripts show that arguments about the status of the interview erupt from the beginning of the trial to its end. On the last day evidence was presented, Judge Halevi, the dark-haired and most flamboyant judge, lost his temper when, despite protesting his desire to reveal the truth, Eichmann still refused to allow the court to consider as evidence the entire interview.[43]

Part One of the *Life* interview opens with the line "I transported them . . . to the butcher," uttered impassively, as a simple matter of fact. It continues with three sets of facing pages that intermingle text with many pictures of Eichmann and his family. On the first set of pages, a large, vertical, almost half-page photo shows a relaxed, smiling, handsome-looking Eichmann in a white suit as he strides in Buenos Aires; it looks like a favorite family photo. Opposite it and also vertical, though slightly smaller, sits a disturbing image of four men about to be shot. "Beseeching victims," the caption says—though, for the record, only one man seems to be pleading. Other photos show Eichmann's wedding, Eichmann's family on Mother's Day 1960 (without Papa), and Eichmann's six-year-old son, peering forlornly through a fence at the spot from which his father had been abducted.

When I began work on this book, I knew that I had read something key about the Holocaust in *Life* decades ago but I did not associate it at first with Eichmann. Then, when I began research on the trial, I knew what I would see in *Life* before I turned each page; with a jolt, I realized that

Life's interview had changed my life. The article had had world historical import, providing facts about the Shoah that had not yet registered fully in national discourse. But, in 1960, as a preteen in Brooklyn, I felt most aware of its impact on my closest friendship.

I remember sitting in my bedroom with Connie, my red-haired, blue-eyed Italian American best friend, who thought that Jews "exaggerated" what had happened to them during the war "to feel special." I remember the incident with great particularity: ruffled bedspread and curtains in three different shades of pink; cheap 45 record-player in the corner, along with my meager stock of books; dolls and stuffed animals all around; *Life* magazine spread on the bed, open to the pictures of the Jews doomed by the Nazis.

See? See? I must have said. It really happened. People like these were killed by people like him, Eichmann. I must have pointed to details— 500,000 killed from Hungary, more than 5 million overall.[44] I must have picked out ripe details: like the time Eichmann saw his first mass shooting of the Jews and says that he wanted to reach out to save a child proffered by its mother—though he didn't.

What I was doing, at age eleven, was using Eichmann as proof that the Holocaust had happened and was every bit as bad as we had heard, and worse. In many ways, serving as proof would be Eichmann's usefulness and purpose in the world and one to which his lack of elegance and his lack of "class" suited him to perfection. Prior to the trial, in several U.S. publications, Israeli prime minister David Ben-Gurion had claimed that the purpose of the trial was less to convict Eichmann than to remind the world of its complicity in Jewish deaths and to rally Israel's teenagers around knowledge of the Shoah.[45] The prosecution called ninety survivors as witnesses, most of whom had had no contact with Eichmann, "to move men's hearts" and display, in richer and more personal detail than had been available before, the full extent of the Final Solution.[46] As recently as 2001, when David Irving sued Deborah Lipstadt for libel for calling him a Holocaust denier, Lipstadt's defense hinged on proving that there had been gas chambers at Auschwitz; as evidence, it requested, and received from Israel, Eichmann's memoir.[47] I was a little younger than Ben-Gurion's target audience—a "gentile" kid in Brooklyn. But I was deeply moved by the concentration camps and committed to raising the subject with friends like Connie and with the nuns at my catechism class. The article about Eichmann hit me like an arrow.

In 1960, *Life* gave me pictures. It gave me documentary evidence of the kind available to the court in Jerusalem. The Eichmann interview and then, later, the Eichmann trial, gave me a sense of having some control of, some support for, what I knew about the Shoah.

Eichmann's capture and trial formed a coming of age for me. But it also formed a coming of age for Israel and for the world. Before the Eichmann trial, public discourse sometimes placed Nazi actions against Jews under the ethnically neutral category of war crimes and crimes against humanity. But, as the record before and since 1945 clearly shows, such crimes rarely occur without ethnic or religious "othering." People understood quite well in private, I believe, that the Nazis had especially targeted Jews, even though they may not have used the word "Jew" out of a misguided sense of politeness. What's more, a greater sense of public reticence about grief and suffering prevailed than prevails today.

Listening to the witnesses at Eichmann's trial, Hannah Arendt felt embarrassed and pained "as witness followed witness and horror was piled upon horror and they [middle-aged refugees like herself] sat there and listened in public to stories they would hardly have been able to endure in private, when they would have had to face the storyteller" (*Eichmann in Jerusalem*, 8).[48] The testimony seemed to her exhibitionist, with the audience as voyeurs, inaugurating what has been called the cult of the survivor.[49] The Eichmann trial entered into the public record histories of the Shoah that had previously been discussed mostly in private. It did not so much provide entirely new information—a claim Peter Novick makes that I find too grand—as break a boundary, or indeed several boundaries.[50] It released a cascade of affect that permanently augmented cultural memory.

Eichmann's Teeth

When Eichmann's testimony began, *Life* magazine saw the accused as "testifying rapidly . . . with towering arrogance," "a good witness, an expert hairsplitter" who dismissed incriminating documents "in a condescending manner with the explanation that some bureaucrat had erred" (June 30, 1961, 46). An earlier article by author Harry Golden had said, "this Adolf Eichmann is really a stranger, a stranger to the human race."[51] Both descriptions stressed control, cunning, skill, haughtiness, inhumanity—pretty much what one would have expected of a major Nazi. They tallied with representations of Eichmann in the popular press, which had moved from substantial reservations about Eichmann's being tried in Israel to a consensus that Eichmann was unquestionably guilty and must be punished.[52] Held in a theater-like setting (the courtroom was a newly completed arts center, converted for the occasion), the trial seemed in danger of proceeding directly to the hanging.

In fact, the night after the trial began—almost half a year before the court would reach its verdict—CBS aired an hour-length docudrama on Eichmann called *Engineer of Death,* which flashed brief historical footage from the Nuremberg trials alongside longer re-creations of testimony implicating Eichmann. It erroneously created the impression that Eichmann had already been convicted at Nuremberg by blurring all lines between fact and fiction. With no verbal or visual disclaimers at any time, it showed an actor playing Eichmann committing acts beyond those with which he had been charged and it provided a motive for why "the second Adolf" had become a fanatic: he looked Jewish, befriended Jews, and spoke Hebrew and Yiddish. In what may have been intended and received as a cautionary tale for America's Jews and gentiles, he supposedly blamed Jews when Nazis beat him. In short, the docudrama added charges and presented "facts" beyond those at Eichmann's trial and it predecided many issues judged there.[53]

In the curious way that media genealogies can work, the 1961 docudrama's view of Eichmann became standard stuff. The landmark 1978 mini-series *Holocaust,* for example, split Eichmann into two characters: the "historical" character named Adolf Eichmann (played by Tom Bell) and an entirely fictional character named Major Erich Dorf (played by Michael Moriarty). Tom Bell's character bears Eichmann's name but appears only briefly and is little more than a cipher. Moriarty's character becomes a central figure in the plot and performs the deeds attributed to Eichmann in the popular imagination, though he is called, on the show, Major Dorf. He runs the show at Wannsee instead of serving as organizer and secretary, as Eichmann had; he invents the language of the Final Solution rather than parroting it like Eichmann; he observes the murders in Poland, as Eichmann did, but is put in charge of the concentration camps, as Eichmann was not. By the end of the show, he's tormented and commits suicide. Splitting "Eichmann" into two characters allowed *Holocaust* to focus on a fictional character who is *like* Adolf Eichmann but who is *not* Adolf Eichmann and could arouse some sympathetic interest in audiences as the convicted and executed murderer could not.

For, by 1978, Eichmann had become a symbol of Nazi genocide, a synonym for evil—that much was firmly established both in the historical record and in cultural memory.[54] He was the demon-Nazi of whom Hitler, Goebbels, and Himmler had denied the world by committing suicide. Who, then, could identify with a monster, like Eichmann? Distancing ourselves from this "outcast from the human race" seemed natural and inevitable—something moral people would do instinctively.

Still, a different image of Eichmann had been evolving from the time of the trial forward that would come to supplement, and to a certain extent to displace, the image of the black-clad master-Nazi. In the evolving image, Eichmann moves from being cruel and powerful in his own person to being a bland, colorless, clerk—a bureaucrat or functionary—even while retaining aspects of the earlier image too. The new image brings Eichmann into line with what I have described as his lack of class—or rather with his possession of the wrong kind of social class.

The pictures. Eichmann's transformation began, I believe, with the pictures. In televised images and in passport-size magazine close-ups, Eichmann's face appeared over and over again, looking not commanding or "toweringly arrogant" as words in *Life* described him, but nondescript. Thin face with sunken cheeks. Some lines, though not deep or dramatic. Sparse hair, sticking up and patted down occasionally by the self-conscious defendant. Middle-aged, middle-European. Ordinary eyes, ordinary build, ordinary though thin and sharp nose, ordinary glasses. Ordinary, ordinary. Except for the mouth, which looked peculiar—like a hole or, alternately, like a twitch or a grimace.

Life gave a concrete, mundane explanation for the mouth: Eichmann's teeth had been removed for the trial, though a puzzle still remains since Eichmann's teeth show in some, but not all, of the photographs *Life* printed.[55] In *The Trial of Adolf Eichmann*, ABC also noted removal of the teeth, though no other video source does and no source gives a definitive reason. Hannah Arendt says that Eichmann's teeth were "ill-fitting" and her remark may help to explain why Eichmann sometimes wears his teeth and sometimes does not: they were probably removed for some portions of the trial but not for others.

The status of Eichmann's teeth may seem trivial. But trivia can influence the way that visual images help to shape public memory, and even history. Grotesque in its mobility, Eichmann's mouth suggests a man who had developed a facial tic long before the trial began. Knowing this man to have been a Nazi who helped to organize the murder of millions, we cannot help but see guilt at work, or perhaps frustration. Either way, the man looks at once sinister but also ridiculous and contemptible. If Albert

Speer's ascot serves as the perfect synecdoche for his image, Eichmann's teeth serve as the perfect synecdoche for his.[56]

The pictures, the pictures. Much as I hate to say it, because it sounds like punditry, I believe that the pictures started the image of Adolf Eichmann as the company man, the dullish war criminal in the gray flannel suit. Writers named the feelings that the pictures produced. Looking at Eichmann, Harry Golden in *Life* identified him, in passing, as having "an ordinary appearance," like "a bland and colorless little functionary" (April 21, 1961).[57] Then, two years later, but much more extensively, Hannah Arendt saw "the banality of evil," words that have become an image and have stuck, though they are frequently misused.

In 1963 and even today, people often miss the disdain with which Arendt invested the word "normal" (the actual word she used to describe Eichmann, not "ordinary"). She meant to suggest that Eichmann exemplified the shallowness of *conscience* under Nazism, where *morality* was synonymous with orderliness and obedience rather than with ethical action or with what the court called "civil courage."[58] As Zygmunt Bauman puts it, "Hannah Arendt had articulated the question of *moral responsibility for resisting socialization*" because "*in the aftermath of the Holocaust, legal practice, and thus also moral theory, faced the possibility that morality may manifest itself in insubordination towards socially upheld principles . . . defying social solidarity and consensus*" (Bauman's emphasis).[59] We have, as a culture, chosen to remember Eichmann's "ordinariness" in a facile act of identification but chosen to overlook the more rigorous moral choices—choices that may well place us outside of social norms—indicated by Arendt and Bauman.

Eichmann Today

Asked today about the Eichmann trial, people are likely to respond with lessons that have assumed the force of clichés. When he is not the Ur-Nazi of our imaginations—"the second Adolf" or "Hitler's right-hand man"—Eichmann is "the man in the glass booth," an "ordinary," "normal" man, a functionary or a bureaucrat. Eichmann was tried and hung as an example and a warning, people say, because "there is a little Eichmann in all of us." He teaches the familiar lesson, "never again."

A spectator at the trial told ABC in 1997 about "a rat, a mouse with frightened eyes"—perceptions far more likely in 1997 than in 1961, when the momentum of convicting and hanging Adolf Eichmann demanded a villain. The most famous witness at the trial, Yehiel Dinur, moved from describing Eichmann as the ice-edged Nazi who had sent him to Auschwitz to describing him as a symbol of humanity: "ordinary" and committing deeds that "anyone could do," "even me!"[60] Publicity postcards for Eyal Sivan's documentary *The Specialist,* distributed in New York in 2000, show Eichmann at age fifty-four in full face, in black outline against a red background (the colors of the Reich). He's tilted to the side and his face wears what I'd describe as a goofy little smile. "The extraordinary trial of a frighteningly ordinary man," the postcard says. All of these descriptions stress ordinariness and all stem from the pictures and from Hannah Arendt's oft-quoted summation of Eichmann as "the banality of evil." But they reduce her formulation to a surprising willingness—given the moral stakes involved, one might even say an astonishing willingness—to see Adolf Eichmann as "one of us."

For, when all is said and done, Eichmann was more than just an ordinary bureaucrat, more than, in 1950s parlance, the man in the gray flannel suit. He was the man in the gray flannel suit who willingly serves the state in an era when the nation-state uses its authority to command immoral acts. He was the man in the gray flannel suit gone over to Big Brother. He was the man who looks out for himself as Number One under conditions when the state has become lawless and murderous.

In this book, I have posited an ethics of empathy and identification that proceeds according to each situation. Under these terms, is identification with Adolf Eichmann a reasonable act? Only, I would claim, under generalizations so large as to be almost meaningless: he was a human being, he did these things; I am a human being, I could do these things, and so forth. But not if identification means what a spokesman like Yehiel Dinur literally says: that every human being, including oneself, would willingly and repeatedly facilitate or commit mass murder.

In fact, the cliché "Eichmann is in all of us," which gets used with good intentions, has become oddly comforting because it is largely meaningless and by and large untrue. Lots of people alive today and, as the court showed, even a small but demonstrable number of people who served the Nazi state refused or would refuse to kill Jews. The court examined at least two specific instances worth revisiting, especially when war crimes are in the air: Anton Schmid and a small number of men in the *Einsatzgruppen.*[61]

Corporal Anton Schmid was a soldier on the Eastern front who, observing what was being done to Jews, felt compelled to help Jewish partisans, despite his reasonable enough concern for his own safety. He provided guns and trucks, even though he knew it was against his own self-interest, and dangerous. Unlike others, he took no money for his aid. With a simplicity that some might be tempted to consider naive, he wrote his wife from prison shortly before his execution as a traitor, "I merely behaved as a human being." In 2001, the German government belatedly honored Schmid as embodying the spirit it hoped for in the new German army.[62]

Similarly, a small but demonstrable number of *Einsatzgruppen* members, when asked to shoot Jews, refused, evaded action, or requested transfer, without penalty.[63] Despite several histrionic gestures toward suicide as his only way out of his situation, Eichmann would have risked neither personal danger nor the safety of his family had he opted out of genocide—though he might have suffered a drop in prestige. Eichmann not only stayed in his job long after he knew what deportation meant, he bragged about his knowledge and took pride in a job well done. Not everyone behaved or would behave like Eichmann. And the judges spent time establishing that fact before they hung him.[64]

I have said in passing that Eichmann was a family man, someone who waited patiently to bring his wife and sons to Argentina and did so to his cost.[65] So was Albert Speer who, we might recall, "betrayed" Hitler by spiriting his family away to safety. So were Nazi officers who brought their families to live with them in the camps and others who organized orchestras at death camps. The family pictures *Life* printed told a partial truth about Eichmann, albeit one most people do not want to hear. As Hannah Arendt says in *The Origins of Totalitarianism*, "family men" like Eichmann can be dangerous under totalitarianism because they sometimes look out first and foremost for themselves and their families, obeying government orders without demurral. To use a somewhat different register, throughout his life, Eichmann practiced the art of looking out for number one—an advertising slogan in our day that percolates through our lives: be the best that you can be; have a better cell phone or better sneakers than others; you deserve it; living well is the best revenge.[66]

Politicians typically conceive of family life as teaching proper values and hence as an unqualified good within democracy. Even hard-edged antiwar literature can turn sentimental about husbands and wives, parents and children: it's part of our cultural wiring, part of our hard wiring perhaps—impossible to tell. But Arendt's insight opens up a startling perspective on the possible demands of family life. For looking out for ourselves and for our families can mean doing anything that serves our own best interests; under certain conditions, it need not lead to moral action at all. How prevalent is the notion of looking out for Number One? Not everywhere, to be sure, in our time; but at least as prevalent as other values.[67]

Yet when people say, "Eichmann is in all of us," they do not mean such ordinary vices as angling for the best place on line or for the nicest house and car on the block. They vault over such quotidian vices to identify with mass murder. It's even likely that quotidian points of possible identification with Eichmann—his social class, his status as a family man, his assiduous desire to please—embarrass us and make us uncomfortable. More so, apparently, than the willingness to avow mass murder! For when we say "Eichmann is in all of us," what we are really saying is, "I could be Eichmann": that is, I would organize, knowingly and voluntarily, year after year, the death of millions. Most of us know that statement to be false—and so we can sleep at night.

But if we said instead, "Anyone could be Eichmann" (even an Adolf Eichmann or, better, even an Albert Speer), we would tell a harder truth, stressing instead the *arbitrariness* of the Holocaust, the *contingency* of everyone's existence. For that is the real shock here, a shock that instantiates the war complex. In the same way, evading contingency and the nervous fates that hold us all, we commonly speak of rights as "human rights" and as "universal." But as we have seen again and again, most recently since 9/11, only states can enforce such rights, and they can pursue or drop enforcement pretty much at will.[68]

While the analogy between ourselves and Eichmann seems to implicate us all as potential perpetrators of evil, what it really does is to exculpate us and to let us off the hook. By repeating that "there is a little Eichmann in all of us," we lay down a voodoo charm of protection that allows the words to slip off of us like Teflon. For we know, among other things, that "we" (the United States at Nuremberg; the Israelis in Jerusalem) held war crimes trials. Could the judges become the accused? Could victims become perpetrators? In two controversial decisions ultimately reversed or undercut by his own government, Judge Halevi, the most flamboyant judge at Eichmann's trial, had ruled that victims could indeed become perpetrators. But Halevi was a maverick—and perceived that way at the time.[69] And, in recent history, the United States has unblushingly sought to exclude its citizens from any possible world court, seeing any charges against Americans as perforce "political."[70] For does the logic of war crimes trials not demand that those who hold them would never commit crimes against humanity?

In fact, the history of genocide both before and after 1945 has been anything but simple or easy. In the 1930s and during World War II, the Allies made choices that left Europe's Jews to their fate—most famously the refusal of refugees and the decision (still a source of controversy) not to bomb German camps. So did Ben-Gurion's party when, as the dominant group in what was then Palestine, it decided to devote its energies and funds to founding a Jewish state rather than to rescuing Europe's Jews (Segev, 18–20, 85). In similarly devious, sometimes unseeing ways, the United States backed the Khmer Rouge before finding Pol Pot murderous; the same for Osama Bin Laden and for Saddam Hussein.[71]

Cultural memory prefers to avoid ambiguities, especially on subjects like war crimes and crimes against humanity. It thrives on black and white, good and evil. The cliché "Eichmann is in all of us" sounds like an immersion in the gray zone, an acceptance of the complexities and ambiguities of identification—but it's not. In fact, it evades the ethical process of identification and empathy I have described, which requires not blanket identification with anyone and anything at all, but parsing the possibilities of empathy and identification situation by situation.

An entry for Eichmann in Flaubert's "dictionary of received ideas"—a compendium of what everybody already knows, the persistence of certain easily repeated ideas and norms—might read: "'The man in the glass booth.' He looks ordinary, banal. He should not have followed orders." Easily repeatable, the ideas blunt reality.[72] Eichmann's ghost remains the undead in our culture. Known, but not known. A cipher rather than a felt reality. The ordinary man, the family man, as war criminal. The war criminal to end all war criminals—except that he wasn't.

CHAPTER THREE

CITIZENS OF
THE HOLOCAUST

The Vernacular of Growing
Up after World War II

Some Memories of Not Getting to Germany

In the summer of 1970, I took a post-college, summer-long, Eurailpass tour of Europe. As I traveled, I picked up books other tourists had left behind. In Lucerne, my husband found Leon Uris's *Mila 18*, a novel about the destruction of the Warsaw ghetto. I found Harrison Salisbury's *Stalingrad*, a detailed history of the vicious siege. Although it was August as I wended my way from Rome to Rimini and back, in the book, winter arrives and the siege gets longer. Details get grimmer. All the cats and dogs have been eaten and it's the rats' and roaches' turn next. Soon even these come to seem like the rarest of delicacies. Human bodies begin to clog the streets.

We board a train heading north for Denmark, expecting to get off in Frankfurt, where my husband's older brother had spent five years in the 1950s, to the despair of his parents, who had lost most of their relatives in Poland. One of the family mysteries is why Vic chose Germany, so soon after the war, and how he could have fallen in love with the much-older widow of a German soldier who, showing great wisdom, refused to marry him.

When the train arrives at the German border, the border police behave brusquely and aggressively. The Italians had said simply, "Eurailpass?" and waved cheerfully without checking either passes or passports. The Germans wake everyone up and inspect each document, bumping some passengers to different carriages for no apparent reason. We exchange glances and agree: we will stay aboard until the end of the line, in Copenhagen.

*   *   *

Now, it's the summer of 1979 and I am once again taking a train from Italy northward, this time into Austria. As we cross the Italian Alps, a man enters our compartment and asks, in a German accented Italian, if he may sit. *Ja. Bitte.* Of course. My eyes keep roaming to his hands, which are missing several fingers and to his eyes, which have a steely glint and a slight but regular twitch. I am twenty-nine that year. The man is well into his fifties with a grim, timeworn look. His age and mien fit, perfectly, those of a veteran from the war.

At the conference I attend in Austria, most of the speakers are the German man's age, or older. At dinners, the topic strays repeatedly to World War II. One man, an Austrian mathematician, now a British citizen, says that he has not been back to Austria since the war. He served in the underground; the Nazis shot his entire family in reprisal. Almost all the conversations are like that: flatly stated reminders of old pain, still present. During the week, conference members have two different choices for a day trip: north into Munich or south, back across the Italian Alps, into Bolzano. Munich has museums, fairy-tale castles, and shops. Although I have just crossed the Alps and have not yet been to Germany, guess which of the two I chose.

*   *   *

Now, it's the spring of 1993 and I am in Jerusalem, taking some tours while lecturing at Tel Aviv University. At Yad Vashem, I wait outside along a road planted with trees for righteous gentiles while my husband finishes the chronological exhibits at Israel's Holocaust memorial. I had started the museum too but stopped at a 1942 photo I have seen before of a naked woman being herded toward a ditch, her soft round flanks exposed, her arms furtively covering her breasts. It's like other familiar photos, including one of a darkly clothed woman bowing her head, her body pitched to the right like a desperate dancer, with one foot raised perhaps six inches from the ground. In her arms is a young child, also clothed in black. Her head bows partly in despair and partly in a protective gesture toward the child. To the left stands a uniformed guard, rifle pointed at the woman. It's a snuff shot, vivid and obscene.

My twelve and ten year olds are with me and, by this time, they are becoming visibly upset. That's why I decide to wait outside with my daughters, giving them a chance to encounter the photos at their chosen time.

A group of German tourists descends from a bus. Perhaps fifty men and women, chattering like any excited vacationers. It's an older group, probably of retirees, with most people well past their sixties. I feel surprised that German tourists that age would come to Yad Vashem. I ask the Israeli guide standing nearby about the group. "Oh, yes. They love to come here. Mostly church groups. In fact, Germans are our largest group of tourists," she says, raising her eyebrows and shrugging, with a tight, wry smile.

What is the source of these erratic decisions, these odd prejudices, so irrational and so unfair many decades after World War II has ended? They jar, to an embarrassing extent, with the process toward an ethics of empathy and identification I espouse with my conscious mind. Why do I recall such snapshots of decisions not to visit Germany? Do I instinctively blame ordinary Germans for the war?

At the conscious level, the answer is, of course, No. If asked, I would say that I have neutral or favorable feelings toward Germany, as most Americans do, although honest social scientists note that the statistics contradict what we might call the vernacular of cultural memory, where feelings remain more complex.[1] I have had German colleagues and German students and, for them, the burdens of being German are clear and present. Some have lived up to stereotypes of cold efficiency (one man even clicks his heels), and some have not—pretty much in ratios like those one might find for stereotypes about other ethnicities. The Germans I know may be guilty of various things; but they are innocent, absolutely, of anything that happened during the war. I do not at all blame, with my conscious mind, Germans under a certain age.

Yet even as I write the words "Germans under a certain age," I have sprung a trap. I am inside a question that galvanized writing about World War II in the 1990s: were ordinary Germans above a certain age responsible for the war and for the Holocaust? Or were they cogs in a machine, unwilling witnesses, even, deep-down, psychological resisters? Were they as surprised as everyone else to be offered the chance, at times the order, to shoot one or two hundred Jews, one or two thousand in a day, close-up with a shot to the neck? Or, more distantly, to use a machine gun alongside a ditch? Or to cram Jews into railroad cars and bring them to the camps? Or to lead them to the gas, knowing what would follow and seeing the results, over and over again? Men, women, and, children de-stroyed—in the gas, especially the elderly and the children. Did they wonder, as almost everyone else has since, how such things could have happened? Were they appalled? indifferent? willing? Even for those clearly guilty of deliberate murder, is it time and more than time, as some would claim, that the world moved on and gave up the idea of pursuit and punishment?

In *Reading the Holocaust,* Inga Clendinnen stakes out an anthropolog-ical view that sees Nazis as different from us but still human; she urges us to put Nazis back into the pictures that remain of the Holocaust since the Jews they killed are dead but the Nazis may survive. I find her reasoning on this point odd—almost a matter of rewarding the perpetrators just for having survived those they murdered.[2] Others have written of the in-creasingly vexed issue of trials for war criminals, especially recent cases like Klaus Barbie and "Ivan the Terrible." Is it time to aim for something like understanding, if not forgiveness? I have no firm answers to these questions, though I do have strong opinions, deep and deep-seated. I am okay with understanding; I do not incline toward forgiveness.

This chapter explores the theme of ordinary people like me who did not experience but grew up with knowledge of the Holocaust, which re-mains a volatile topic. It consists of discrete but linked sections that ex-plore the state of private and public discourse among what we might call citizens of the Holocaust. I include under that term, whose usefulness I would like to test, all those who feel involvement, connection, responsi-bility, and a sense of belonging with regard to the Holocaust—and also, therefore, not just the possibility of or imperative for ethical thought and action, but also more disparate and covert feelings of possessiveness, ob-session, shame, guilt, secretiveness, hesitancy, and blockage. Two of the sections are analytic. The rest fall under the categories of oral and per-sonal history, which have been important to this book's attempt to track emotions as they interact with public discourse and with recorded history. The final section returns to the theme of ethical action, working with Alain Badiou's concept of the immortal.

Growing Up with the Holocaust: My Own Memories,
Followed by an Analytic Turn

All my life, I have thought about what it meant for men, women, children, families to have had their lives disrupted by the war—working in factories, drafted into the special world of the military, or, far worse, forced to leave their homes, abused, and subject to arbitrary death—living suspended lives for a period of five to seven years. The disruption of ordinary lives was my emotional point of entry into World War II: the way that "home" ceased to be a place of safety; the way that no place was safe for many people for a protracted period of time. The first documentary I saw about the concentration camps (at the age of seven or eight) made me throw up and ask questions at catechism that got me, usually a "good girl," into trouble. My favorite fantasies about the war were being a resistance fighter in Norway or France or a righteous gentile.[3]

I felt a deep, visceral reaction to the Holocaust—a topic that reduced me for years, quite literally, to tears. Although I never planned it, it is perhaps not entirely accidental that I have always had friends who are survivors' children and that I married at a young age into a Jewish family. If asked, I might have attributed the intensity of my feelings to my marital family, in which my husband and I, after thinking about choices like Unitarianism, decided to celebrate the traditions with which we had grown up, giving our children their choice of religion or the choice to have none at all. As a result, and without any disagreements or discomfort, my husband and older daughter are Jewish, I am a lapsed Catholic, and my younger daughter has no religious affiliation but considers herself half-Jewish and half-Catholic by acculturation, an identity that, if avowed in public, would have been considered Jewish under the Nuremberg Laws. Those laws, almost always prefaced by the adjective "infamous" but little read or even understood today, underwent a long process of revision and negotiation before being promulgated in 1935. They inscribed the so-called "¾ rule" by which people who had three Jewish grandparents were automatically considered Jewish, whether or not they practiced Judaism. Those with two Jewish grandparents and two non-Jewish grandparents (*Mischlinge* grades I and II, depending on further details) were Jewish if they practiced Judaism, were the product of a Jewish/non-Jewish marriage or extramarital affair, or were married to a Jew.[4]

If asked, I might have attributed my deep feelings about the Holocaust to identifying imaginatively with how my family might have been torn apart under Nazi law. In doing so, I would have fallen into a syndrome Peter Novick describes for Jews, but is in fact much broader, in which the fact of *not* having experienced the Holocaust constitutes a bond with those who died.[5]

But as I researched complex issues like the Eichmann trial, the subject of chapter 2, I realized that the Holocaust has been cosseted by sentimentalizing and by taboos, some of which I shared. As 2000 passed into 2001, the Irving-Lipstadt trial—in which Holocaust denial, whose victory was much feared as the trial began, proved a paper tiger—and the volatile issue of reparations for survivors' heirs suggested that our culture is moving rapidly through different stages in its understanding of the Holocaust. The transitions come naturally from the passage of time and the death of survivors—facts often noted but surprisingly little processed. But they also come from the accumulated burden, the direction and the tenor, of the work that has been done to date.[6]

Early survivor testimonies, like Primo Levi's, had questioned the right of survivors to speak, noting that they were not always the best or the good—those who most *deserved* to speak. Luck would intervene, and craftiness. So that all survivors, Levi claimed, bear a burden of guilt—at the very least, for "having omitted to offer help" because, quite naturally in the camps, "you take care of yourself first of all."[7]

Levi's voice, so rough, so eloquent, stilled itself in death and, since the time he wrote, a very different and almost entirely laudatory sense of the survivor's voice has emerged.[8] Alan Mintz puts it well when he notes that "the shift from silence to salience is surely one of the most stunning developments in American culture in our time."[9] Indeed, a hierarchy exists for narratives of the Shoah, a hierarchy that both publishing and the academy continue to observe but rather more rarely mention or question. Survivors, like Elie Wiesel, come at the top and sometimes zealously guard their position. Those survivors who claim, as Levi did, only modest agency or authority can get drowned out in our culture's will to applaud survival in and of itself. The authority accorded to survivors can make itself felt even on weighty scholars like Zygmunt Bauman, author of the award-winning *Modernity and the Holocaust,* who felt the need, as I have several times, to claim a Jewish connection through a spouse or a spouse's lost European relatives—even while protesting both the feeling and the need.[10]

When, as in the recent Wilkomirski scandal, survivor testimony proves false, the situation tests the ethics of identification. If someone who mourns the Holocaust as deeply as Wilkomirski does could falsely claim to have survived the camps—the scandal made people ask—how can we be sure that our identification with the Shoah is real and not deluded or self-serving? The problem with the question is that it assumes absolutes in situations where grays often prevail. For, despite repeated calls for analysis, we have currently no means of *evaluating* survivor testimony beyond accepting it as true or rejecting it as false, even though it can quite easily be something in between, or both.[11]

Raul Hilberg has recently shown that Holocaust testimony is "a personal account with selected revelations." It is not the same thing as a full and accurate picture of the Holocaust, or even an accurate rendition of personal experience, or even a full and accurate record of personal memory. As Hilberg further notes, survivors represent only a small fraction of those affected by the Shoah and differ demographically from any norm that might be established using country of birth, social class, language skills, degree of religious belief, physical properties, and temperament.[12] What's more, testimony, and especially testimony made long after the fact, often includes what people have heard as well as what people saw— as Hilberg puts it, "rumor, which is itself always a fact" (*Sources*, 162).

In the hierarchy of Holocaust narratives, after testimony by survivors, writing from what is usually called "the second-generation" counts next, whether the second generation is reckoned as the children of those who actually lived through the camps or, more loosely, as those with some kind of genealogical connection to the Holocaust or to World War II more generally—often a parent's experiences or deeds.[13] Art Spiegelman records the phenomenon with wit and wisdom in the dual time frames of *Maus*. In the two-page Preface to Part I, for example, young Art wants to play outside with his friends when his father needs some help indoors. "FRIENDS? Your friends? If you lock them together in a room with no food for a week, THEN you could see what it is, FRIENDS," his father says, applying lessons that had served him well in the camps but seem over-the-top in ordinary life.

Although some of Spiegelman's narrative (the scenes concerning his mother's suicide; those narrating his reluctance to begin his book) record his sleeplessness and stress, the book clearly distinguishes between being traumatized, having short-term trauma-like reactions, and being influenced or even in thrall as one grows up to someone else's trauma. *Maus* maintains what seems to me an appropriate distinction between survivors and their children. But, in practice, the boundaries between these conditions, like the purview of the word *trauma* itself, remain quite vexed.[14] In 2000, the Holocaust Memorial Museum mounted a major conference on and for "the second generation" in which "passing the torch" was a frequent image. The Modern Language Association and other professional organizations endorse the same tendency when they organize, as they do with some regularity, panels on "the second generation," a term that assumes that the Holocaust is a legacy, a heritage, an inheritance.[15]

But how, one might ask, do some people born after 1945 inherit the Holocaust while others do not? And what, one might ask, is the Holocaust a legacy of? What should we make of the very term *the second generation*—a term borrowed from immigration narratives, where it describes degrees of ethnicity and proximity to "natural-born" citizenship? Is the Holocaust in fact a "citizenship"? If so, who is born a citizen and who can be "naturalized"?[16] Ironically enough, history shows that the Nazis' denial of "citizenship" to Jews helped to facilitate the deportations that fed the camps. Does "citizenship" as a fact and a metaphor make things happen but short-circuit issues of causation?[17]

Secrets and Hesitations

When I began writing this book, I sent an experimental survey to a variety of people—most of them children during the war or, like me, in the postwar generation—asking them to tell me their memories of learning about World War II. It was an informal rather than a scientific experiment, but it produced several striking results.

Many of the differences in the responses I received were based on factors I had expected, such as age, ethnicity, nationality, and parents' histories during the war. But, more surprisingly, some were based on where respondents born in the United States had grown up. Those from the West Coast seemed, for example, far more likely than those from the East to mention the Japanese internment camps. Reiko, a former stockbroker whose family business was confiscated during the war and who spent her youth interned on a farm in Utah, was one example; Chris, an academic not of Japanese descent and at least twenty-five years younger than Reiko, was another.[18] Perhaps not surprisingly, almost all those from the East Coast or of Jewish descent, or both, responded with a memory about growing up with the Holocaust. The pattern seemed to confirm how cultural memory begins in the family and moves out into the proximate community, with memory of the internment camps strongest on the West Coast and memory of the Holocaust strongest in the Northeast.

One man spoke for others when he said, "I cannot remember a time when I did not know that the Nazis had slaughtered the Jews," a topic he found both "taboo" when he was growing up and "fascinating." A second man gave a minority response, citing his sense of outrage and shame that the Jews had not fought back. A third man recalled, "the horror and fascination [that word again] of piles of corpses" and spoke of "memories of horror [that] have become seasoned, distorted, glamorized, even vaguely eroticized." A fourth man who had grown up in New York only after emigrating from Germany told me that 1945–46 "was like attending a year-long wake."[19]

I was unsure how, or even if, I would ever publish the survey I had gathered—which is admittedly unscientific and based on a small sample of fewer than two hundred people, overly skewed toward professionals, and especially people who write or teach, some of them quite well known rather than ordinary people—though they are, of course, ordinary people too. But social scientific surveys, especially those on sensitive topics like sex, politics, and, for that matter, feelings toward Germans after World War II, have problems too. A survey of attitudes toward Germany showed, for example, that Americans say they are overwhelmingly positive about Germans and have been since 1961, the year the Berlin Wall went up, but notes that different attitudes emerge "around the water cooler." What's more, the way questions are asked almost always influences responses, and respondents may give faulty or even false information.[20] So that, small as it was, my survey still seemed worth preserving as part of the vernacular of growing up after World War II. The story of the survey begins with a chance encounter.[21]

*　　*　　*

Shortly after sending out my questionnaire, I met an American acquaintance in London. Not knowing anything about his background, I was surprised by the intensity with which he said, "I owe you a letter but I haven't been able to write it." Fearing the usual story about a busy schedule, I began to murmur some remarks in that direction. But he shook his head and said, "No, I mean I *could not* bring myself to write it though I've been thinking that I'll have to take your invitation and write it sometime." As we talked, I understood the reasons for his hesitation, which, although powerful and unusual, also indicate hesitations many people feel.

My acquaintance taught literature at a large and prestigious state university for many years before his recent retirement; his brother is a journalist.[22] Both were children aboard the *St. Louis,* the ship of Jewish refugees infamously turned away from Havana and New York and forced to return to Europe. His family had moved from Germany to northern Italy after the Nazis rose to power. It was not an entirely good choice, but one good enough to earn them Italian passports and hence the right to disembark in Cuba, where the family lived for two years before securing visas to the United States. This man told me about a Fulbright fellowship in Germany he later won and his mother's reaction, which was to throw out the acceptance letter. Later, she came to visit him during his Fulbright year and set a snotty waiter back on his heels by surprising him with her impeccable German. But, from the various things he told me, I have chosen the story about the *St. Louis* because it resonates strongly with other statements I received.

Poet Alicia Ostriker, for example, similarly recalls an experience from childhood that she has not previously mentioned, one I will quote in full because it is skillfully written:

> One of my earliest childhood memories is the memory of how I "learned"— but that is not the right word—of the destruction of European Jewry. I was six and in the first grade, in the fall of 1944. . . . Sitting on my grandfather's lap as I often did, I asked him who he was going to vote for, for President. . . . My grandfather was silent. Then he said that he was not going to vote. Shocked, I . . . gave him a lecture on his duty to vote. His reply was that he was not going to vote for any President because no President would save the Jews in Europe.
>
> It was the first time I had heard the phrase "the Jews in Europe." . . . My family belonged to a leftwing freethinking strand of Jews and I had never been inside a synagogue or been told about the Jewish holidays. Nor had I been told about anti-Semitism. So I was mystified. But only with one half of my mind. With the other half, as I sat on my grandfather's lap and sensed that he was holding back tears, I seemed strangely to understand exactly what his words signified, and more. . . . This moment changed me permanently, though I never spoke of it to anyone.

"This moment changed me permanently, though I never spoke of it to anyone": I hear in Ostriker's words an echo of the professor's "I owe you a letter but I haven't been able to write it . . . I *could not.*" Both memories involve the family circle and the murder of the Jews in Europe. Both involve an element of things unspoken or sensed, and a contrapuntal movement that both connects children to their elders and marks moves toward independence. Both involve abstractions, like "the Jews in Europe," or "the Germans" or "Germany," abstractions that veer toward recognizable stereotypes. The child is father to the man, insofar as the recollection comes from long ago but the effects have continuing vividness and power.[23]

Novelist Joyce Carol Oates similarly remembers forbidden topics in and around the family circle about the murder of the Jews in Europe:

> In my novel *You Must Remember This,* the young heroine is appalled by an issue of *Life* magazine, and I think this was probably my personal memory, but it was a confused and ahistoric vision (of death camp survivors), with no context to explain it; nor did I have anyone to talk with about it. My family was a warm, close-knit family but my parents weren't comfortable with such discussions, perhaps like many people whose educations have been abruptly terminated, and they would never have initiated them. The Holocaust may have simply been too horrific to speak of; my father's mother was the daughter of German Jews who'd come to the United States in the 1890's and assimilated, changing their name, and it seems to me that the very words "Jew"—"Jewish"—were never uttered in our household.

Quite by coincidence, like many of those who supplied me with memories, Ostriker and the literature professor are Jewish.[24] With just one assimilated German Jewish grandmother and a secular past, Oates would not be considered Jewish, even under the racist Nuremberg Laws. Her family's way of dealing with the Holocaust was to avoid it as a distant and unpleasant topic. But it would not be too much to say—indeed, Oates hints as much—that knowledge of the death camps became a resonant fact in her imagination, one that helped to form her often-scary image of the human mind and sympathy with the outsider's point of view.

And so, I will want to say outright that not all of those who were children during World War II or are in the postwar generation and had their lives changed by the Holocaust are Jews. That may seem like a kind of nonstatement, except that even good books, like Peter Novick's recent *The Holocaust in America,* ignore, and even denigrate as superficial, "gentile" (Novick's word) interest in the Shoah.

I'd like to use a famous photograph to illustrate what I mean. The photograph shows two young girls aboard the *St Louis* as it sailed from New York after being denied entry. The girls are well dressed and pretty, obviously well cared for. Their faces wear expressions of great sadness. Glimpsed through a porthole, framed by it, they look angelic, but also trapped. Their sadness mirrors ours and creates a sense of shame at their possible fate. The writing professor's connection to the photograph is intimate; he may even have played aboard ship with these very children.

But few observers can regard such images with blank indifference. Most will immediately identify with the photograph from spots in the middle distance: not immediately or genealogically connected but connected nonetheless through a pervasive feeling of identification based on a feeling of belonging akin to that of a citizenship. Most people alive today share vantage spots on World War II in the middle distance. The closest of these middle distances, as Art Spiegelman's *Maus* quite brilliantly attests, is, of course, that of survivors' children.

Now I am sitting with an old friend in her house in Tel Aviv. While we were still students, this woman wrote one of the first pieces I had read in which the critic assumes a fully autobiographical voice. She was born after the war, as I was, in the United States, though she is now married to an Israeli and a long-term resident of Israel. I knew, because she had told me early in our friendship, that her parents were survivors. Her essay describes her feelings about an Anne Frank necklace she received at age thirteen, which always made her feel as though Anne's death reproached her own happy life.[25]

Her father adored his only daughter and made her life as magical as possible. But he had a peculiar habit of taking her out and then abruptly disappearing in public places. If my friend called out to him, he would mimic her cry and then cradle her protectively; afterward, he loved to repeat the story of these scenes. After his sudden death from a heart attack, the mystery of his actions revealed itself.

Cleaning out his wallet, Hana found, folded behind his papers, a soiled and worn black and white photo of a five-year-old boy: her half brother, of whose existence she had known but whose picture she had never seen, the product of her father's first marriage. Hidden from the Nazis among Christians, the boy had also had a doting father, but one who just could not resist visiting. His visits revealed the secret. One day, "he arrived to find that his son was gone" and, Hana speculates, the "little boy's imagined pleading cry for his missing father must have tormented him every day of his life as he looked at the photograph. And perhaps being able to 'rescue' me during those moments when I called out to him for protection were necessary reenactments for him."

The son and his mother died in Treblinka; my friend does not specify (or perhaps does not know) details. It is 1993 when we sit in her house discussing a book proposal she had written for expanding her wonderful essay into a book about Anne Frank, probing the idealizations and oversimplifications, the possessiveness and feuds that surround her story—a book since written, but not by my friend. For at the time, she spoke about not being able to begin her book, despite being so obviously prepared to write it. When I asked why, she mentioned the sensitivity of the topic in Israel, where she lives and works. But there was something else, a something she could not specify, which I suspect has to do with her father: more secrets and hesitations, which emerge as a theme, a major theme, in childhood memories about the war and the question of who can talk about it, and how.

Now it is 1999 and I am sitting in a restaurant with a woman I have known since elementary school. Like my other friend, she is the only child of survivors and I have been aware of that ever since we were very young. Her feisty mother, now in her nineties, wore the first faint blue tattooed number on her wrist that I had ever seen, an object I found fascinating. Rosa knows about my project and is willing to share. When I ask about the fact that so many survivors have just a single child, she says, "Partly, it was age. My mother was in the camps during her twenties and she was in her thirties by the time she got to the United States. But I think it was the feeling that they had to have a child—to have a stake in life—but just one since having more would be risky. My mother always says that she felt dead after the war. That she didn't give birth to me, I gave birth to her."[26]

It's a fragile moment, one that brings lumps to both our throats. And, like many such moments, it goes toward story. "My mother likes to tell how, when I was around eighteen months, she heard a crash from the living room and raced in to find me holding the cord of a lamp, standing in the middle of broken glass. 'Lamp gone, lamp all gone' I said. And my mother says that was the first time she remembers laughing since the war. You and I have children. We know how funny they can be as babies. But it took until I was *that* old, and the broken lamp, for her to laugh." It is, of course, a wonderful story. "Lamp gone. Lamp all gone": humor only a survivor could love.

At this dinner, I ask Rosa about two of the texts I planned to write about—*Hitler's Willing Executioners* and *Fragments*. She's an operations research engineer and business school dean, with a literary bent, and knows about the books but hasn't wanted to read them. At an earlier meeting, I'd asked her about Art Spiegelman's *Maus*, which she had not read either, though they speak, so clearly, to her complex feelings about her parents. Now Rosa elaborates, saying that she's fascinated by World War II and the Holocaust, but also can't come too near them, probably because she heard about them so young, and from her parents. "It makes my parents feel special that they're survivors," she says, "But, you know, survivors' children aren't necessarily the best people to speak about the Holocaust. Maybe they're even the worst—because it's too close."[27]

By 1999, I had begun to draft several portions of this book and was surprised to find that some people I respect did not want me to write it. One friend was even willing to rupture our friendship over the issue: it did not play to my strengths, she said; it was not consistent with my earlier work; I could write about World War II but should not tackle the Holocaust as a subject—a limitation I tried to accept but found I just could not. What these people may also have meant but did not say was that I am not Jewish, have no direct connection to the Holocaust by life history, and am not a historian, the kind of writer everyone agrees can address the topic. Sensing connections with my earlier work, and feeling that identity politics had misfired, I resisted, but then spent several years reading history. I began to see some flaws in available archives but nonetheless armed earlier versions of this chapter like an armadillo. In the end, as the current chapter will attest, I felt willing to let go of some of the armor, though I felt and feel nervous—a secret and hesitation of my own—as I drop each chink. Part of the process of breaking through my blockages about the Holocaust came (as the Prologue describes) after 9/11; but part came from the experience of finally getting to Germany.

Ordinary Germans: An Oral History Followed by a Second Analytic Turn

In 2000, I decided it was time to visit Germany and made two separate trips to Berlin and then, in 2001, more extensively into Franconia and Bavaria, including Munich. Most of the cities I visited had been bombed extensively during the war; different decisions had been made about how to rebuild them—modernization in the former West Berlin; replication of historic cities in Nuremberg and Würzburg. Everywhere I went, I encountered polite people. Helpful people. Efficient people. People admiring of the United States, even on my second trip, during the trying first year of the Bush presidency. Cultured people. Musical people. Food-loving people with large street markets and stores and with numerous ways to capitalize on leisure and on pleasure.

Still, in every city and on many streets, I saw telltale signs of one of the underlying attitudes that made National Socialism attractive: as W. G. Sebald puts it, the Germans' "unquestioning work ethic" and celebrated love of order show up even in the countryside, where everything is "straightened out and tidied up as it is up to the last square inch and corner" ("Natural History," 12; *Vertigo,* 253). Germans stand and wait long minutes at street corners rather than cross a completely empty street on a red light. When it rains on Sunday, no street merchants crop up in Berlin (as they do in New York) to sell cheap umbrellas; finding an umbrella took me the major part of a day, since only certain stores sell *schirms* and these stores are uniformly closed on Sundays. Trains are clearly and almost obsessively marked. They are rarely late and never early. An early train waits outside the station until the clock coincides with the posted hour so that everything works on time, just perfectly. On multiple occasions, I recognized with a start signs of what, following Claudia Koonz, I call in chapter 2 "the Nazi conscience," whereby Hitler appealed to Germans by making prejudice against outsiders seem not just rational but also virtuous. The "Nazi conscience" helps to explain Nazi history, which otherwise in Germany today seems so . . . well, unthinkable.

In summer 2001, I attended a conference in Bamburg where, in tantalizing ways, conversations supplemented the survey I had taken about growing up with knowledge of the Holocaust. On the most dramatic occasion, I found myself at an extensive meal and wine tasting with two men, both apparently German, at which the conversation took a startling turn. At first, the men bantered in what seems the universal manner of professors. But when I commented on the rebuilding of cities like Würzburg and Nuremberg as replicas of their prewar selves, the dialogue became explosive.

"Oh yes, the Germans like to say that they lost 100% in the War. But Poland lost 150%," the younger man (who was fifty-four, in my own postwar cohort) said. Sensing for the first time that the man was Polish (he had seemed German and spoke the language impeccably), I asked one of the questions I had asked on the questionnaire I described earlier in this chapter: what did he remember learning about the war when he was growing up? The thoroughness of his answer overwhelmed me.

His parents, he said, had come from large families—eight sisters and eight brothers, few of whom survived the war. One was a Resistance fighter, shot in an action. One was apolitical but was shot in reprisal as one of fifty Poles seized at random to avenge a German death. ("Polish trash, you see" the man says, his lips contorting.) The grim catalogue climaxed with the story of a sailor on a Polish submarine submerged when the Germans invaded that did not surrender until its supplies ran out. The Germans accepted the surrender but then took the sailors back out to sea on a barge they sank in the Baltic. One man was allowed to swim to shore and survive if he could—as he did, to bear witness—though that man was not the Polish professor's uncle.

Not wanting to get in the way of his recollections—which fleshed out the devastating ethnic persecution Poles experienced, a frequent ellipsis in American and European cultural memory—I murmured something noncommittal about having thought he was German. He erupted in an unexpected direction. "No; no. But we're all friends now," he said, gesturing expansively to the other man on my left, with whom he indeed had an old friendship. "It's all global now. Has to be. So we have this amnesia," he said, tapping his head.[28]

My husband, my collaborator on such occasions, turned to the German man to my left and asked when he had been born: 1934, he said—a significant date since he falls into the prewar generation, though he would have been eleven at the war's end—too young to be held responsible. But, rather than leave it there, he continued—almost as a kind of compulsion.

He and his mother, he said, left Berlin in 1942 to escape the bombing. He talked briefly about the countryside where he lived but said nothing about the bombing itself. What he recalled most was how his father, who did not like the National Socialists, would be solicited to join: "every Sunday, every Sunday they would come and say that he must not be patriotic. That he must dislike Hitler because he would not join." A pause. "We like to think we would be heroic," he said, "that we would stand out, but who knows, really?" Then he went on, musingly—or was it out of practice: "And then, after the War, the Communists came and arrested my father for being a National Socialist."

One person who read this manuscript suggested, plausibly in the abstract, that the remark testified only to the no-win situation at the time: the man's father was in danger for not joining the party; then, after the war, he was in danger, even though he had not joined. But my dinner companion's tone, facial expression, and body language were unmistakable, especially around the phrases "we like to think that we would be heroic, that we would stand out, but who knows, really?": the German man had said more than he had intended before the Americans and his Polish colleague; he wanted to conclude his confession with an ellipsis.

My next questions might have been: so *did* your father join the party?

When? Was he in the military? Why did the Soviets single him out? But I was at a dinner and a wine tasting, not an inquisition. The conversation had flown pretty deeply in the direction I had steered it, and, in the perhaps misguided interest of politeness, I did not press further. Still this man—this perfectly nice, highly intelligent man—had given himself away. What did your father (or grandfather) do during the war? Such simple, homey questions. Questions that send shock-waves through Germans and generate secrets, hesitations, and blockages of their own that can and do erupt into huge public controversies, like the fascinating recent dispute about ordinary Germans and the Holocaust.

*   *   *

When Daniel Jonah Goldhagen published *Hitler's Willing Executioners: Ordinary Germans and the Holocaust* in 1996, German reviews appeared even in advance of European publication. Most reviewers took positions already marked in the United States but took them far more strongly. Goldhagen tells us nothing new, critic after critic said, and the author does not sufficiently acknowledge his indebtedness to other scholars. Goldhagen gives just one cause for the Holocaust (anti-Semitism), reviewers complained, and such explanations remain blunt, but insufficient. Goldhagen asserts rather than proves, critics maintained, and the book suffers as a result from overwriting, repetition, and faulty, circular logic. To begin with men one *knows* participated in murder (as Goldhagen did, working only with the *Einsatzgruppen*) and then show that they were "ordinary Germans" does not justify the leap that ordinary Germans, all of them, were willing murderers of Jews.

But despite the book's flaws—and even Goldhagen acknowledges it has some—vehemence pervaded the German reviews that everyone, including many German commentators, found troubling. The reviews identified Goldhagen's Jewishness as instrumental to his book, labeling him as the "son of a Jewish historian from Rumania," citing "Old Testament rage," and eying suspiciously "Jewish columnists" and "nonhistorians" in the United States. Although the German scholars hated how Goldhagen had revived notions of collective German guilt prevalent immediately after the war, they moved with shocking speed to stereotypes about "Jewish" temperament and Jewish media conspiracies that have proved so much more dangerous.[29]

The story of what happened next, of Goldhagen and his book in Germany, forms the stuff of legend. Goldhagen went to Germany to debate his critics in public: Daniel in the lion's den, a pundit quipped. But the ordeal quickly turned into what Volker Ullrich called "A Triumphal Procession."[30] Seated among his gray-haired critics—pale from years spent in archives and visibly angry—sat the boyish, Tom Hanks–like, assistant professor from Harvard, looking like a movie star and nodding politely as his critics spoke. The young man emerged as *likeable,* it turned out, and the German public liked him. What's more, what Goldhagen had to say appealed deeply and profoundly to German audiences, especially to those under the age of forty who had lived entirely in the new, democratic Germany that Goldhagen praised.[31]

In Holocaust scholarship, a lot of heat surrounds the issue of intentionality versus functionalism: the issue of whether Hitler had always planned genocide or whether circumstances combined after the invasion of Russia to prompt mechanized destruction. Most of Goldhagen's original German critics cut their scholarly teeth on functionalism, which began as a useful extension of historical studies, but, over time, became more and more an orthodoxy, focused on details that came to serve as a buffer from the emotional force of the Holocaust.[32] Goldhagen named names and described actions with narrative impact. He supplied details about murder and visceral horror of the kind functionalists shun. Norman G. Finkelstein attacked Goldhagen for writing Holocaust "literature," which repeats familiar motifs, rather than Holocaust scholarship; his co-author, Ruth Bettina Birn, objected to how Goldhagen brings his narrative around, time and again, to himself and to his own opinions.[33] Such criticisms function within larger debates among historians about whether history is a narrative art or a science—a debate in which Goldhagen's book seems in some ways an unlikely participant since it is not an especially well-written book. Still, *Hitler's Willing Executioners* plumbs the scope and effects of anti-Semitism, facts that all have known, but not always spoken. Although it didn't really include completely new material, the book kept its readers reading and reminded them strongly of events that tend to be elided.

The gray haired scholars writing the reviews and surrounding Goldhagen in debate stressed systemic, functionalist explanations. The funny thing—not so funny, really, for the older scholars—was that young Germans did not want to hear any more about systems and structural causes.[34] Rebuttals of fact and substance sounded like pedantry, obfuscation, and sheer nastiness born of professional jealousy. At one notable moment in the debates, Hans Mommsen, "the doyen of German Holocaust research," claimed that, "many perpetrators were themselves unclear about their motives." Goldhagen turned to the audience and asked, "Is there anyone here in the audience who agrees with Professor Mommsen that the people who were murdering Jews did not know what they were doing?"[35] At such moments, audiences approved. Thumbs up for Daniel.

After Goldhagen's popular success, German critics were forced to reverse themselves. Rudolf Augstein's interview with Goldhagen, originally published in *Der Spiegel* (August 12, 1996) and reprinted under the title "What were the murderers thinking?" in *Unwilling Germans?* helped mark the turn. In the interview, the interviewer displays a curious tic. For though the information is not, strictly speaking, relevant, Augstein veers several times into family history.

"But here's how it was," Augstein says, drawing upon experience, or rather, upon his father's experience:

> The citizenry thought—I learnt this from my father—"Now [after the SA purge] the regime is on a better path, now the hooligans have been killed." Hardly anyone was interested in the Jews back then. Then along came the draft, anti-Versailles. That got a lot of people excited. . . . Today, it's no longer so easy to appreciate that the majority of the populace back then was on his [Hitler's] side, and one didn't worry about the Jews. (Augstein, "What were," in *Unwilling Germans?*, ed. Shandley, 154)

Nor is the allusion to his family's history isolated. Augstein returns, almost irresistibly, to the past. At one point, for example, he makes the classic "some of my best friends" defense:

> We had Jewish acquaintances in Hannover at that time. We could speak openly with them. They said: "It's clear to us that there is going to be a war." We said: "Yes, there'll be war." . . . Then they said: "But we have a slim chance of coming back. Please take our Lovis-Corinth pictures. When we come back later on, or when one of us comes back, then give us half a share." We replied: "Unfortunately, that's something we can't do. The war will be lost, and we don't want to be found in possession of Jewish property." That was the attitude then. (Augstein, "What were," in *Unwilling Germans?*, ed. Shandley, 155)

Despite their air of spontaneity, Augstein's comments display an odd total recall in their recreation of dialogue. And despite his credentials as a historian, the author feels the need to air his and his parents' credentials as opposing the Nazis in their hearts. So do many Germans, once the topic becomes the war. As John Cleese repeatedly says while receiving German guests in a classic episode of the old BBC comedy *Fawlty Towers*, "Don't mention the war!"[36]

The Immortal

Earlier in this chapter, I asked whether the Holocaust could be conceived of as a citizenship and, if so, who is born a citizen and who can be naturalized. Two answers spring to mind. First: the common idea that the Holocaust "belongs" to Jews as the largest and primary group of victims (though gypsies, homosexuals, dissenters, and others were, of course, victims too) and to Germans as perpetrators. And, second: the idea that the Holocaust belongs to everyone in the near or middle distance, anyone who feels an emotional response, and not just those who have a biographical or genealogical connection—an idea that carries with it the belief that the Holocaust belongs to all of us as a test-case of modernity. I have used both models in this chapter, though I incline strongly toward the second.[37] Both come together around the idea of identity, and the need to specify what one identifies with and how. For me, they come together around Alain Badiou's concept of the immortal.

Again and again in narratives of the Holocaust, there appear not just depressing stories that inspire horror, guilt, and shame, but random stories that strike us, immediately, as bright, shining, immortal: marking the place where we would like to reside and the kind of citizens we would like to be. Resistance fighters. Righteous gentiles. Or, at a quieter and more quotidian level, often one of spontaneity and simplicity, ordinary people who, when confronted with the needs of Jews, opened their doors or took other risks to help those they perceived as ordinary people too.

I feel the tug of such stories strongly and always have, or at least as far back as I remember. That tug made me at first reluctant to write about it directly, lest sentimentality creep in—or worse. For Holocaust literature is riddled with instances like Wilkomirski's of an inappropriate, even warped identification with the Holocaust that usurps others' sufferings as one's own. Even well-intentioned books like Frederick Kempe's *Father/Land*, a personal view of contemporary Germany, can track down a sense of family guilt and responsibility until it seems . . . what? inappropriate? obscene?[38] And even some Holocaust narratives, like Yehiel Dinur's

FIGURE 1. "When the subject is war, Vietnam and now Iraq produce substantial dissonance; the American role in World War II does not. Still, perceptions of these wars run interference with each other continually." The cover of *Saving Private Ryan*, a novel by Max Allan Collins, based on the screenplay by Robert Rodat (New York: Signet, 1998).

FIGURE 2. 9/11: "A photograph was somehow required, somehow a necessary gesture if one had a camera on hand that day": an ordinary photograph, taken by the author. Witnesses felt keenly the lack of information about what they had just seen.

FIGURE 3 George W. Bush speaks at the American cemetery at Colleville-sur-Mer, during ceremonies marking the sixtieth anniversary of the D-Day landings in Normandy, on June 6, 2004, as the American adventure in Iraq stalls. World War II has been a useful rhetorical touchstone in the "war on terror." Photo courtesy of AP/Wide World Photos, John McConnico.

ADOLF
EICHMANN

The extraordinary trial
of a frighteningly
ordinary man.

The
Specialist
A film by Eyal Sivan and Rony Brauman

a Kino International Release

FIGURE 4. "From the landmark historical drama *Holocaust* (NBC, 1978) to Eyal Sivan's *The Specialist* (1999; 2000), our culture has shown a repeated, almost continuous, interest in Adolf Eichmann. Why the fascination? And what changes have occurred over time?" Publicity postcard for Eyal Sivan's film, with a description of Eichmann based on Hannah Arendt.

numbers on them in red paint were ranged against the walls of
the back yards. What I found most uncanny of all, however, were
the gates and doorways of Terezín, all of them, as I thought I
sensed, obstructing access to a darkness never yet penetrated, a
darkness in which I thought, said Austerlitz, there was no more

movement at all apart from the whitewash peeling off the walls
and the spiders spinning their threads, scuttling on crooked legs
across the floorboards, or hanging expectantly in their webs. Not

FIGURE 5. "Star shapes, doorways, tangled roots: in W. G. Sebald's books such objects
become images of time, change, decay, and ruin—memento mori." Here, two black-and-
white photographs of Theresienstadt, a key transit camp in the "Final Solution," are inte-
grated into Sebald's *Austerlitz* (2001).

FIGURE 6. "Civic centers littered with corpses and turned into breeding grounds for maggots." Civilian deaths from the Allies' incendiary bombings of German and Japanese cities are an aspect of World War II that has remained below the threshold of American consciousness. Here, the *Altmarket*, Dresden, February, 1945.

FIGURE 7. Hiroshima, August 6, 1945, from underneath the mushroom cloud: a topic and a point of view surprisingly under-represented in scholarly literature in English. Photograph by Seizo Yamada.

FIGURE 8. "Doomed lovers": the cover of a 1996 Vintage edition of *The English Patient* capitalizes on the movie, which eliminates what author Michael Ondaatje called "the original country" of the novel.

Shivitti, contain not just moving testimony and at least one glimpse of the immortal but also a more pervasive and disturbing sense of self-display. I'd like to use Dinur, the witness about Auschwitz we've met before who fainted at Eichmann's trial, as an intriguing and, indeed, as a fascinating, example.

Beginning in 1955, Dinur published five linked family-chronicle novels called *Salamandra: A Chronicle of a Jewish Family in the Twentieth Century*. He published under the name Ka-Tzetnik 135633—slang for concentration camp inmate, followed by his tattooed number—bypassing both his given name (Yehiel Finer) and the already-symbolic name he had adopted in Israel (De-Nur or Dinur, "from the fire"). The best-selling author wrote as a citizen of the Holocaust, as a voice from the concentration-camp universe that he called Planet Auschwitz. He made himself into, and has been designated by others, as a survivor who represents all survivors. [39]

Many years after *Salamandra* and more than a decade after the Eichmann trial had made him a spokesman for the Holocaust, Dinur began to write a memoir called *Shivitti*. In contrast to the novels, which he claims he wrote in just two and a half weeks, *Shivitti*, a very short memoir, took Dinur ten long years to write and was only able to be written under the titillating sign of LSD. [40] During an unconventional therapy for concentration camp survivors in Holland, Dinur experienced a series of LSD visions that constitute the subject of *Shivitti*. The book reports wild and wooly stuff that interacts with Dinur's fictions, framed by a straightforward narrative of how he arrived at the therapy, what he did and thought while he lived in Holland, and how he felt after he returned to Israel.

In the process, Dinur identifies a Rabbi he had seen at Auschwitz who accepted death with spiritual tranquility. He recalls looking into the eyes of a yawning S.S. man and thinking—in a transposition of earlier utterances about Eichmann—"I am terrified of the S.S. man—he is me." He sees mountains of corpses, fire, chimneys, flame, and ashes. He sees Asmadai (Satan) and his minions Shamhazai and Azael. He sees divine figures from the Kabala—Shekina (the female principle) and Neshama (soul) who elevate him on a throne and call him Nucleus. He sees the face of God. He sees camp guards, including "the German Blonde" from *House of Dolls*, who identifies him as Christ. In the final vision, he sees his sister, his brother, and his mother, who accuses God of the fate suffered by Danielle and Moni (characters in Dinur's novels). At a climactic moment, he feels himself within his mother's mind in the gas chamber and at that moment "splits" from his own identity. That splitting forms the root trauma that has led him to LSD therapy. Accepting the identity of "Nucleus" as both a burned object and a living self, he imagines reentering the mass of corpses from which he had emerged after the *Einsatzgruppen* decimated his village and then, like "a flaming salamandra . . . like a missile bound for the upper spheres, I shoot up from the launching pad of skeletons into the tempest of my own cry of passion—And re-enter my body."[41]

Dinur rambles fairly wildly in this book, often in ways that even an admirer, like Omer Bartov, calls "anguished, at times almost insane" (*Mirrors of Destruction*, 197). But although the book circles around and around Yehiel Dinur, taking his pulse as a representative survivor obsessively, I finally found him a less compelling person than a minor figure who appears in *Shivitti* in a section devoted to Dinur's nondrug-induced experiences. That minor figure, or so it seems to me, is an immortal.

Dinur recalls a Dutch Jew who worked with him on a "labor crew" in Auschwitz. The man seemed ordinary, even weak, muttering "Kan niet lopen," ("I can't walk") over and over as he and Dinur marched along in Auschwitz. Dinur never knew the man's name. He never even knew Dutch—though he sensed the meaning of the man's "Kan niet lopen" and "will never forget the rebellion contorting his face when he refused to execute the German's order."

One memorable day, Dinur tells us, the crematorium "could not cope with any more and the holding barracks were filled beyond maximum capacity." A truck arrived from the train station carrying "a living load of gypsy women and children" who were dumped into a pit, presumably dug by the "labor crew," though the agency by which the pit was dug remains (as is characteristic of Dinur) unspecified. Ordered to empty a container of kerosene over the women and children, the Dutch Jew said "'No! No!' . . . A 'No' of that kind had never before been given to a German in Auschwitz."[42]

Like Dinur, the Dutchman had probably become habituated to his duties—digging ditches, tossing in dead bodies. Burning living people in a pit forms a novelty that defamiliarizes the situation and prompts his instinctive "No, no!" That the "No" refuses to kill gypsies, that it is an act directed toward those outside his ethnic grouping, is significant but may or may not be a simple matter of chance. The essential thing is that the Dutch Jew's "No" is situated in the specific moment of being asked to kill and is something of which he might never have been capable before and might not have been capable again.[43]

As the women and children catch fire, the S.S. man kicks the Dutch Jew's "skeleton-body, like a piece of driftwood . . . into the flames" (47). Although completely ineffectual in stopping the murder and a peripheral moment in *Shivitti*, the Dutch Jew's "No, no!" nonetheless echoes in the text. It illustrates something Hannah Arendt wrote: how "under conditions of terror, most people will comply but *some people will not*"—a motif whose exceptional status prevents it from seeming like a cliché. His "No, no!" marks an act of ethical resistance and, as Hannah Arendt puts it, "no more can reasonably be asked, for this planet to remain a place fit for human habitation" (*Eichmann*, 231).[44]

The Dutch Jew's conduct recalls the essence of ethical thought in Buber and Levinas, in which establishing vital contact via dialogue or via recognition of the other's face is of the essence. He becomes, in Primo Levi's words, one of "the few bright examples of those who had the strength and possibility to resist," someone who shows that "it is not permissible to admit that this pressure [of the modern totalitarian state] is irresistible" (Levi, *Drowned*, 29). His example recalls as well a moving episode in Levi's *If This Is a Man*, a book that explores areas of guilt and responsibility that Dinur does not. "Part of our existence lies in the feelings of those near to us [in proximity, not in familial or loving relationship]," Levi writes; "[t]his is why the experience of someone who has lived for days during which man was merely a thing in the eyes of man is non-human." It is also why, for Levi, the ability to give a slice of bread to someone else on the eve of liberation marked more effectively than liberation itself "the first human gesture."[45]

Focusing on Dinur, I feel convinced of his sufferings but sometimes feel as well that I am in the presence of fishy business: he develops his reaction to the story of the Dutch Jew, for example, by a series of histrionic gestures and utterances that call attention to himself and away from the Dutch Jew, all the while avowing his trademark "muteness." Focusing on the Dutch Jew, I feel: here is the real thing. Here is a man whose "No, no," while it did not save any lives, nonetheless changes the universe.[46]

The somber fact that such acts are small and that they often lead to failure should not, as Arendt reminds us, obscure that they exist. We have become accustomed to identifying Nazism with evil—which it was—an identification that has been diluted by all too frequent comparisons between Hitler, Qaddafi, Saddam Hussein, and others. But, as Alain Badiou suggests, we are perhaps too willing to accept evil as our fate. The impulse toward goodness cannot be prescribed. And, as I am much aware when the rhetoric of "evil" flows so freely ("the axis of evil," "the bad guys," America seen abroad as a demon), the very vocabulary of Truth, Goodness, and Evil belongs not just to philosophers like Badiou, who can use it judiciously, but also to politicians and to extreme religious fundamentalists, who generally do not.[47] Still, as Badiou argues, we need not for that reason discard the concepts, so long as we situate them in specific contexts rather than attach them to abstractions like "Democratically elected governments always protect the good" or "Having suffered, all Holocaust survivors are to be believed equally and absolutely"—principles that prove wrong at least some of the time.[48]

The impulse to goodness (the Truth, Badiou claims, insofar as evil presupposes goodness) will take different forms in different contexts. It will activate itself through individuals, rather more rarely through communities, which must be provisional or else are liable to ossify into a new and singular truth that will ultimately belie the truth of a particular situation. The person who achieves the truth, however briefly, however ineffectually, achieves a defamiliarization, an epiphany, a secular grace, a moment of being-ness, a shining.[49] The Immortal, Badiou calls it. A saving radiance that arrives by chance, "beyond any principle of the management or calculation of existence," and disappears as soon as it manifests itself, but names a sense of possibility. A possibility, a chance "of being a little more than living individuals, pursuing our ordinary interests."[50]

We know it when we see or hear it. And we see or hear it, if only from time to time, even in so dim an event as the Holocaust.

CHAPTER FOUR

UNEXPLODED BOMBS

This chapter moves to a different register of cultural representation—that of fiction, and especially elite fiction made into popular films—and it begins with two observations. First: if one excludes novels about the Holocaust, there are far fewer important postwar novels written in English about World War II than one might expect. And, second: the recent novels we do have generally sidestep combat, often by using dual settings or dual timeframes that motivate (in the sense of making seem natural) movement to a different place or time and, consequently, displacement onto a different subject.[1]

After a spate of novels about combat in World War II through the mid-1960s—Norman Mailer's *The Naked and the Dead* (1948), James Jones's *From Here to Eternity* (1951) and *The Thin Red Line* (1962), for example—the number of important postwar novels about combat becomes surprisingly scanty.[2] Joseph Heller's *Catch-22* (1962) takes place near the end of World War II and is among the best-known examples, as are Kurt Vonnegut's *Slaughterhouse Five* (1969) and Thomas Pynchon's *Gravity's Rainbow* (1973), with its mad chase for the V2 rocket. But none of these novels especially sticks in the mind as about combat or even, despite their settings, as especially about the Second World War. *Slaughterhouse Five*, for example, registers as science fiction or even, given its date of publication and Billy Pilgrim's son's status as a soldier, as about Vietnam, though it announces its topic quite clearly as the firebombing of Dresden—even as the way our culture has *forgotten* the firebombing of Dresden.[3] Like many novels published during the war, the novels by Vonnegut, Heller, and Pynchon are what Paul Fussell calls "blunder books," about the bureaucratic, technological norms of military life, which became common in postwar life.[4] They fit a model described by Peter Conrad, with which Paul Fussell agrees: both during 1939–45 and in the decades since "This was a war to which literature conscientiously objected."[5]

In the relatively rare recent novels that deal with combat in World War II, the front has generally moved elsewhere so that the novel enacts a time and a place somewhere in-between war and peace. Or, in a device that similarly displaces combat, the novels' dual time-frames (one close to the war and the other far removed) or dual settings buffer the war years by always providing a some-other-time, a someplace-else where the narrative can go. The rhythm provides escape from the intensity of the war. It also establishes a counterpoint found in other recent novels between events in Europe and events elsewhere, often colonized locales, that extends geographical space in a way that undermines belief in the norms of "the mother country" as natural and inevitable. I find the projection into other geographical space an important aspect of contemporary novels that deal with world war. Indeed, I will want to claim that, by linking imperialism and war, the novels may explore what we might call the theory of world war, a field of thought under-realized in our time, and one that requires grasping how both the spirit of world war and the feelings behind imperialism espouse control over others and a will toward violence.[6]

Georg Lukács says that great historical novels bring "the past to life as the precondition of the present" and usually address events thirty, forty, or even Sir Walter Scott's "sixty years past." If he's right, a wave of historical novels about World War II may be just ahead of us, and is overdue.[7] But it seems to me possible that important historical novels have already been written about World War II but have not yet been recognized as such. We have not yet uncovered the principles by which they *re-imagine the past to make "the past the precondition of the present."*

I want to suggest that one such principle may be the uneasy, sometimes inchoate perception that imperialism and the attitudes of subjection expressed through imperialism motivate, parallel, and resemble the forces behind world war in their lavish expression of violence. I will further want to suggest that cultures that experience imperialism and world war as the media in which they live—*media* in McLuhan's sense, as the mechanical or verbal technologies that control the scale and pace of everyday life—experience a hunger, a need, for dialogue with others, not yet satisfied in the social world, which is why fiction is the best place to look for it. In revulsion against the wholesale and anonymous death world war produces, literature posits and explores, tantalizingly, other possibilities.[8]

The chapter that follows employs close readings, psychological approaches, and approaches via the media to offer new or different interpretations of Michael Ondaatje's *The English Patient* and Kasuo Ishiguro's *The Remains of the Day,* novels about which I frankly felt surprised that there remain new and pertinent things to be said. For although these novels have been discussed by critics—Ondaatje's within the rubric of postcolonial criticism, Ishiguro's under the rubric of point-of-view and narratology—they remain unplumbed for anything but the surface content of material about world war.

These two novels may seem slender bases on which to build a theory of imperialism and world war—books whose greatness and survival in the future I would not even be willing to guarantee. But I will want to claim that they point, nonetheless, sometimes in ways beyond the actual words on the page, toward a host of elisions concerning aspects of World War II outside of Europe, where European and American cultural memory has tended to focus. They point toward Asian and postcolonial contexts elided not just in cultural memory but also in scholarly writing about the novels and in films based on them. I call these contexts unexploded bombs.

Most people know, for example, that Ishiguro's *The Remains of the Day* is "about" appeasement in 1930s Britain. Stevens's passivity during the 1930s has been read, in fact, as the "real" or "hidden" topic of the text. But appeasement and passivity as topics are almost as clear in the novel as the protagonist's, Stevens's, manifest obsession with being a butler; in fact, for any thoughtful reader of the book, they are hard to miss. Far fewer people (in fact, I have found virtually none) take seriously the novel's 1956 setting, a factor I explore here, or can even identify its historical contexts when asked.[9] In the same way, but more pointedly, I address the novel's meanings in the context of the atomic bombings—a topic absent from *The Remains of the Day* but present in *The English Patient* in novel form, though elided from the film. Representing Hiroshima and Nagasaki remains, as I discuss in the Introduction, one of the more surprising elisions in cultural representations of World War II. What do these novels have to add? Potentially, I believe, a great deal.

In this chapter and the next, which will explore W. G. Sebald's small but impressive canon, I take up questions raised in previous chapters, questions that literature can broach outside the frame of the social world:

what would it be like to think of "self," "family," and "group" in some ex-tended sense—as a metaphor for relations with others? When contem-plating the memory of World War II, what would it mean to exist within that sense—to be a citizen of the world? And I add some additional ques-tions: what should we make of the postcolonial themes that so often dog the subject of war in recent fiction? What are the implications of pairing imperialism and World War II as themes, beyond the obvious historical proximity of these events and the clear role the war played in undermin-ing empire? Given that world war provokes disordered states of mind and produces physical devastation, does it also open up, at least poten-tially, different senses of the word "community"? What would such a community look like? Would it survive transition from the hypothetical world of fiction into the social, historical world? How would the subjects raised in fiction show up, even by omission, in society?

On Fire

I begin with a story that has become familiar—so familiar that we have, in a sense, ceased to really read it. After the success of the 1996 film, *The English Patient* became part of the contemporary imagination, a bit of the public vernacular, even a joke on the television series *Seinfeld*.[10] Lush and lovely, sexy and exotic, the movie swept the Academy Awards and made the novel a bestseller. If you are the rare person who has not read the book or seen the movie (or not at all recently), the plot, summarized in the next three paragraphs, goes like this:

Katherine and Almasy, an elegant young Englishwoman and an older Hungarian archaeologist who reads Herodotus, meet in the desert and begin an affair in Cairo just before the war. Bodies mesh; tempers clash: they are doomed lovers, like Cathy and Heathcliff in *Wuthering Heights*, where the characters also express fated passion in an idiom of violence.

They part—but Katherine's husband discovers the affair and crashes his plane into the desert in an attempt to kill all the members of the trian-gle. When Katherine survives but is too badly injured to travel, Almasy houses her in a nearby cave where they had previously discovered a mural of Egyptian swimmers that proves the desert once existed below the sea: it is one of a series of motifs in the book that stress major geographical shifts in climate and in political power.[11] She later dies when the British arrest Almasy as a German spy and he cannot return, as promised, in time to save her. Almasy then retrieves her body by airplane but, when the

Germans shoot down the plane, is spectacularly burned. All of these events take place in memory and occupy much more space in the film than they do in the novel.[12]

Time-present in both the novel and the film is 1944 and 1945, in Italy, where Hana, a young Canadian nurse, takes care of Almasy in an abandoned Italian villa, once a nunnery. Two additional hangers-on reside in or near the villa: Caravaggio, a Canadian thief, and Kip, an Indian assigned to the engineers who is billeted at the villa while defusing German bombs. Almasy becomes friends with both Caravaggio and Kip; Hana and Kip fall in love. But both men are far more complex in the novel than in the film.

In the novel, Kip's background and history occupy pride of place and control the climax in August 1945, while the film omits Kip's background completely and ends on V-E Day. In the novel, Caravaggio knows Hana well through her adopted father, Patrick, the hero of *In the Skin of a Lion*—a dropped link that I will find consequential. In the film, Caravaggio pursues Almasy as a spy who betrayed him; he did not previously know Hana, and her father is never mentioned.[13]

Normally, it seems ho-hum when films alter novels, for films do it all the time. But *The English Patient*, the film (1996), ends up revealing a great deal about the novel and about elisions in cultural memory by what it chose to omit—most strikingly, the novel's references to Hiroshima and Nagasaki and to everything in the novel that might lead one there: Kip's history; the story of Hana's father, Patrick; some key passages that give an unconventional view of World War II; the epilogue that offers glimpses of Kip and Hana later in life. Surprisingly, there is a new interpretation of *The English Patient* waiting to be written.[14]

* * *

In the film, Kip is basically a piece of male cheesecake or eye candy: attractive and young, and often letting down his long dark hair to wash or comb it, he's there to serve as Hana's love interest and to add a bit of exotica. In the novel, he's a key, a lynchpin character, whose history is given as richly, indeed, more richly, than either Almasy's or Hana's and whose revulsion at Hiroshima and Nagasaki forms the turning point of the plot. Why the omission of most of Kip's story and especially of the atomic bombings?

The screenplay's preface says that the movie had to change the complicated plot to meet the demands of the screen and that important changes were made as the material underwent its final cut.[15] That explanation seems true enough but begs the question of what cuts were made, and why. The director, Anthony Minghella, no doubt followed his personal interests in shaping the film, as any writer or director needs to do, but he also may have felt that American and European audiences would relate best to European central characters like Almasy and Katherine and would reject the novel's strong emphasis on Hiroshima. Is there historical evidence in the public record to suggest that a director could safely omit the atomic bombings—and indeed should do so if he wanted to be safe? In the Introduction, I said that there was; now I need to flesh out that point, adding a few salient examples to drive it home.

In 1946, when John Hersey published *Hiroshima* in the August 31 issue of *The New Yorker,* the magazine sold out in a few hours. Newspapers in the United States and abroad reprinted the text, which was reissued as a book and remains available today. A complete translation appeared in September in *France-Soir,* prompting striking reactions by noted French intellectuals like Albert Camus and Georges Bataille, which—surprisingly and as one sign of our desire to look-away—were not translated into English until the 1980s and 1990s.

Hersey's journalistic method was to follow a small group of Japanese citizens—a doctor, a mother at her home, a secretary, a Methodist minister—and a German missionary through the day of the bombing and the days and weeks afterward. As Mary McCarthy pointed out in a scathing review, the group is disproportionately Christian relative to the Japanese population and clearly chosen either to suit Western tastes or because Hersey's contacts in Japan led him most readily to Christians.

Hersey's book went through multiple editions. It was, by any rational measure, a success. But, by and large, Hersey's book was read, and then forgotten or processed in a key that by-passed Hiroshima and its victims almost completely.[16] Its continuing life as a cheap paperback, without critical apparatus, marks it as most likely aimed at junior and senior high school students: like Dickens, Hiroshima and the Holocaust have entered school curricula, potentially with the same numbing effect.

Moral debate about the atomic bombing surfaced during 1945–46, but in isolated pockets around the United States: among intellectuals like Dwight Macdonald and Mary McCarthy, among African American leaders, and among many theologians and churchmen. Racism formed a theme for W. E. B. Du Bois and Roy Wilkins, who pointed out, as was indeed the fact, that the bomb had been developed for use against Germany but had been dropped, twice, on Japan. Commentators in the *Saturday Review, U.S. News and World Report, Commonweal,* and many religious periodicals stressed how callous Americans had grown about civilian bombing since 1940–41 and the London Blitz. They warned of excess pride. They spoke of "apprehension" about the future—a common word, even a theme word—now that the United States had unleashed, for military purposes, the energy of nature.[17]

There were social and political reasons at the time, to be sure, for the relative absence of dissent. The United States entered the war after Pearl Harbor; the years since had been long and difficult and most people felt exuberant joy when they ended. From President Truman's first announcement forward, the government explained the bomb in terms of avoiding a much-feared invasion of Japan.[18] But it remains surprising that our culture has maintained, for almost sixty years, a spirit of denial and displacement with regard to the atomic bombings.

In 1995, for example—around the time that *The English Patient,* the film, was being finished and re-cut—an exhibition at the Smithsonian (discussed in the Introduction) was scheduled to include photographs of and quotations from the atomic victims but was truncated to omit the Japanese. In 2003, the Smithsonian permanently installed the Enola Gay in a similarly sanitized exhibition. And, as I discuss more fully in the Introduction to this book, relatively few major books of nonfiction in English tackle Hiroshima and Nagasaki head-on as historical realities, and they have appeared at widely spaced intervals, most in the 1990s. A great deal of writing in English treats related issues, such as nuclear disarmament. But relatively little examines the bombings, their background, or their immediate effects on cities and the humans within them. It is worth repeating that the paucity seems obvious if one compares the numerous books on the Holocaust and on aspects of the Holocaust to materials about Hiroshima.[19]

The facts suggest, then, that a big budget film like *The English Patient* could omit Hiroshima and Nagasaki with relative safety. Indeed, leaving out Hiroshima and Nagasaki was the uncontroversial thing for director Minghella to do—the very thing least likely to provoke any protests. After the dismal fall of 2001, the irony is that Kip's plot should seem relevant to us all.

Elided Histories

Kirpal Singh was the second son of a Sikh family that had, by long family custom, dedicated its first son to the British army. When his older brother refused to serve, Singh felt moved to save the family honor and took his place. The army never considers using him as a doctor, though he has a medical degree; the novel does not explore that decision—and the film does not even mention it, since Kip is not a doctor—but we can assume it has to do with Kip's ethnicity. Instead, the army uses synecdoche to place Singh: as a surgeon, he has skilled "hands"; therefore, he should become a sapper, an infantryman who defuses bombs.[20]

Historically, as one can discover in sources outside the novel, this family background rings true. From 1780 to 1839, the Sikhs under Ranjit Singh established an empire up to the Khyber Pass that disintegrated after their leader's death. There was an internal power struggle; British forces massed on the border. Between 1845 and 1849, the British lured the Sikhs into two disastrous and bloody wars and the British annexed their land in northwest India, the Punjab. Later, the Sikhs won favor during and after the Mutiny of 1857 by putting their militaristic traditions to the service of the British Crown. In World War I, the highpoint of good relations between the British and the Sikhs, Sikhs formed one-fifth of the British Indian Army. Relations between 1918 and 1939 deteriorated so badly that far fewer Sikhs signed on for World War II. Sikh history up to the setting of *The English Patient* helps to explain Kip's "in-between-ness" and shifting identifications with Britain and South Asia: he is a kind of "Tory" Sikh, still attracted to and serving British institutions.

Once Kip arrives in England, he becomes part of an elite bomb squad led by an eccentric Englishman who respects Sikh customs; when this good man is killed in a devastating explosion, Kip seeks the anonymity of the sappers in the Italian campaign. (The movie omits completely Kip's sojourn in England and the explosion that killed his mentor.) As a sapper, Kip works intensely, wearing a radio to help him concentrate. He lives with death; he saves lives. In the novel, his relationship with Hana begins around a drama of wires held and cut. She breaks through his defenses, and he breaks through hers. Like Othello or Aeneas, he tells her of his homeland, which includes Amritsar and The Golden Temple, sites to which Kip especially imagines taking Hana. The film omits the Sikh holy places completely, substituting a visit to murals in a Catholic church. But historical sources reveal important background information about Amritsar and The Golden Temple not included in the novel, but available to an audience familiar with Indian history, the audience Ondaatje's novel addresses.[21]

Amritsar was the site of a famous massacre in 1919, when economic depression fueled civil unrest and the British killed thousands of Sikh civilians. Afterward, many Sikhs (like Kip's brother) joined Gandhi's freedom movement and refused to fight for the British in World War II, even though, as the novel notes, the Japanese abused Sikhs in Malaysia. Because of their privileges under colonialism, Sikhs became the target of resentment at the 1947 Partition: when 2.5 million Sikhs were forced to leave Pakistan, there were Sikh-Muslim riots; the Indian government revoked special privileges. With such large-scale changes, resentments remain and have overflowed from time to time, up to today.

Resentments. Overflowing up to today. During the 1970s, Sikh activism (usually directed toward independence and statehood) and religious fundamentalism grew, parallel to nationalist and fundamentalist Islamist movements in Pakistan, though obviously quite different in intention and methods. In June 1984, roughly six years before publication of *The English Patient,* Sikh nationalists made a stand at The Golden Temple. When Indian forces led an assault against the badly outnumbered Sikhs, some seven hundred Sikhs were slain. In October 1984, Sikh guards killed Indira Gandhi in reprisal, loosing further violence. In 1997, the massacre became a renewed source of embarrassment for Queen Elizabeth II when her consort Prince Philip questioned the number of Sikh victims, mostly on the basis of what he had heard from an old school chum.

Does it matter that many, even most, readers in the West do not, by and large, know these histories of events in India from the nineteenth century on? (American readers, even graduate students trained in postcolonial approaches, generally do not.) Does the novel thereby lose some of its historical resonance and some of its meanings? I believe it does—and that our lack of understanding reflects the generally parochial sense in the United States of which events affect "us" and which do not. For the Sikh territory claimed by England, which began the processes I have described, was the Punjab, where Kashmir is located. And Sikh nationalism has repeatedly conflicted with the claims of both the larger Hindu India and the larger Muslim Pakistan.[22]

In 2001, after the World Trade Center attack and collapse, al-Qaeda referenced Palestine and Kashmir as twin sources of grievance.[23] Those in the West began to understand that of course histories converge and matter not just to "them," but to "us." In June 2002, a flurry of publicity in the West surrounded India's and Pakistan's confrontation across the border of Kashmir, with its accompanying nuclear threats. Then, in the rhythm typical of news in the West, and especially the United States, the publicity disappeared, even though Kashmir remains a source of tension, war, and possible disaster.[24]

In a 2002 speech, former President Bill Clinton laid out several ways that the United States could meet long-term concerns for security after 9/11 by seeking a foreign policy that aimed at peace, not war. He stressed increased international aid to improve education and to increase the wealth available abroad, more international cooperation, and the need to know wider histories and to see them as linked to ours before terrorists make us confront them. One statistic in Clinton's talk seemed especially telling. Currently, Americans believe that the United States spends 10 to 15 percent of the national GNP on foreign aid but should spend closer to 3 to 5 percent. In fact, the United States spends less than 1 percent of GNP on foreign aid—less than any other developed country.[25]

Clinton's speech may seem like a digression but it is, in fact, quite pertinent to *The English Patient*—for the novel has been saying similar things all along. It is, I would claim, at least in part a novel about what we in the West have conveniently elided or have never known about Asian histories we deem minor but are really part and parcel of our own. Once again, the differences between the novel and the film make the point dramatically.

In the novel, after a series of dramatic incidents in which he rescues Europeans from bombs, the climax occurs when Kip hears over his radio that the United States has dropped atomic bombs on Hiroshima and Nagasaki. The personal and the world historical intersect as Kirpal Singh's life, devoted to defusing weapons for the Allies, ceases to make sense because so many bodies, so many Asian bodies, have been consumed by heat and fire.[26] As he puts it, in a passage that overwhelms the senses, the racism in the reaction to the events, even more than the events themselves, unsettles him: "All those speeches of civilization from kings and queens and presidents . . . such voices of abstract order. Smell it. Listen to the radio and smell the celebration in it" (ellipsis included in original, 285). Kip reacts first with violence toward Almasy—still thought of as "the *English* patient" and hence as a Master who has betrayed him—and then with flight. He recoils toward India and an Asian identification that will make him, in the epilogue that ends the novel, a family man and doctor in his native land, only comfortable at a table where "all of their hands are brown."[27]

In the novel, the news from Asia shocks Hana too but effects a movement outward toward an ethics of empathy and identification. It coincides with the news that her beloved adoptive father, Patrick, has been killed in France, set afire in a dovecote where he had taken cover during combat.[28] Patrick died of burns, as Almasy will: the personal connection justifies in retrospect Hana's spontaneously and already-conferred love and care for Almasy, as though he were her father or her lover. As Hana writes to her stepmother, "From now on I believe the personal will forever be at war with the public" (292), by which she means that she mourns both her father's death and the bombings. Although the Anglo world is indifferent to her father and was, by and large, not thinking of Japan's dead on V-J Day, the two events will reside together in her mind. At the end of the novel, in the epilogue, Hana becomes a shadowy figure dedicated to good works, but nunlike, perhaps—and this would be worth exploring, save that the novel does not go there—as the price paid for the ethical actions she performs.

Almasy, Patrick, Kip's friends and comrades in England and Italy, those killed in Dresden, Tokyo, Hiroshima, Nagasaki, and those reduced to ashes in the camps: World War II has specialized in charred and incinerated bodies. Although *The English Patient* focuses so intensely on Almasy, I believe that he should be understood not just as a romantic icon but also as an emblem and a symbol of all the burned bodies of World War II. In the Introduction, I suggested that visual representations—photographs, films—tend (as W. G. Sebald puts it) to "displace our memories completely, one may even say they destroy them." In this instance, visual images from the film—which more than double the novel's attention to Almasy's romantic plot in Egypt and eliminate references to Hiroshima—displace history.

The movie opts for a more conventional ending than Hiroshima to Kip's plot: he feels devastated when his buddy, Hardy, dies when he sets off a bomb on V-E Day—not, one should note, V-J Day, a distortion consonant with the current emphasis on the European war. Kip's grief seems entirely personal and he leaves the villa simply because he has been billeted elsewhere. There *may*, however, just *may* be a hint of Hiroshima in the film—not at its end, but at its beginning. The screenplay, published before the film's final cut, indicates that Almasy's plane "ERUPTS IN

FLAMES" and "THE MAN FALLS OUT OF THE SKY CLINGING TO HIS DEAD LOVER. THEY ARE BOTH ON FIRE."[29] What we see on screen instead is a blinding white light, like the blinding white light, "a tremendous flash . . . whiter than any white . . . the terrible flash . . . [like] a large meteor colliding with the earth . . . like a gigantic photographic flash" described several times near the beginning of John Hersey's *Hiroshima* (5, 8, 12, 14). The blinding white light may be just a cinematic device—a coincidence, and completely inadvertent. But it might, just might, derive from descriptions of Hiroshima.[30]

I feel almost done with *The English Patient*, except to unpack some further implications. In a passage often quoted by critics, what we might call a canonical passage, Caravaggio offers a cynical, postcolonial reading of World War II in which "the good war" was better for some on the Allied side than for others: "The trouble with all of us is we are where we shouldn't be. What are we doing in Africa, in Italy? What is Kip doing . . . fighting English wars?" (122).[31]

In the film, the character who comes closest to articulating Caravaggio's meanings is Katherine, in her diary, written while she lies dying in the desert cave, a diary that Hana later reads aloud: "we die rich with lovers and tribes. . . . We are the real countries, not the boundaries drawn on maps." In the novel, those words belong to Almasy (261), and they receive embodiment in the novel's epilogue (also omitted from the film), where Hana and Kip enact mental telepathy from Toronto to Delhi—she drops a glass, he catches a fork—bypassing the imperial center. The strong sympathies that develop among the characters delineate a hypothetical territory founded on transnational cooperation and communion.

Two Canadians, a Sikh, and a Hungarian have been brought together by chance amidst the ruins of Italy: in their villa, stairways end in midair, ceilings have been blown away, buildings stand open to the sky—the images convey war's destructive effect but also the removal of boundaries and the lability that can characterize what we might call warspace.[32] In both novel and film, the characters establish a non-nationalist sense of community and enact rituals of conversation, touch, and play (Hana's hopscotch; the shells Kip uses to create candles; the gramophone sessions) to create the sense that, when war has eroded other norms, *community* and *family* are where you find them. Like snakes in the desert, the characters are "shedding skins." They are casting off the sense of possessiveness and national identity that produced the war.[33]

It all comes crashing down with Hiroshima. But, here again, the setting amidst ruins remains consequential. In his study of the postwar Italian film, a genre perforce set amidst ruins, Gilles Deleuze describes an "any-space-whatever" (*espace quelconque*) that has lost, or never had, a social function: "The experience of any-space-whatever by human beings is, according to Deleuze, terrible but potentially liberating through the power of estrangement effected by the functional vacuum it creates."[34] If times of war produce temporal violence, shock, and trauma (as they do), what remains after the war has passed can foster different and more hopeful reactions—reactions that take account of destruction but experiment with new and creative ways of belonging "through impropriety and unbelonging."

It sounds attractive, even glitzy: a revolution in consciousness born out of war but more positive than Freud's wartime consciousness or than the omnibus term *trauma*—an opening up of creative potentials, phoenixlike, out of destruction. In fact, the kind of zone described here may exist only within the space of fiction. For actual warspace (like that Sebald discusses, the subject of the next chapter) also typically contains death, decay, danger, deprivation, and exploitation—and should end with reconstruction. Still—and that gives the argument a final turn whose implications I will want to explore in the Conclusion—art's removal from the exigencies of history can be a strength in this instance insofar as art is, by definition, "non-actualized, a reserve of betrayed potential" but also, and therefore, a laboratory for exploring new potentials.[35] I have, several times in this book, referred to the power of *defamiliarization*. If this interpretation makes sense to you, as it makes sense to me, the "estrangement" characteristic of postwar space provides yet another example.

Masters of Repression

"Of those things we could not speak, we said nothing"

As anyone who has read the book or seen the film will immediately know, *The Remains of the Day* is not at all a war novel in the sense that *Saving Private Ryan* is a war film or even in the sense that *The English Patient* is a war novel. No combat takes place, nor have any of the main protagonists been in combat. The book makes no reference at all to the Blitz or to D-Day or to any of the motifs most common in discussions of World War II in Britain. In fact, the actual years of the war, 1939–45, constitute a kind of black hole in the novel, somewhere the plot, which is coextensive with the thoughts of the first person narrator, will not go.[36] And yet I will want to claim that the war impinges on the novel in ways beyond its obvious references to appeasement.[37]

For anyone who has not read the novel or seen the film somewhat recently, the plot (which I will summarize in the next two paragraphs), goes like this: in 1956, Mr. Stevens, butler at Darlington Hall, drives west to Cornwall to visit his former head housekeeper, Miss Kenton. He tells himself that he wants to lure her back into service now that he has a new employer, an American who has purchased the Darlington estate. Having heard that her marriage is ending, he also wants, though he does not articulate this goal, to recover the romance he missed in their youth. Both attempts ultimately fail.

Like Stevens himself, the book seems much more attuned to the memory of the 1930s, and hence to the ambiance of pre–World War II Britain, rather than to 1956, the year in which the action unrolls. The 1930s included important turning points in Stevens's personal life (his father's death, his meetings with Miss Kenton) but these events seem, at least on the surface of Stevens's mind, less important than his professional life, which was at its height when Darlington Hall hosted Nazis and those who urged appeasement. Although he continues in his mind to defend his former employer, Stevens feels uneasy when he recalls how, around 1932, intimates of Mosley's Fascist party in the United Kingdom frequented Darlington Hall and the tone turned anti-Semitic. Still, he remains proud of how he organized dinners and of how well the dinners turned out. And he does not consider the discredited policies the dinners helped to promote.[38]

For anyone who has worked on Adolf Eichmann, as I have, Stevens echoes, in a suitably reduced key, Adolf Eichmann at Wannsee, proud of how well he had organized the ninety-minute conference that set the contours of the Final Solution. His foolish pride resembles Eichmann's when he asked his judges to consider "the fact that I obeyed, and not whom I obeyed."[39] But while Stevens does not explicitly remember the war or any of its details, he recoils so thoroughly from even the most casual allusion in the years afterward that we can see its impact in the trace of the recoil. Three times on his journey west, people he meets casually mention the war and identify Darlington as a collaborator. Three times, like Peter, Stevens denies having served him.

In this context, the novel's setting in July of 1956 is hugely significant.

The date coincides with the Suez crisis, an important boundary to British imperial and political ambition—and one marked by dubious actions. Along with the United States, Britain and France tried to rein in Egypt's Nasser, who had established friendly relations with and was buying arms from both the Soviets and the Czechs. He was initiating what came to be called the third-world movement of "non-aligned" nations, a consortium of governments that the superpowers wooed for support. When Nasser refused, Britain, along with France and the United States, withdrew loan commitments made earlier for construction of the Aswan dam, a key to Nasser's plans for modernization. On July 26, 1956, Nasser responded by nationalizing the Suez Canal and imposing a fee to use it. Britain and France then used Israel as a surrogate invader, in an attempt to manipulate the United Nations into banning all troops, including the Egyptians, from the Canal Zone. The ruse backfired when the world body voted to create a buffer between the Israelis and the Egyptians and, with strong support from the United States under Eisenhower, pressured Britain and France to withdraw.[40]

The event formed a turning point in twentieth-century history, perceived at the time as a blow to British and French imperialism and as signaling the rise of Arab secular nationalism. After 9/11, one can perceive it as one of many steps that would later lead (as fundamentalism vied with secularism) to militant Islamisms hostile to modernization and to the West. Suez has not been referenced as often as one might expect in the decades since, though it dominated the news in 1956, much as the war on terrorism dominated the news after 2001.[41]

When discussing British accounts of World War II in Burma, historian Barbara Tuchman notes that "no nation has ever produced a military history of such verbal nobility as the British. Retreat or advance, win or lose, blunder or bravery, murderous folly or unyielding resolution, all emerge alike."[42] Paul Fussell notes how the British used euphemism in World War I in which the adjectives "sharp" or "brisk" described attacks or retreats in which many men had died or raids in which "about 50% of a company had been killed or wounded" (Great War, 176). Communiqués issued on the disastrous first day of the Somme stressed merely "continuing fighting." As Conrad Aitken said, "A future historian, if he leaned at all on these carefully sieved accounts, would be quite misled" (cited in Fussell, Great War, 176).

Part of Britain's chipper-ness and moral clarity came from an ingrained rhetoric of British pastoralism and the idealization of rural, country life—two tendencies Stevens typifies in the novel. "I have seen in encyclopedias and the *National Geographic Magazine* breathtaking photographs of sights from various corners of the globe," he says, but a quality "will mark out the English landscape to any objective observer as the most deeply satisfying in the world, and this quality is probably best summed up by the term 'greatness'" (28). Stevens's tastes and knowledge are, to put it mildly, quite parochial.

Yet Stevens lived through World War I and saw the consequences of fascism in Europe. The son of servants, his brother died in the Boer War, an important prequel to world war in the twentieth century (40).[43] Closer to home, Stevens has experienced on a daily basis how the servant class, his life's milieu, shrunk after 1916 and became almost archaic after World War II. That contraction formed part of larger changes in the world, like decolonization—a topic alluded to by Dr. Carlisle on Stevens's travels (192). Stevens registers all these facts at the fringes of his mind, though he chooses, he always and characteristically chooses, to look away. A master of repression who practices derealization as second nature, he identifies with the master class and its days of prewar glory.[44]

The Remains of the Day has been read as a tour-de-force of narrative technique and as a masterpiece of point-of-view in fiction. It has been read as a parable about social class. In the most political readings, it has been read for its attention to the years between the wars and for its condemnation of appeasement. The book justifies all these readings.

And yet, I want to claim that the book represents something more, something part and parcel of the British emphasis on "greatness," on "sharp," "brisk" action at all costs. I want to make a claim—unusual for me insofar as it is based on evidence entirely outside the text and noticeably absent in it—that just as the novel evokes, by its 1956 setting, Stevens's neglect of Suez, it evokes by omission the neglect in the West of Hiroshima and Nagasaki. That claim may seem hyperbolic, since the novel will not speak the names *Hiroshima* and *Nagasaki* any more than Stevens will say the word *appeasement* or even seems to know the word *Suez*. But the thematic and technical parallels between Ishiguro's first two novels and *The Remains of the Day* suggest such a view rather strongly.

Like *The Remains of the Day*, Ishiguro's first two novels feature first-person narrators who are masters of repression. In *A Pale View of Hills* (1982), a housewife named Etsuko represses her memories of Nagasaki and her feelings about her older daughter's suicide, displacing them onto the story of another mother and daughter who remain shadowy in the text. In *An Artist of the Floating World* (1986), an artist named Matsuko Ono, who made imperial propaganda, cannot understand why he and his daughters lost prestige after 1945, even though he lost his wife and son during the war. In style and substance, Etsuko and Ono resemble Stevens, maintaining a superficial cheerfulness and self-esteem undercut at many points by the stories they tell.

Etsuko and Ono are Japanese, and, through them, we come to see Japan as a culture of decorous repression, par excellence. Stevens is English and, through him, we come to see England as a culture of decorous repression, par excellence. The three novels illuminate one another and should be read together as the first, and (so far) major phase of Ishiguro's career.[45] Together, the novels explore how, after disaster, most Japanese, most British, *most people* chose willful forgetfulness and what one character in *Hills* calls "the business of life." For individuals, and within a culture, "the business of life" determines what is remembered, what is elided, and how. One can see that in many sites of official memory in the United Kingdom, including the Imperial War Museum in London, a place where one imagines Kasuo Ishiguro, born in Nagasaki in 1954 in the aftermath of the nuclear destruction, though he has lived since 1960 in England, is likely to have seen.

The Imperial War Museum dedicates most of its permanent exhibition space to the two world wars. But the exhibit on 1939–45 overwhelmingly emphasizes the Blitz and British bravery during the Blitz and virtually excludes the Asian war. Visitors can read about RAF pilots—their amazing pluck, how so many owed so much to so few. They can see posters distributed at the time, enlisting full civilian support for the war effort. They can identify with native British courage and hear the stirring words of Winston Churchill. They can sit in a recreated bomb shelter and sing cheerily along with the soundtrack.

Within London, the emphasis on the Blitz remains strong and has been augmented by the recent opening of the War Cabinet Rooms and the Docklands Museum, impressive sites that devote substantial space to the topic. Having been in my childhood an addict of *Their Finest Hour*, a documentary based on Winston Churchill's memoirs, I understand the strong emotions that surround the Blitz. I listened, on many summer nights, to the stories told by Rose Cohen, a white-haired neighbor who had lived through the East End bombings. Still, one might notice that the Imperial War Museum devotes the overwhelming majority of its space— in fact, fully ten of eleven rooms on World War II—to the European war.

The Asian war, which marked the end of British empire and was a crucial arena, occupies by comparison only one room that is disproportionately small and, given the spatial layout, possible to bypass entirely. While it is represented in that room, the dropping of the atomic bomb is described on a single small placard alongside a staircase that leads to the next exhibition. Quite literally, I had to sit down on the stairs to read the following description: "Although devastated by the Allied bombing offensive, Japan's defences threatened to make an amphibious invasion extremely costly. It was therefore decided to use the recently developed atomic bomb to force Japan's surrender. On 6 August 1945 an atomic bomb was dropped on Hiroshima and, three days later, a second fell on Nagasaki," leading directly to unconditional surrender. Notably, the wording uses the passive voice to evade all agency. In the same evasive way, the museum's section on the postwar period includes a large photograph of a mushroom cloud that does not mention Hiroshima or Nagasaki, functioning instead as a generalized image of apocalypse and accompanied by references to the need for nuclear disarmament.

While museum exhibitions must be brief, even terse, the representation of the atomic bombings in this instance is unusually so, without any mention of casualties or any display of photographs. It contrasts vividly with the much fuller, indeed excellent, displays about the Soviet front and about postwar crises such as Suez. As one sign of the larger entity called British culture, the exhibit at the Imperial War Museum does not exactly falsify World War II. But it does clearly favor some events over others. Like the narrator of *An Artist of the Floating World,* it prefers a glamorized image of the past to a more complex present.

Uniqueness

In Europe and North America, considerable heat surrounds the issue of whether the Holocaust was "unique" and whether it can or cannot be mentioned in the context of other mass annihilations in our time, including Hiroshima and Nagasaki. The issue forms part of the policing of World War II in the publishing and academic worlds I allude to in the Introduction and in chapter 3. In general, the orthodox view stresses the uniqueness of the Holocaust, an event well represented in public discourse, and downplays Hiroshima and Nagasaki, seeing them as regrettable but as absolutely necessary to end World War II. The most extreme version of this view sees the mention of other catastrophes as an insult to the 6 million. What might have been the effect of our cultural self-censorship for Ishiguro and Ondaatje when writing about World War II?[46]

Both men are, of course, Asian born: Ishiguro, in Nagasaki in 1954; Ondaatje, in Sri Lanka, of mixed British and Tamil stock. Both are also long-term residents of the West: Ishiguro in London, England; Ondaatje in Toronto, Canada. Both have written about their countries of origin: Ishiguro in his first two novels; Ondaatje in his autobiography and in *Anil's Ghost*.[47] It seems likely that these authors, while very aware of Asia's devastation during the war, would have been equally aware of the bias in the United Kingdom and North America toward the European arena and of sensitivities toward the Holocaust. It seems possible that they tread carefully as they wrote.[48]

But the "uniqueness" of the Holocaust seems, on any balanced assessment, to be a classic instance of a debate that yields more heat than light. Of course the Holocaust was unique and it is not that difficult to articulate its uniqueness. What sets the Holocaust apart is the Nazi fixation on Jews as primary victims both in and out of the camps (a feature also of pogroms and other anti-Semitism) *in combination with* (as Edith Wyschogrod puts it) "the character of the mechanisms of destruction. the bureaucratic and technological means used to assure the annihilation of the maximum number of persons in the least possible time."[49] I would add two important codicils to Wyschogrod's distinction: that the mechanisms of destruction proceeded under government auspices and that they aimed, as genocide does, at the genealogical eradication of a people.

But, of course as well, the twentieth century was a century of "mass annihilations" in which technology and the speeding-up of death played their part and continue to play their part wherever such technology exists. Can we end a competition among catastrophes that should never have begun? Can we prevent the masking of one catastrophe by another, or, worse, an overall numbing of the postwar imagination?[50] The writer I want to consider in the next chapter, W. G. Sebald, offers in his novels some compelling insights.

CHAPTER FIVE

"THEY ARE EVER RETURNING TO US, THE DEAD"

The Novels of W. G. Sebald

"When we turn to take a retrospective view, particularly of the years 1930 to 1950, we are always looking and looking away at the same time," W. G. Sebald wrote, "the need to know . . . at odds with a desire to close down the senses."[1] We experience "individual and collective amnesia," or, something more primal, a "preconscious self-censorship," an "almost perfectly functioning mechanism of repression"— a silent fascination, a voyeurism that, in its attraction to death as a destructive sublime, has a "pornography" effect (10, 12, 14, 98). Sebald speaks of historical facts that operate like family secrets (10)—known but never said, disciplining individuals into "self-anesthesia" chosen by the group because "the population decided—out of sheer panic at first—to carry on as though nothing had happened" (11, 41). Although eyewitness testimony emerges, it has an inherent inadequacy and a "tendency to follow a set routine and go over and over the same material" (80). People experience "overload . . . paralysis" (25) and forget what they do not want to know (41). So that events, even though they influence an entire culture, never seem to cross the threshold of the national consciousness (11).

Sebald's words might apply to many aspects of my topic. But, in fact, he wrote with a German "we" in mind and, as the dates 1930–50 will suggest, with reference to Nazism's rise, World War II, and Germany's postwar devastation. Most specifically, he refers to German memory of the destruction of Germany's cities in World War II and to some of the following historical facts: 131 cities and towns bombed, with many "flattened almost entirely"; roughly 600,000 German civilian victims, often killed in the gruesome form of suffocation as firebombs sucked oxygen out of cities; civic centers littered with corpses and turned into breeding grounds for maggots; horror stories like mothers, stunned by the inexorable and rapid events, carrying dead babies in suitcases, or families caught at their dinner tables and turned into ashes.[2] If you feel that you have heard these kinds of details before, I would say: of course you have. On a larger scale, with the ethnic group changed from German to Jewish, and with more direct volition by the perpetrators, you have heard similar details in connection with the Holocaust.

Sebald knew, and felt acutely for most of his life, the connection between the Holocaust and the destruction of Germany's great cities. Born in Germany in 1944, he left in 1967 and never again lived long-term in his native land except for one brief try. Although he wrote in German, he chose to live and teach in East Anglia. Behind his choice flash hints of a family past not inhospitable to Nazism: a father in the *Wehrmacht*, drinking like all good burghers on his nights off with the boys; parents who never discussed the Holocaust or the Allied bombings in the family home; countrymen he has encountered who express a persistent anti-Semitism.[3]

In *A Natural History of Destruction*, Sebald speculates that Germans intuitively felt the fire from the sky as a just retribution for the destruction and desolation Germany had caused: "the majority of Germans today know, or so at least it is to be hoped, that we actually provoked the annihilation of the cities in which we once lived" (103). After the war, they turned their willingness to work, their love of good order and their civil ethos of obedience—equivocal virtues that Sebald placed at the core of his theory of Nazism and, more generally, at the core of the limitations of human reason—into the single-minded rebuilding of their cities. Still, they knew or (what is not quite the same thing) they had the knowledge available to them that the cataclysm that had destroyed their cities had arisen, as Sebald suggests, from the very same love of order that had led in the past to their embracing Nazism and abandoning what the judges at the Eichmann trial called "civil courage." Sebald recalls that German leaders once contemplated with delight the possibility of firebombing London and complacently anticipated success at Stalingrad. The destruction of Germany forms part of history's recursive patterns, in this case, the visitation of fire-bombing upon those who had destroyed and fire-bombed others.

I have begun this chapter with "Air War and Literature" because in it Sebald left a skeleton key to his canon, an insight into its sources. "At the end of the war I was just one year old, so I can hardly have any impressions of that period of destruction based on personal experience," Sebald wrote: "Yet to this day, when I see photographs or documentary films dating from the war I feel as if I were its child, so to speak, as if those horrors I did not experience cast a shadow over me, and one from which I shall never entirely emerge" ("Air War," 71). After "Air War and Literature," references to the bombing that seem casual on a first reading of his earlier works leap forward with new prominence.[4] Indeed, with this essay, the settings of many of Sebald's books amidst ruins and abandoned places—and especially ruined fortresses and civic buildings—emerge as Sebald's secret code for postwar Germany, a subject flashed before the reader of his novels and withdrawn in a simulacrum of the toddler's game Freud called Fort/Da.

But "Air War and Literature" is, I believe, a key and a code that we should use with caution. For I will want to claim that a broader sense of *process*—of gradually making and testing connections between individuals and themes—forms the very essence of Sebald's fertile prose. The process leads not just to the ashes of his native Germany in 1945 or to camps such as Theresienstadt, which the title character of *Austerlitz* visits toward the end of that book, but also to a broader vision of repeatedly accessing memory, repeatedly perceiving connections, repeatedly parsing and refining the possibilities of identification—and then beginning the process again. Process forms the essence of Sebald's work—his theory of the novel as well as his theory of history. His books are process books, leading to a place—the novel, the world—defamiliarized and seen anew but never safe, never settled, never complacent. They record a meditative state of mind in which "unbelonging" merges seamlessly into belonging and in which geographies of space and time expand.[5]

*   *   *

Although Sebald's major books—*Vertigo, The Emigrants, The Rings of Saturn,* and *Austerlitz*—are usually called novels, only *Austerlitz* resembles a conventional novel at all, and even it tests the form's boundaries. Indeed, with their many striking black-and-white photographs, all his books resemble extended photo-essays, with the photos sometimes illustrating what is said in a fairly literal way and sometimes initiating for the writer and the reader consideration of new and additional connections. The books have the air of outsiders, observers, and *flâneurs,* assembling bits and pieces of other genres and often linking them, quite literally, by the narrator's journeys or by a set of chance encounters. They seem both objective, like a mirror or a camera traveling down the road, and obsessively selective, returning over and over again to the same places or to similar motifs layered carefully, like mosaics.[6] Casual and even contingent-seeming in their linkages, by the end, through luminous prose, they have transformed reality.

Testing. Probing. Sebald's books weigh the meaning of what it means to be a "narrator," what it means to be a "character," what it means to "tell a story."[7] They test the limits of how information can and cannot be put together and of how histories circulate from one person or book to another. In fact, I believe that Sebald tests the viability of the novel after 1945 because (although he would never put it so baldly), the genre thrived within the same systems of rational thought and modernity that have given us industrial excess, imperial hubris, and world war.

An annotated summary of the books follows in the next few paragraphs, omitting *Austerlitz*, Sebald's final novel, which will be discussed in more detail below.

In *Vertigo*, Sebald's first novel but published third in English, an unnamed narrator moves from the battle of Marengo (via Stendhal), through an evocation of Vienna as if through Kafka's eyes, to the narrator's small hometown in Germany where an avalanche killed a heroic mountaineer and his dog, to the recollection of his father's Nazi uniform and past—each a "token of some great woe that nothing in the world will ever put right" (228–29). The very form of *Vertigo* marries the novella and the travel memoir; it also portrays vivid attempts to see and imagine events through another's eyes.

In *The Emigrants*, Sebald's narrator relates four encounters with Jews and others displaced from Europe for whom the war years may be "a blinding, bad time . . . about which [they] could not say a thing even if [they] wanted to,"[8] but a blank which nonetheless colors their lives and sometimes, as in the first two sections, leads to suicide. The book's four sections chronicle: the narrator's encounter with a Lithuanian Jew who hides, even from his wife, his Jewish identity, whose closest friend, an Alpine mountaineer, disappeared into a crevice shortly before World War I; the narrator's search for his German grade school teacher's past; the narrator's quest to learn more about Great Uncle Ambrose, a German émigré bachelor who worked and had a strong affinity for wealthy Jewish families and experienced, late in life, profound depressions; and the narrator's sense of responsibility toward a Jewish artist named Max Ferber whose family once lived in a German town and whose mother entrusted him with a lengthy memoir. [9]

All the narratives include lost lives and supplemental histories—sometimes quite literally in the form of written manuscripts, which impose on the narrator duties and obligations. The narrator meets Max Ferber casually, for example, befriending the artist largely because he is new to Manchester. But he returns to Manchester years later, once he realizes that he had failed to ask Ferber about what happened to his parents after they sent him away from Germany in 1939. Entrusted on that occasion with Ferber's mother's memoir, the narrator includes it word for word in his tale. Then the narrator feels moved to visit sites in Franconia the memoir mentions, including a Jewish cemetery. The narrative becomes, in effect, a stone of remembrance, evocative of those Jews place on cemetery headstones when they visit. Over the course of his canon, such rescuing of lost lives and lost histories proves to be Sebald's special gift—his mission and his achievement as a writer.

In *The Rings of Saturn*, the unnamed narrator—who seems, as is usual in the books, a version of Sebald himself—is an inveterate reader and walker, who seeks out and traverses books and expanses of the land that chronicle disaster. [10] A walking tour provides the loose narrative framework of *Rings*, a meditation attuned to mutability in the manner of Sir Thomas Browne, that narrates in ten discrete chapters some of the following events: Sir Thomas Browne and his work; the history of Lowestoft (an easterly port) and its decline; the herring trade and the writer Borges; Napoleonic sea battles and massacres in World Wars I and II in Bosnia; Roger Casement and Conrad; the murderous Taipei Rebellion and the erosion of a coastal city called Dunwich; a maze in the landscape; the rise and fall of the English port of Orford; Chateaubriand (the French author), and a hurricane in East Anglia; a history of the silkworm and the production of silk in England and Germany.

What are we to make of such a miscellaneous, such a motley list of subjects? For, putting aside the luminous quality of Sebald's style, which keeps one reading, the list is indisputably motley. Finding the links—or at least trusting that they will emerge—becomes the reader's task, for which literary critics are particularly suited.

Imperialism, war, and wartime consciousness link many of the chapters, which come together thematically around a 1936 proclamation by the German Führer "that Germany must become self-sufficient within four years . . . [a goal that] self-evidently included silk production" (292–93).[11] But the thread that links the whole is, finally, the filament of the lowly silkworm, which figures in the book both as a literal fact—the Dowager Empress at the time of the Taipei Rebellion loved and cultivated silkworms, when the Huguenots fled France they settled in East Anglia where they wove their fabulous silk, Sir Thomas Browne's father was a silk merchant, and so forth—and as a double metaphor. First, the silkworm is a metaphor for the human mind, ceaselessly forming channels and connections, spun out and registered, and then sometimes effaced. But, second, the silkworm is a metaphor for the self as worker, chained to the machinery of his own making, which will ultimately self-destruct.

Sebald stresses that the Victorians and the Nazis both advocated the cultivation of silkworms as a model for sanitary procedures and for human conduct. He uses the silkworm as a model too, though more cautiously, aware that industriousness entraps us within systems of our own making. Near the end of the book, the killing of the silkworms "batch" by batch "until the entire killing business is completed" tacitly evokes, as much of the book does, the Holocaust.[12]

Within each of the book's ten chapters, the linkages can seem—as the summaries I have given will suggest—capricious and specific to W. G. Sebald. But they often engage the power of place to organize experience. Sites in *The Rings of Saturn*—Lowestoft, Orford, Dunwich, Norwich—are both extremely precise and specific (all of these being cities or towns in Southeast England) and more generally resonant and even symbolic, insofar as each place bears within it, as part of its constitutive history, the trace of everyone who has passed through it: hence, Chateaubriand actually lived for a time in a region called "The Saints"; his work is read by a woman who lives there now and talks to the narrator of *The Rings of Saturn*, who has read additional work by Chateaubriand and others. Sebald's methods of linkage thus allow grand historical themes to express themselves not so much through historical figures or fictional characters (as in historical novels) as through the resonant and textured histories of sites and of individuals, whether historical or fictional, associated with those sites.

Caterpillars and cocoons, metamorphoses and hatchings, historical debuts and endings, hopeful beginnings and horrors. The book ends with a record of facts that occurred on a single day, Thursday, April 13, 1995,

"Maundy Thursday, the feast day on which Christ's washing of the disciples' feet is remembered" (294). The list includes an account of catastrophes interspersed with happenings of joy:

> On this very day three hundred and ninety-seven years ago, Henry IV promulgated the Edict of Nantes; Handel's *Messiah* was first performed two hundred and fifty-three years ago, in Dublin; . . . the Anti-Semitic League was founded in Prussia one hundred and thirteen years ago; and, seventy-four years ago, the Amritsar massacre occurred, when General Dyer ordered his troops to fire on a rebellious crowd of fifteen thousand. (294–95)

Surprisingly, and against all odds, we arrive in Amritsar—the Sikh holy place I stressed in the previous chapter, while writing on *The English Patient,* because "silk cultivation . . . was developing . . . in the Amritsar region and indeed throughout India," undermining trade through China. Sebald then loops back to the Germans and the defeat of their imperial ambitions "in headlong retreat from the Red Army" on April 13, 1945. It concludes with a domestic event: the death of the narrator's father-in-law on the day from which he writes, April 13, 1995.[13]

Sebald's list may sound trite in summary, but the passage is quite wonderful in the narrative, achieving the kind of lift-off that writers dream of. It reveals how historical time —if examined and parsed—always includes a modicum of joy but an undertow of sadness and a series of catastrophes, some recalled by history, some forgotten, some willfully elided. As in Herodotus, individuals thrive and die, empires rise and fall, sometimes capriciously and sometimes with the predictability of the tides.

"And so they are ever returning to us, the dead": no insight was more typical of Sebald's open, generous sympathies. Sebald's narrators rescue lost histories by the patient investigation of lost lives, an investigation that includes sympathy with place and networks of objects and things as the contexts for the human.[14] He writes, as he says in *On the Natural History of Destruction,* as "a child" of World War II but also as someone attentive to the plight of other children of the war—to theirs in fact far more than to his own, to theirs as a way, perhaps, of laying to rest his own. He also writes as a citizen of the world, one with sympathies for all war's victims, but especially for the Jews, someone whose work enacts and tests the process toward an ethics of empathy and identification.

The key book, the indispensable book in this context is *Austerlitz,* Sebald's last novel, and as good a swan song as any writer could wish.

In *Austerlitz*, an unnamed narrator who, like all of Sebald's narrators resembles Sebald himself, talks at intervals over thirty years to Jacques Austerlitz, a scholar who shares the narrator's fascination for decayed architecture and other things once solid gone to ruin. They meet at the Antwerp railway station, covered by a dome with an intricate glass ceiling. The plot, the action consists of discussions of "star-shaped fortresses" and other official buildings all over Europe whose elaborate shapes "clearly showed how we feel obliged to keep surrounding ourselves with defenses until the idea . . . comes up against its natural limits" (14).[15]

The shapes of the fortresses echo the decorated dome of the railway ceiling and repeat many times in the words of the narrative and in the multiple black-and-white photographs that accompany it. Over time and over many pages, the characters' conversations lead to Terezin, Theresienstadt, the star-shaped fortified town in western Czechoslovakia that the Nazis used as a show camp but where many people died and from which many more, including Austerlitz's mother, were shipped east and vanished.

Star shapes, stairways, grids, doorways, railway stations, tumble-down fortresses, tangled roots: in Sebald's books such objects become images of time, change, decay, and ruin—memento mori. Star shapes, stairways, grids, doorways, tangled roots: the replication of shapes resembles tessellation, the way that nature repeats an underlying pattern multiple times with variations, so that nature seems both infinite and unified, random and precise—a nonmechanical computer.[16]

Austerlitz, the title character, lost all memory of his Jewish roots after he was sent from Prague to Liverpool Street Station in London and then to Wales in 1939, as part of a *Kindertransport*.[17] Adopted by a dour Calvinist missionary and his wife, and raised in isolation, he experienced his home as an oppressive place where "they never opened a window" (45). It made him sad "to wake up early in the morning and have to face the knowledge, new every day, that I was not at home now but very far away, in some kind of captivity," like a bird or an animal in a zoo.[18] In his dreams, he felt "overwhelmingly immediate images forcing their way out of him." But in his waking life, he "tried to recollect as little as possible, avoiding everything which related in any way to my unknown past" (139). Then, as an adult, Austerlitz embraced the sadness, burrowing irresistibly toward his history.

Research on his last name leads him to Prague.[19] His visual memory of streets, doors, and stairways brings him to Vera, the servant of his childhood home. The scene when they meet forms a model of understatement: "Vera covered her face with both hands, hands which, it flashed through my mind, were endlessly familiar to me, stared at me over her spread fingertips, and very quietly but with what to me was a quite singular clarity spoke these words in French: *Jacquot,* she said, *dis, est-ce que c'est vraiment toi?*" (153). (A friend recalls visiting unannounced, after fifty years, the farm in the Dordogne that hid him as a ten-year-old after his parents had been deported from France. "Eh, tu est Marcel," the farmer who opened the door said, not missing a beat.)

With Vera, Austerlitz visits spots in Prague that he did not know were so familiar and hears from her, in a complex interweaving of voices—a choral effect that captures the theme of shared catastrophe—the history of his parents up to their disappearance.

Theresienstadt, the camp where all traces of his mother end, becomes the apotheosis of the star-shaped fortresses and ruins that Austerlitz and the narrator discussed or visited near the start of the book. Built "in the eighteenth century to a star-shaped plan," the town now appears as an abandoned ruin and exists as a museum, frozen in time. The narrative records certain key images, some of which recur from Sebald's other books, like a rococo figurine of a dancing man and woman, which stands in the window of a deserted shop. The statue "rhymes" with a photograph Austerlitz has found of himself in Vera's house, dressed in eighteenth-century garb as a tiny page to his mother's "lady" at a costume ball they attended shortly before the war.[20]

Being there, in the place, Austerlitz "for the first time acquired some idea of the history of the persecution which my avoidance system had kept from me for so long, and which now, in this place, surrounded me on all sides" (198). As so often in Sebald's work, the site compels the process of making connections: "I understood it all now," Austerlitz tells the narrator, "yet I did not understand it, for every detail . . . far exceeded my comprehension" (199).

In some remarkable narrative sequences, Austerlitz finds a film made by the Nazis to sustain the illusion that Terezin had harbored a normal life. The inmates of the camp labor in workshops; they sit and watch a concert. Austerlitz scans the crowds for his mother, cannot find her, and hits upon the device of slowing down the film, "creating, by default as it were, a different sort of film altogether" (247).

Suddenly, people in the workshops "looked as if they were toiling in their sleep"; music at the concert "had become a funeral march dragging along at a grotesquely sluggish pace." The film emits "a menacing growl" that reminds Austerlitz of big cats he had once heard in a zoo who "lament hour after hour without ceasing" (247–50). In slow time, the film reveals things and meanings not ordinarily perceived. But Austerlitz does not find an image of his mother until one tumbles by chance from a book in Vera's house. As he pursues his mother's face, persistence and chance, effort and contingency work together, in a process that reaches an end but then begins again as Austerlitz sets off to find traces of his father. The sequence forms a keystone element that both stabilizes the narrative and opens up the whole.

Because *Austerlitz* moves so dramatically toward Theresienstadt, it seems to be about World War II more directly than Sebald's other books. It's tempting, at least at first, to use "Air War and Literature" as a scrim through which to read it. If one did so, the title character's preoccupation with ruins would mask his sense of childhood loss through the Holocaust in a way that parallels the author's or the narrator's hidden preoccupation with Germany's destruction. (As I note previously, I assume that the narrator resembles Sebald in some respects but is not identical with the man himself in all or even in most particulars.) The narrative would then reveal the title character's past but continue to mask the narrator's or author's secret obsession. In turn, the masking would help to explain why Austerlitz's recovery of his past and the image of his mother does not end either his restless questing or the narrator's.

The explanation I have just given may seem a little complicated, so let me also put it this way: if one used "Air War and Literature" as the key to *Austerlitz*, the tragedy closest to Sebald's own past—the destruction of German cities—would still remain unaccessed and unprocessed at the end of the book. Yet the narrative would have gone pretty deeply into some aspects of the Holocaust (the *Kindertransport;* Theresienstadt), which also engage the narrator's interest and emotions, even though he did not experience them personally or through any direct genealogical connection.[21]

There's a nicely devious, layered quality in the narrative sequence I have just described. But I would not, finally, want to push this reading of the novel too far. In fact, I need now to turn on the interpretation I have just given, expanding it further. For I believe that Sebald's interest in the catastrophes of others has, finally, more ineffable secrets.

"Listening to the roar of traffic, with a mounting sense of panic. . . ."

There are at least three ways to read Sebald's obsession with catastrophe. The first, but my least favorite by far, reads it as depression, as the effects of a personality trait that led to the episodes of debilitation and treatment alluded to at the beginning of *The Rings of Saturn*. I do not like this explanation because it seems too narrowly biographical, conflating the narrator and the author completely, which seems to me unjustified, and reducing the fictions to the by-product of illness.[22] But, finally, I do not like it because to brand the books as pessimistic or depressing misses the overall mood and tone of Sebald's novels, which I find more exhilarating than depressing.

I have mentioned Virginia Woolf and, if severe depressions there were in Sebald's life, they would be both as relevant and as irrelevant to the final effect of Sebald's books as her depressions were to hers.[23] They would be biographical facts, alluded to in the work. But they would not be coextensive with the work or its effect, which exceeds any personal illness.

A second way to read Sebald's obsession with catastrophe, while also biographical, seems somewhat less confining. Born in Germany, in 1944, Sebald's great topics—mutability, change, loss, and memory—always suggest to the modern imagination the Holocaust: the mutation, the change, the loss closest to his / our time, into whose milieu Sebald was born. Under this second interpretation, Sebald comes to his themes "naturally" since the Shoah, when it is not thought to "belong" to Jews—in the sense of having happened, as victims—is thought to belong to the Germans, in the sense of responsibility, as perpetrators. Even if it seems, as it does to me, ultimately too narrow, there are many factual justifications for this interpretation, enough to use it as a tentative rubric: Saul Friedlander notes, for example, that many Holocaust historians are Jewish and many others are non-Jewish Germans and that these two points of view have shaped Holocaust studies.[24] I like this view better than a strictly biographical approach, though it also depends, rather too specifically for my taste, on identity politics.

But there is a third and still better way to read Sebald's persistent meditations on catastrophe, one that uses the Holocaust as a starting point but identifies with its histories not as a Jew, or as a German—two connections based on identity politics, which always limit as well as expand the imagination—but *with* Jews and *with* Germans, identifications based not on what one might call a biographical imperative but on an ethical relationship to the world's dead. I need to be absolutely clear here: I am not talking in Sebald's case about a glib view of perpetrators as "victims" or about any kind of equivalence set up between Germans and Jews—an equivalence Sebald would, I believe, entirely reject.[25] I am talking instead about an open, generous, fully examined set of relationships—one alert to small-scale as well as to mass catastrophe, one in which Otherness (alterity) does not preclude a sense of connection, but demands it.

Sebald perceives the Holocaust as a profound recent historical catastrophe, even as a "unique" event that marks an important "before and after" in human history.[26] But he also perceives it as an emblematic event for European modernity—one possible consequence of the ordered, "sanitary," industrialism so fascinating to Austerlitz.[27] At the same time, he perceives it as the disaster that crystallizes most completely for our time the common, but profound human catastrophe: to be caught in time, which will obliterate all that can be accomplished in time, even the arduous work of memory. The process can be slow and gradual, quick and surprising, natural or manmade. But it is always most terrible—because arbitrary and avoidable and obeying no natural law—when it is manmade.

"And so they are ever returning to us, the dead," the narrator says in *The Emigrants;* "the living and the dead can move back and forth as they like," he says in *Austerlitz* (185). Sebald's mission as a writer is to seek out the dead and to make them welcome. It's a responsibility, a task, but also and ultimately second nature. For pervasive identification with the dead of the kind usually considered "premodern" augurs a kind of immortality. A labile current, it overflows into identification with animals and with things.

Understanding Sebald in this way makes his unusual techniques as a writer sing. As a narrator, he has an obsessive interest in many subjects but perhaps most consistently in people uprooted from their native place and from the sense of being "at home." He also burrows, with extraordinary persistence, into the history of natural events—hurricanes, avalanches, floods—histories that might be seen as meaningless given the inevitability of catastrophe and the scale of man-made devastation in our time, but which he also rescues in words from the moraines and abysses of time. He seems attuned to catastrophe's effects not just (and most) on humans, but also on nature: a landscape altered by a hurricane; eroded shores and submerged villages; trees dug up and replanted in a library courtyard, away from their native setting. At times, he even seems to perceive such events from the trees' point of view (*Austerlitz*, 278–81). Similarly, he seems aware that objects *participate in human catastrophe:* the lost mountaineer's boots in *The Emigrants,* Austerlitz's backpack, the rococo figurine in Theresienstadt. His imagination enriches the human by seeing it as part of nature, part of a network of things, albeit the part we privilege.[28] But he never commits anything as pathetic as the pathetic fallacy; he anchors his perceptions in his narrators / perceivers, the only ones able to articulate regret or sadness.

When he turns to world-historical catastrophe, as in *Austerlitz,* Sebald's themes require an extraordinary interpenetration of narrative voices. One voice—Vera's, the servant in Prague—reaches us, the readers, through the medium of Austerlitz's voice, which has been transposed onto the page by the unnamed narrator who, since he does not exist, can only speak through the author, W. G Sebald. In the following passage, for example, Vera's subject is how Austerlitz's father, Maximilian, gradually came to understand the sentiments of *Volk* mass feeling as a consolation for the humiliations of the First World War, driving Nazism in a dizzying, quasi-mystical spiral. It's a long passage, but a rich one that repays attention:

Maximilian, in spite of the cheerful disposition which he shared with Agáta [Austerlitz's mother], had been convinced ever since I knew him, said Vera, so Austerlitz told me, that the parvenus who had come to power in Germany and the corporate bodies and other human swarms endlessly proliferating under the new regime, a spectacle which inspired him, as he often said, with a sense of positive horror, had abandoned themselves from the first to a blind lust for conquest and destruction, taking its cue from the magic word *thousand* which the Reichskanzler, as we could all hear on the wireless, repeated constantly in his speeches. A thousand, ten thousand, twenty thousand, thirty-seven thousand, two hundred and forty thousand, a thousand times a thousand, thousands upon thousands: such was the refrain he barked out in his hoarse voice, drumming into the Germans the notion that the promise of their own greatness was about to be fulfilled. Nonetheless, said Vera, Austerlitz continued, Maximilian [Austerlitz's father] did not in any way believe that the German people had been driven into their misfortune; rather, in his view, they had entirely re-created themselves in this perverse form, engendered by every individual's wishful thinking and bound up with false family sentiment, and had then brought forth, as symbolic exponents of their innermost desires, so to speak, the Nazi grandees. . . . From time to time, so Vera recollected, said Austerlitz, Maximilian would tell the tale of . . . a trade union meeting. . . . Maximilian had told her, said Vera, that in the middle of this crowd, which had merged into a single living organism racked by strange, convulsive contractions, he had felt like a foreign body about to be crushed and then excreted. . . . It was in just the same vein, said Vera, that Maximilian later repeatedly described the spectacular film of the Party rally which he had seen in a Munich cinema . . . [which showed] the Führer's airplane descending slowly to earth through towering mountain ranges of cloud . . . [and] the ceremony honoring the war dead during which, as Maximilian described it to us, Hitler and Hess and Himmler strode down the broad avenue lined . . . by the power of the new state out of a host of immovable German bodies . . . and the huge forests of flags mysteriously swaying as they moved away by torchlight into the dark. (166–69)

This spectacular passage alludes to many theories of Nazism that I cannot pursue here as a perverted form of the oceanic, a prodigy produced, in part, by Germany's more typical love of orderliness and rationality. It alludes as well to Nazism's use of the mythic and the occult in mass rallies that enacted visually symbolic dramas of national unification unto immolation.[29] Indeed, the passage not only alludes to the perversion of oceanic unities but also prescribes an antidote, embodied in Maximilian's detached, witnessing, defamiliarizing eye. For while Sebald's themes require an extraordinary interpenetration of narrative voices, a suspension of the individual within the narrative that might efface individual judgment, as Nazism did, they also require a careful parsing that allows the thoughtful individual to be distinguished within the whole. Maximilian distinguishes himself from what is happening around him; Vera marks Maximilian's voice from her own; Austerlitz marks Vera's, and so forth. The process of following Sebald's prose will annoy some readers, but it will thrill and excite others. I am one of those who feel thrilled: that is why I enacted, in a small way, the interpenetration of my own words with Sebald's at the beginning of this chapter.[30]

Sebald's narratives within narratives (often with quotation marks omitted) can be hard to follow, like Faulkner's. But distinguishing one voice from another beyond a certain point proves to be quite unnecessary. For, after noting the disjunctions and gauging the tenor of what is being said, the reader can, finally, allow the voices to sound together. All of Sebald's speakers use the same images; all speak the same language—a language "wondering at the nature of the foundations on which our world is built" (180). The interpenetration of minds, the choral voice, seems the perfect technique to embody Sebald's themes.[31] For, as an author, Sebald is the master of lability, of intimate identification with the fate of others, an author who *feels* rather than mouths the familiar words, "do not ask for whom the bell tolls. It tolls for thee." The common images, the common effort, reflect an underlying sympathy profoundly part of Sebald's vision in which history becomes a version of the sublime—terrible and uncontrollable, and obliterating human lives—but linked to human experience through the recognition of relation.[32]

"The border between life and death is less impermeable
than we commonly think"

W. G. (Max) Sebald died at fifty-seven in a car accident on December 14, 2001. The event occurred within months of the publication in the United States of his most acclaimed novel, *Austerlitz*, a book that had illuminated the otherwise bleak fall of 2001. I never met the man, but I have found his books a revelation. I see him still or at least (to echo a typical Sebaldian phrase), I imagine that I see him still in my mind's eye: tall and sensitive-looking, his body outlined by a tree against which he leans (much as my father leans in a favorite family photo), slim, though his later photographs suggest a visible thickening around the waist, with a shock of receding white hair brushed back from a furrowed forehead, or eyes framed by glasses that greet the lens and yet squint into the camera's eye.[33] Looking into the distance unflinchingly, Sebald expressed what some critics have called "pessimism" or "angst" but seems to me more aptly called felt contingency, the accumulated tenor of history.[34] His work as a novelist emerged quite late in life, when Sebald was in his late forties. Before then, he had published very decent scholarly essays and books mostly read by other professors of comparative literature.

In what I have just written, in this chapter as a whole, I have performed what for me is an unusual and public act of identification with an author that takes me back to the need for specifying what one identifies with, how, and why—an issue crucial to many chapters in my book and crucial also to Sebald's novels, which give full rein to the act of identification until it seems time to rein it in.

No one could deny, for example, that Sebald's interest in the Holocaust and in Jewish characters as windows into the Holocaust is obsessive. Although the Holocaust is rarely mentioned in his work, as one critic quipped, the reader thinks of nothing else—an unusually deft transfer of obsession from writer to reader. But I would distinguish Sebald's obsession strongly from the delusional claims of someone like Bruno Dossekker (pen name, Binjamin Wilkomirski) or from the kind of identification via self-interest Peter Novick describes,[35] in which the fact of *not having experienced* the Holocaust forms a bond with those who died. Sebald's narrators do not call attention to or serve themselves; nor do they usurp others' suffering as their own. They facilitate others' stories; they are alert and present to them and willing to assume the duties and responsibilities that being in the middle distance implies.

In this sense, the passing of stories from speakers (characters) to listeners (narrators), and from authors to readers becomes the very subject of Sebald's work. The essence of these relationships in and around Sebald's writing is contact, dialogue, responsible listening, careful relating, and alert reading. The process demands careful attention to, and respect for, others—identification versus objectification. It confers responsibility but maintains a distance between oneself and another self. Such linking of self and other by dialogue, awareness, respect, and responsibility forms the core of many ethical theories, especially those of Buber and Levinas. In Sebald, looking, listening, and memorializing what deserves to be memorialized emerge not just as appropriate but also as necessary for the condition of being human.

In fact, the narrator in Sebald's writings proceeds very much in consonance with the model of Alain Badiou's *Ethics*. He works situation by situation toward an ethics of identification or away from it, as the situation demands. In *The Rings of Saturn*, for example, the narrator speculates on the Dowager Empress's motives as he tells her story, but he extends to her neither sympathy nor an act of identification. He identifies with Austerlitz as a connoisseur of ruins and as someone bereft of his native land; but he remains aware of being German-born and therefore always and already in a different relationship from Austerlitz to sites like Theresienstadt or Liverpool Street Station.

There is a *generosity*, a *shining* at the core of Sebald's work that readers know when they see it. In fact, such generosity and shining motivate the composition of Sebald's books. Almost everyone knows that Sebald founded a Center for Translation in Norwich at the University of East Anglia. But I learned on a recent visit there that the Center bases itself not just on the pragmatic need for teachers of literature to teach English students in the English language but on the loftier goal—now part and parcel of a lecture series renamed after Sebald in 2002—of reducing the claims of nationalism in literature, so often used (think of *The Aeneid*) to vaunt the goals of the imperial state. Translation as a generous act, undoing the violence of imperial nationalisms: Sebald's perspective may account for why he has had such good luck with his translators and they with him.

"Do you have any photographs of when you were at school? on sports day?": Sebald's colleague Clive Scott told me that some of the photographs in Sebald's books were found in archives (most likely by an assistant that a government grant made possible for Sebald in the last five years of his life), but also that he often asked friends to raid their personal archives for his books. In that way, friends' photographs made their way into texts that may become immortal. The level of collaboration, the level of community involved in Sebald's work can be that specific: two men, collaborating in adjacent offices. But his vision never defines communities so narrow as to be based on family connections or on friendship alone. Sebald's narrators pursue connections where they find them, often through chance encounters whose responsibilities they do not evade, but take further. As in Primo Levi, relationship is conferred by proximity, not relationship; as in Badiou, it begins by chance and proceeds situation by situation—with the imperative of keeping up, of seeing things through.

It is of the very essence in Sebald's books that readers participate in the process too, in a dialogue, a collaborative effort that plumbs the under-acknowledged potential of narrative to generate strong emotions as well as aesthetic pleasures of perceiving pattern and form.[36] The author . . . the narrator . . . the characters . . . the plot . . . the reader: the chain forms Sebald's theory of the novel—a Möbius strip from which no one element can be separated, each folding into the other with just a subtle twist. Connections. Twists. A theory of the novel and also, I believe, a theory of history highly relevant to the themes of this book.

Sebald richly understood, and he reminds us, that every disaster remains distinct and yet part of a whole—and that no one can win a competition for disaster. For catastrophe is a common process—a process we dread and yet one in which we are always already involved: alive but, in Austerlitz's words, "in some kind of captivity." Hiroshima, the Holocaust; the Holocaust, Hiroshima: one can define differences between the two of cause, of scale, of motivation, of victims—so that the differences between the events and their uniqueness are never in doubt. But both suggest the arbitrariness with which death can come, the man-made quality and the technological speed of mass death in our time.

CONCLUSION
Toward an Ethics of Identification

In the last two chapters, I turned to fiction, a turn that might have seemed jarring, even evasive, after a beginning grounded in statistics and in history. But the turn was, finally, quite deliberate in order to probe the kind of imaginative projections that novels can provide, their opening up of a space based on social realities, but not determined by them. For what we imagine, what we *are capable of imagining* bears, though not always directly or in anything like a definable straight line, on what we do and on how we enact the future.[1] At the beginning of this book, I used Freud's essay "Thoughts for the Times on War and Death," and I would like now to return to it to map some of the ways that it anticipates and to some extent *brings into being* the myth of the modern that emerged after World War I. With the twists, turns, and detours we have seen as typical of cultural memory, that myth became our myth too.

Like Hannah Arendt, Freud linked imperialism with the destruction of world war—a logical and intuitive connection and one based on historical propinquity, though one surprisingly under-theorized in our critical literature, where thinkers and critics tend to deal with one topic or the other rather than with both.[2] Under the pressure of world war, Freud's notion of civilization eroded and his feelings of membership within a clubby group of "white nations upon whom the leadership of the human species has fallen" became equivocal at best.[3] Then as now, economic interests linked Europe but they did not help to prevent, indeed they had seemed to foster, murderous rivalries. Once the sign of progress, technology increasingly made war more efficient, but not less brutal. Freud noted with dismay that the distance from which we now kill seems to diminish both respect for the enemy and remorse for his death, producing a fundamental alienation and abstraction. But, at the same time, the sheer number of deaths and their cumulative effect undermines customary euphemisms about, and the tendency to look away from, death.

"Our habit," Freud noted in his 1915 essay, "is to lay stress on the fortuitous causation of the death," to ask, as people always do, What did he / she die of? In this way, "we betray our endeavor to modify the significance of death from a necessity to an accident" and to treat the dead with "something like admiration for one who has accomplished a very difficult task" ("Thoughts on War and Death," 223). That's the way it is, that's the way it always is—we want to know the cause of death, as though death always has a definable cause that could be prevented. One sees that still in the common parlance of obituaries: people "battle" cancer; they die valiantly "after a long fight." In the same way, we try to portray all soldiers' deaths as brave and meaningful, even if some occur outside of combat or on senseless missions. After 9/11, it was common to describe all the World Trade Center dead (every one of them, without exception) as "heroes" and any demurrals from that view could be roundly censured.[4]

If World War I made polite fictions about death difficult to sustain, World War II made them even more so. What did people die of during the world wars? They died "in the war"—yes, they did. But, in addition to all the usual causes, they died by machine-gun fire or bombardments, their body parts dispersed like projectiles; they died by gassing; they starved or froze to death; they contracted typhus, or diarrhea, life oozing away with bodily fluids; they were burned or suffocated in "routine" and then in area or incendiary bombings; they were evaporated by the atomic bomb; they died of radiation sickness. The things people died of in world war made euphemism difficult to sustain—and so, in a sense, even more necessary. As Freud recognized in 1915—when the situation was still quite decorous compared to what came later—world war ignores "the distinction between civil and military sections of the population, the claims of private property." What is more, it trades not in single deaths— already hard to bear—but in "a multitude of simultaneous deaths" that "appears to us exceedingly terrible" ("Thoughts on War and Death," 211, 223).

What soldiers experience at first hand, even cultures by and large protected from the harshest facts of war, like the United States, felt too in expanding circles.[5] As world war more and more frankly involved civilians as a significant, sometimes the dominant, number of those killed, fear and apprehension became prominent emotions. As it became harder and harder to put death out of mind, our defensive formations grew ever more elaborate until (as Sebald might say) they reached their "natural limit."[6] As Freud put it: "in our civilized attitude towards death we are once more living beyond our means, and must reform and give truth its due" ("Thoughts on War and Death," 234).[7]

In the context of world war, Freud's exposition of Eros (love and sexuality) and Thanatos (destruction and death) in *Beyond the Pleasure Principle* becomes indispensable.[8] Freud speculates boldly, almost breathtakingly, that living matter emerged for unknown causes from inorganic matter and always seeks to return to its earliest state. Because death is always immanent in the living being, self-preservation from accidental or premature death (for example, in war) seeks only to remove the contingent in order to allow the immanent to unfold. The death instinct, the will of living matter to return to an inanimate state that existed prior to life, exerts a pull toward what seemed to Freud a form of "perfection," albeit one that we "cannot admit" (*Beyond the Pleasure Principle*, 37). His insight goes a long way toward explaining the fascination people feel alongside the horror of war: the display of destruction, the reduction to the inorganic, not only inspires fear and apprehension, it also provides the vicarious satisfaction of a goal and an endpoint reached.

"'The aim of all life is death,'" Freud speculates in *Beyond the Pleasure Principle* (32). It's an echo of "If you would endure life, be prepared for death," the final sentence in "Thoughts for the Times on War and Death."[9] War, Death, Life: Freud being Freud, sexuality cannot be far behind as the fourth term in an ongoing human drama.

In *Beyond the Pleasure Principle*, Freud describes the sexual instincts, always a privileged site in his theories, as an attempt to recapitulate the transition between death and life and so as an attempt to repeat and prolong the moment when "life" emerges. Although they can only prolong the process that leads to death (most concretely through the moment of ejaculation or the secondary life of reproduction), the erotic instincts forestall the movement toward individual death.[10] One reason Freud moved from speculations about sex in his early work to speculations about the origins of culture and religion is, I believe, that both channel the urge for individuals to join physically with another into larger and larger entities.[11]

Freud was always aware that literature, philosophy, and science can reach similar conclusions by different means; he often refers to having discovered some of his most important theories in great literature. And, in fact, many modern writers, some of whom read the same materials as Freud, raise similar concerns.[12] In 1922, for example, the same year *Beyond the Pleasure Principle* appeared, T. S. Eliot published *The Waste Land*, a poem often and openly read as a lament about the state of culture after World War I. Notoriously complex, Eliot's poem can't be fully explicated here, any more than Freud's work can be. But the essential point I need to make about the poem is not a contentious one. The poem alludes to the Great War from its opening lines—"April is the cruelest month, breeding / Lilacs out of the dead land"—a quite direct reference to World War I's spring offensives and to fields of death in France, through spectacles of the dead ("I had not thought death had undone so many"), to the poem's fascination with Eastern religions as a source of renewal and regeneration for a debased and debilitated West (*Shantih shantih shantih*).[13] Eliot saw the degraded state of modern life as permeating sexuality and as writ large in sexual crises.[14]

The poem's large network of allusions cycles regularly through Shakespeare, Jacobean drama, Christianity, Dante, the religious East: it's a long, rich list. But its most frequent cycle and the one immortalized in the poem's original notes is "the wasteland" as it figures in the Parsifal and Grail myths, with their Theban echoes of nature offended and the erotic urge corrupted or destroyed. Lurking just behind the poem, and lurking too for Freud, are massive works like Sir James George Frazer's *The Golden Bough*, with its armchair compendium of myths and ethnographic reports about kings who die and queens who mate with the new kings, cyclically, in patterns that align with the seasons.[15]

I could add other examples of postwar narratives linking world war, death, life, and sexuality, but I need to get to my immediate point: Freud and Eliot articulate the basic elements of myths that their culture would adopt and elaborate in diverse forms after World War I, myths that represent both primitive and civilized societies in terms of sexuality, violence, war, and death, with attention as well to economic systems, such as gift-giving.[16] These elements repeat again and again in the philosophical, historical, psychological, and literary materials of the day, making the myth of the primitive resemble the myth of the modern. Westerners often attribute to primitive others a constant need for ritual to pacify violent nature, to offset human violence (patricide, blasphemy, or the killing that comes with war), and to assure fertility. After World War I, the same anthropological categories permeate accounts of and fictions about contemporary life.[17]

It's no accident that, in Ernest Hemingway's *The Sun Also Rises* (1926), the protagonist / narrator has a thigh wound like Tristan's, but higher up and causing impotence—a sexual wound caused by and symbolizing World War I. Jake and his love, Lady Brett, can't stand thinking about it and so they don't. They go clubbing instead and talk in brittle-speak, a language of banter and thrill-seeking that forms a self-protective language to hide the pain—and wouldn't it be pretty if it could?

Always sour on industrial modernity, D. H. Lawrence experienced World War I as the apocalyptic realization of his worst fears. The revised version of *Women in Love* (1920) encoded the principles of Eros and Thanatos in the metaphors Lawrence used to structure his book—the African and Arctic ways to cultural dissolution. Like so much modernist work, the book manipulates symbols that link the primitive and the modern, sexuality and death: Gudrun's curious carved wooden figurines, the sadomasochistic thrill of Winifred's rabbit, Gerald and Gudrun in love, Minette (Pussum) and the African statues, Gerald's frozen death in the snow in Germany. According to Lawrence, the African way is sensual and the European Arctic way is rational, but both lead to individual and cultural death.[18]

"The bitterness of the war," Lawrence claimed in the 1919 foreword to *Women in Love*, "may be taken for granted in the characters," whose dialogue rattles like machine gun fire. The appearance of such images in civilian representations of postwar life should, I think, be taken seriously. They are signs of the unnatural prolongation of World War I in the modern imagination. They signal what I believe in fact to be true: that the twentieth century consists almost entirely of a state of mind tinged, and sometimes dominated, by wartime consciousness.

It's tempting to think of modernist writers as having one huge crib sheet—something like Frazer or Freud—always before their eyes. And, in a sense they did. But what they really had was a culture of war and the cultural myths that grew up around their culture of war. The myths were already nascent when the war began and largely traceable to Freud but were strongly inflected by the particular disillusionments and losses of World War I. Myths, being myths, any particular version has flexible and variable elements, but the myths in question always involve sexuality in contest with the death impulse.

Sexuality can be, and usually is, corrupted by social class or by economic factors. It often veers into violence and death—though, of course, it need not. Influences float free—strong but inchoate in a culture. Does the deferral of, "the shelving" of death via sexuality become our myth too? Is that why we have increasingly emphasized sexuality to the extent that talking about sex, which, at the beginning of the twentieth century, was overly censored and mostly absent from public discourse, had become by century's end not just open but also so pervasive and so casual that sex can seem a joke or punch line rather than something mysterious and ineffable?

"If you would endure life, be prepared for death": Freud's final statement in his 1915 essay enjoins a view of life that includes, indeed requires, awareness of death.[19] We live in a culture in which sex-talk is everywhere but also and simultaneously one both isolated from and afraid of death. At the same time—the simultaneity being not a bit surprising—we have become a culture fond of *sentimental fantasies about death* on the one hand, and, on the other, what I would call *spectacles of death*. The sentimental fantasies involve prettified versions: *The Lovely Bones* kind of thing that one sees over and over again in contemporary culture, in which the dead are not really dead but people like us, only better, and involved in life on Earth as presiding spirits or angels. Sometimes, as in popular reenactments of ancient myth, characters visit the underworld and find either that it holds no fears or can be overcome as the ancients could not overcome it. Each time I see this motif in contemporary culture, part of me feels intellectual contempt; part of me wonders whether it does not represent our culture's wish to come into more intimate contact with death, to spin-out some contemporary version of ancestor-worship.

But far more important and, I would say, almost definitive for our time, are what I call spectacles of death—fictional or distanced enactments that have numbed us and left us unprepared for the actuality. The trailers for what I call "bang-bang" movies (bullets spraying, cars leaping, buildings exploding, blood spurting) form spectacles of death and we can't avoid them unless we come very late to the local Cineplex and skip certain movies entirely. Television shows like *ER* enact with regularity a hovering between life and death and the transition between one state and another. Although no one to my knowledge has said so, many shows later incorporated emergency room scenes as a matter of course to cash in on the appeal of the motif.[20] Shows like *CSI* and *CSI Miami* have moved the spectacle one step further—beyond the transition between life and death and firmly into a hard-to-look-at, hands-on immersion in, even parsing of, the dead, or, to be precise (for the difference is important), of the pseudo dead. With their graphic autopsies and their simulated computer images of death, the shows can be hard to watch, although America is clearly watching.[21]

At the same time, our culture reacted with the strongest possible horror to the World Trade Center disaster and counted, one by one, these and other American deaths. Events around the war on terrorism—the immolation of bodies, the desecration of body parts, the beheading of hostages—and their dissemination on television or via the Internet violate typical boundaries and generate strong responses. Like the inflated fears around anthrax in 2001 and SARS in spring 2003, such reactions may reflect an imbalance between our fascination with death in the abstract or at a distance and our personal apprehensions about death that (Freud's words) "has fallen on some person whom we love" or with whom we identify.[22] Fascination, the "pornography effect," vicarious satisfaction, extreme horror, fear, and avoidance meet and mingle when death as spectacle becomes death close to home, a felt reality.

*   *   *

How do we count the dead in World War II? The victims of the Holocaust? What does it mean that, in many instances, we cannot name or even number the civilian dead? That we cannot bury them according to tradition? How do such realities affect the way we live now?

The United States lost relatively few civilians as a direct result of World War II; in England, 60,595 civilians were killed as a result of the war, most in London, with 82,182 seriously injured. The USSR lost approximately 6–7 million civilians among its total casualty figure of some 20 million (total estimates now being raised to 25 million or even 50 million, as Soviet archives open); civilian losses in Poland were also in the range of 6 million and included huge numbers from both Jewish and non-Jewish populations. Estimates of civilian casualties in China range from 2 to 10 million—a mind-bogglingly wide swing—with some estimates of the civilian dead in the Second World War not including China at all. On the losing side of World War II, estimates of German civilians killed range from lows of 500,000 to highs of over 3 million, the median being 1.6 million and the most reputable trying to separate those killed in Allied bombings (roughly 600,000) from those killed in other ways. German military losses are estimated at between 2.8 and 4.7 million, with the most reputable sources citing 3.5 to over 4 million dead.[23] By way of contrast, between 1941 and 1945, the United States enrolled over 16 million troops, with 292,131 battle deaths and 115,187 outside of battle—though one sees in print some variations in those numbers and hears, surprisingly often, much higher figures cited too. One of the asymmetries of war is that the larger the number of the dead, the more the chaos involved and the more unlikely that precise records will exist. And so we have figures like 3–5 million versus 292,131; 6–7 million versus 60,595.[24]

The number killed in the Shoah has become by convention "the 6 million," though that figure is partly guesswork like any other. It's largely based on Nazi records, including deportation figures kept by Adolf Eichmann, which counted human cargo in names but also in the aggregate— seven hundred to a car, a thousand. Estimates of the total number of Jews killed range from 4.5 to 10 million—and the figure chosen can be fighting words.[25] But when all is said and done, no single source is totally reliable; 6 million has lodged in cultural memory and will do.

Roughly 70,000 died in Hiroshima at impact and during the first days, though that figure too remains partial guesswork and others died over the next several weeks, months, and years. On the day the bomb exploded, people walked around dazed, knowing that something unprecedented had happened but having little way to understand the harnessing of energy that had actually occurred.[26]

In the context of such statistics, a 1947 essay on Hiroshima by Georges Bataille slaps us in the face with an opening that functions like an insult, a provocation: "Let's admit it," he exhorts, "the population of hell increases annually by fifty million souls. A world war may accelerate the rhythm slightly, but it cannot significantly alter it." He buttonholes his reader with the proposition that "To the ten million killed in the war from 1914 to 1918 one must add the two hundred million who, during the same period, were fated to die natural deaths."[27] By the same measure, to the standard, conservative figure of 50 million dead between 1939 and 1945 as a result of World War II, we would have to add roughly 300 million.

Bataille, with whom I'd like to linger just a bit, is both serious and ironic in bringing normal mortality figures to bear against those produced by world war. On the one hand, there *is* nothing special about mass death; it keeps the Earth afloat and the greater horror would be the multiplication of lives ad infinitum. On the other, as Bataille also recognizes, "the death of sixty thousand [the figure he used for Hiroshima] is charged with meaning, in that it depended on their fellow men to kill them or to let them live" ("Residents of Hiroshima," 226). For Bataille, "the atom bomb draws its meaning from its human origins," origins that swirl around "a core of darkness [that] remains untouchable," by which he means the omnipresence of death (221). In a passage that bears comparison to Freud, he writes, "misfortune's profound nonsense" remains "a basic component of human life," but one that most people do "not dare look in the face" (229). If Bataille is right, the atomic bombs formed a grotesque imitation, an intolerable simulacrum, of natural death. And because, as Freud puts it, "a multitude of simultaneous deaths appears to us exceedingly terrible," the emotions the bombs generated had to be bracketed under some category such as "the alternative to an invasion of Japan" or "civil defense" or "nuclear disarmament" —anything other than, Death: see also, the inevitable.

In these times of ours, which have only gotten worse, "the military art of destruction gains unprecedented means" and, according to Bataille, human sensibility "experiences this [as] new proof of its own useless-ness" ("Residents of Hiroshima," 231). What's more, Bataille claims, when forced to choose "between the horrors of war and giving up any of the activities through which it believes it must secure its future, society chooses war." As we have seen once again in the new century, individuals look toward the State for security in times of crisis even though, as Bataille speculates, the State, knowing that individuals can be expended, "immediately diminishes the individual's security and chances of survival" (229).[28] In effect, in the kind of paradox Bataille loves, "the need to make life secure wins out over the need to live" (229), producing a kind of stasis or paralysis in which the patterns of apprehension I have traced in this book prevail. Bataille's observations go a long way toward explaining America's reactions to 9/11, a date that brought death home and seemed to require, for many Americans, including most members of Congress, who voted in huge numbers for the Patriot Act, a trade-off between safety and civil liberties and truncated, for almost two full years, the kind of debate one might have expected about government policies.[29]

In the September 2002 *Harper's,* Mark Slouka said that 9/11 jarred the myth of American exceptionalism, the feeling that the blessed nation was, somehow, immune from death. We could get over, more or less, what happened "over there," an anywhere-but-here that includes Rwanda, Bosnia, and (though he does not mention them but should) Kampuchea, Israel and the former Palestine, Afghanistan, and now Sudan and Iraq. He said that American culture does not live with death but puts it quickly away, unlike many more traditional groups, like the rural Czechs he mentions and the many others he does not, who tend graves, store bones, access ancestors in ceremonies and dreams, even (among the Punan and the Asmat of Irian Jaya), sleep on their fathers' skulls. Each of Slouka's observations is true enough, in its way.[30]

But he was wrong to say that America "sailed over" Auschwitz to focus on 9/11 as a "world historical event." Rather, I would say that reactions to 9/11 were conditioned by Auschwitz and the other death camps and also by Hiroshima and Nagasaki and the cumulative events of World War II. Mass death, coming quickly and even arbitrarily; quick and simultaneous deaths, produced by technology's baneful side: 9/11 brought those facts home, though they had been with us for some time. Mass death is different from individual deaths—as Freud recognized long ago. *Both* are difficult to accept and process—and not just for Americans. Like Auschwitz, Hiroshima, Nagasaki, and other massive technological deaths, 9/11 had an added twist that heightened our fear and our initial paralysis: it left no bodies, and few bones. No bodies. Few bones. Mass death caused quickly rather than natural death in slow time. The "normal" coping mechanisms did not pertain. Even cultures intimate with death might be stumped and stymied. Death is always out here, and in us, but the war complex thrives most in such special conditions.[31]

If "worrying about the future is from now on the only foundation for worrying about the future," Bataille concludes, all we have is "a morality of the instant . . . that says: 'I am. In this instant I am. And I do not want to subordinate this instant to anything'" ("Residents of Hiroshima," 234). Bataille's conclusion might be a version of the contemporary witticism, "I shop; therefore I am." But it might also be a version of the destructive sublime, a secular transcendence modeled on religious transcendence, itself often based on the acceptance of death and a realization of life's fragility.[32] Bataille's conclusion loops back to Freud but rewrites him in a postwar, existential key—bringing me full circle, save that the circles have overlapped and spread. For Bataille's 1947 essay might seem merely eccentric except that *history*, including history since 9/11, has made his ideas about how modern people behave in the face of death seem not idiosyncratic but on-point and irresistible.

* * *

In the introduction to this book, I said that the war complex is the difficulty of confronting the fact of mass, sometimes simultaneous, death caused by human beings wielding technology, in shorter and shorter periods of time, often on religious or ethnic grounds and under government or other political auspices—a fact urged upon us repeatedly by World War II but as insistently deflected. I stand by that as this book concludes. But we cannot finally process death in the millions or even in the thousands. Facts and statistics lay bare the natural rhythms of the world—Bataille's "core of darkness"—too starkly. And so we particularize mass death through our imagination of nations and groups, but most of all through our imagination of families and of individuals. The numbers in my last sentence—nations, groups, families, individuals (a great many, many, relatively few, just one)—revisit but reverse those in the conjunction of self, family, and nation that I raised in the Introduction, a conjunction that seems to me of the essence. The cultural memory of Hiroshima and the Holocaust in the United States, as well as the evolving memory of 9/11, have followed very different paths, but they merge on this point: the war complex grows as we grow and lives where we live, in families. It begins by imagining historical disaster in the home.[33]

When I think back over the materials I have examined and the memories I received about World War II, I am struck by how almost all led back to families. When John Hersey wrote *Hiroshima,* he focused on individuals, including, in striking sections, a mother and her children in their home when the bomb fell. Similarly, a turning point in many Holocaust testimonials is the separation of families at the camps and, for those who survive, the abandonment at some point of a weaker friend or relation. From Elie Wiesel's *Night* (1961), through William Styron's *Sophie's Choice* (1979), to Anne Michaels's *Fugitive Pieces* (1996), fiction frames the Holocaust with narratives about families: Sophie choosing which of her children will have a chance to live; Michaels's hero bereft forever of his sister Bella. In the same way, television dramas like *Holocaust* (NBC, 1978) were structured around families, as were major films about the Holocaust, like the Academy Award–winning *The Pianist* (directed by

Roman Polanski, 2003). Our focus after 9/11 was not just on the individuals lost, even though the numbers involved, relative to World War II, were small enough to allow that focus, but also on their families. We process catastrophe as it afflicts the individual, through families. The point of maximal emotional vulnerability for the individual is as the survivor of a lost family.[34]

Is the emphasis on the family or on the loving couple a convention and a sentimentality? Possibly—though it's hard to know for sure how we would know, so pervasive is the value we attach to love and family feeling, though they can be differently defined. Is such a narrow basis of empathy contemptible? Yes, in a way, especially when we bypass, as we tend to do, the deaths of others, especially others who are enemies. Or are such reactions only natural or so culturally conditioned as to seem natural and, so, inevitable? Does the answer matter, since it's all we have? Jewish services look beyond the individual death to emphasize the will of God; Christian renunciation and Buddhist *samadhi* bypass the personal at the end. Hinduism sees attachment to those we love and to life itself as *kleshas,* things that hold us back from recognizing and participating in the energy of the universe. The religious teachings are consistent but the lessons they teach are the hardest of all to learn. For our culture to exit from the war complex, we've got to start from our reality, project a future—even if it is, at first, only imagined—and build from there to an ethic large enough to include others as though they were our families or ourselves.

But that would make war impossible, one might say. And I of course would say, Exactly so—though I would also add that such a total revolution in human consciousness seems not just hard work but also unlikely, at best. Consider the evidence even within this book: the difficulties of identification, its pitfalls—even around a subject like the Holocaust. But consider also the way that certain deeds emerge as shining: Anton Schmid's, the nameless Dutch Jew's, the narrators in Sebald's fictions who, when faced with impossible and even self-endangering feelings of empathy, press onward. "Immortal" Alain Badiou calls the process of ethical action based on the simple acceptance of otherness. Immortal. But also present among us in ways we cannot always predict.

The "I" that says so makes another point as well. Cultural change never arrives all at once and spontaneously through a unit as large as a nation or a society. First, there must be individual convictions and actions; then those of groups; then the forum of public discourse, followed by some degree of cultural consensus in which the original impulse for change must repeatedly be perceived and felt anew—a tricky proposition at best—rather than simply mouthed or repeated.[35]

For now, the processes of empathy and identification I have been tracing exist mostly in isolated but demonstrable instances, in theory, and in fictions. But they may, just may, be gestating within the individuals who form our culture. At certain points, they surface in communities that come together for a specific purpose and then disband. To give some recent examples from 2003 and 2004: in the large and, to some extent, unlikely (given the initial lack of media coverage they received) antiwar rallies in America and around the world that preceded the U.S. invasion of Iraq; in the best moments of Howard Dean's campaign; in Madrid in March of 2004, when the public turned out in multitudes flashing whitened palms to say, No more. In all these instances, large segments of the general public shook off the paralysis that gripped public discourse after 9/11 before most politicians and most media did.[36] Such impulses will not end all war—a utopian goal at best—but they may prevent some wars some of the time: a modest goal and one realistic enough to aim at. The task, to cite Badiou one last time, is to show that "something else is possible, but not that everything is possible." For us, for now, the task is "to propose a few possibilities" and to show "how the space of the possible is larger than the one we are assigned."[37]

For though our actions may not be entirely unfettered by the societies in which we live, though "not everything is possible," what we do, what comes next, is always and truly up to us. I have stressed movement toward an ethics of empathy and identification that proceeds not in knee-jerk fashion but situation by situation. Where do we go from here? We continue, we go on, taking chances as they come to us.

AFTERWORD

Childhood memories of watching World War II documentaries were at the origin of this book—rituals of family bonding that made me a connoisseur of World War II long before it became a professional interest. Dismay over the invasion of Iraq saw *The War Complex* through to its end, changing me and my book in the process.

Because its origins ran deep, *The War Complex* has been in many ways a stealth book, taking shape gradually, over a period of years with, atypically, no publication of parts along the way. In its early incarnations, the book met with resistance that both surprised and dismayed me. In the end, I'd like to give my thanks to those who resisted, who made me more thoughtful and certainly more careful. My thanks also, and more publicly, to those who read or heard versions of early drafts or offered instinctive encouragement: Geri Thoma, Priscilla Wald, Alex Roland, Alicia Ostriker, Karl Kroeber, Martin Meisel, Deborah White, Michael Wood, Jan Radway, Chris Newfield, Maryanne O'Farrell, various members of a seminar I taught at Emory University, and lecture audiences at Emory, the University of Wisconsin–Milwaukee, and the University of Akron. Three unnamed readers for the University of Chicago provided wonderful insights that very much improved the book. Clive Scott of the University of East Anglia kindly spent some time with me to talk about W. G. (Max) Sebald; his observations helped me round off chapter 5.

A 2003 seminar at Duke University called Wartime and graduate students in a Contemporary Fiction class provided food for thought and, sometimes, for citation. Because this book celebrates collective work, I feel especially grateful for their insights. Joe Fitzpatrick, who co-taught with me the Duke in New York in the Arts and Media program in 2002 read some drafts and made good suggestions. Caleb Smith, whose dissertation I was advising, offered me the kinds of focused, intensely helpful readings that writers dream of; always on target, his suggestions improved several chapters. David Gardner, my assistant in fall 2003, displayed proofreading skill that I especially appreciated when I proofread later chapters myself.

Friends and family were sustaining joys. Rosa Oppenheim, Elaine Showalter, and Joyce Carol Oates proved outstanding in their support and friendship. Alan Thomas, an editor who has become a friend over the years, showed caution laced by grace throughout. My thanks to him and to the many outstanding people at the University of Chicago Press, including Randy Petilos and Dawn Hall, who helped bring the book to life.

My husband, Stuart, and my older daughter, Kate, were their usual exemplary selves, reading various drafts and helping me to think through certain problems. My younger daughter, Lizz, undertook two photographic projects in 2002 and 2003 that interacted with my book: *Warbooks* and *Evidence,* the first an artful representation of what libraries hold on the subject of war, the second a compendium of graffiti, signage, and other ephemeral marks of public response to the 2003 invasion of Iraq. My thanks to her for her passion and for her suggestion as to the title of this book.

One final note as I send this book off. I had hoped that John Kerry would be president when *The War Complex* appeared and that new directions would lead somehow to peace. But the 2004 election suggests that our current culture of war will be ongoing, perhaps even extended. I would still answer the question, Where do we go from here? as I do at the end of the book: we keep up, we go onward, taking chances as they come to us.

Marianna Torgovnick
November 2004

NOTES

Prologue

1. Two troubling signs of slippage in the public mind between Iraq and al-Qaeda: the persistent belief among Americans that at least one Iraqi hijacked planes on 9/11, even though the fact that none of the hijackers was from Iraq has been fully documented and widely reported; the erroneous belief that the capture of Saddam Hussein (or, for that matter, that of Osama bin Laden) would end Islamist attacks. On Iraq and al-Qaeda, see Tom Zeller, "The Iraq-Qaeda Link: A Short History," *New York Times,* June 20, 2004, section 4, 4. See also the accompanying sidebar, "What the Bush Administration Said."

A note about spelling: al-Qaeda, like al-Jazeera, is sometimes spelled differently in different sources and even within different parts of the same source: one often sees Al Qaeda; sometimes, and increasingly, al-Qaida, which is relatively more correct because it conforms to the fact that there is no letter "e" in Arabic transliteration. Qaeda remained standard as this book went to press. Following advice from scholars and the most frequent usage of the *New York Times,* a source frequently cited in this book as a newspaper with national distribution, I use al-Qaeda and al-Jazeera (lower case *al;* hyphen), but use different spellings if found within titles or quotations.

2. When I first wrote the phrase "the politics of fear," it seemed dangerous and "out there" to do so. After the candidacy of Howard Dean, Democrats and others began to articulate the idea quite freely.

3. Widely hailed as a triumph at the time it was given, the 2003 State of the Union later came under attack for a substantial error concerning Iraq's having sought nuclear materials from Niger. The implications thickened when officials within the administration were accused of having leaked the name of a CIA operative in order to punish her husband, who had helped to expose the original misinformation; as of this writing, an inquiry into the leak remains ongoing. See Paul Krugman, "Waggy Dog Stories," *New York Times,* May 30, 2003, Op-Ed.

In another event hailed initially as a media triumph, the president landed on an aircraft carrier on May 1, 2003, to declare the end of major hostilities and appeared in a flight suit, even though, respecting the difference between the military and its civilian commander in chief, not even Dwight D. Eisenhower donned a uniform as president (see Paul Krugman, "Man on Horseback," *New York Times*, May 6, 2003, Op-Ed, A-31). His choice (followed by subsequent appearances in quasi-military garb) was perceived differently as hostilities in Iraq persisted and disaffection with the war grew.

4. The first quotation comes from David E. Sanger, "Threats and Responses: News Analysis; A New Doctrine for War," *New York Times*, March 18, 2003, A-1; the second comes from Tony Judt, "America and the World," *New York Review of Books*, 50:6 (April 10, 2003): 28; www.nybooks.com/articles/16176, 13 of 16. I had perceived connections between the cultural memory of World War II and 9/11 as early as November 2001; by spring 2003, they had become fully legible. With regard to Munich, Judt's word choice was well advised: Munich, as most people should remember, was about *opposing* one nation's aggressive action against another sovereign state; Saddam Hussein had taken and proposed to take no such action in 2003.

5. On the bluntest statement, a commencement address at the Air Force Academy on June 2, 2004, see Elizabeth Bumiller, "The Reach of War: The President; Addressing Cadets, Bush Sees Parallel to World War II," *New York Times*, June 3, 2004, A-16. Throughout summer 2004, as support for U.S. policies in Iraq eroded, the president often chose to address military or other highly screened audiences, a decision that might have been seen as isolating him from the popular mood. Meanwhile Michael Moore followed his best-selling *Dude, Where's My Country* (New York: Warner Books, 2003) with *Fahrenheit 9/11* (2004), a film that had to overcome powerful obstacles to reach audiences. Books that had exposed the Bush administration to criticism and opened public discourse continued as best sellers, including Bob Woodward's *Plan of Attack* (New York: Simon and Schuster, 2004) and Richard A. Clarke's *Against All Enemies: Inside America's War on Terror* (New York: Free Press, 2004).

6. Always active among those who demonstrated in favor of a diplomatic solution in Iraq, the Vietnam analogy reentered wider public discourse in July 2003, when General Abizaid used the words "guerilla combat." While many specific differences exist between Vietnam and Iraq, (the terrain, political contexts, etc.) the analogy suggests both combats as "quagmires."

7. See Sarah Lyall, "Threats and Responses: Human Rights; Amnesty Calls World Less Safe," *New York Times*, May 29, 2003, A-13 and Don Van Natta Jr., "A World Made More Dangerous as Terrorism Spreads," *New York Times*, April 18, 2004, section 4, 1. The issue was raised again by the 9/11 Commission, whose general sense was that al-Qaeda had been able to recruit substantially after the invasion of Iraq and had become more diffuse, making its future actions more difficult to detect.

8. Sigmund Freud, "Thoughts for the Times on War and Death," reprinted in *On Creativity and the Unconscious: Papers on the Psychology of Art, Literature, Love, Religion*, ed. Benjamin Nelson (1915; New York: Harper, 1958), 223. Freud's title in the original German is "Zeitgemäßes über Krieg und Tod." See Samuel Weber, "Wartime," in *Violence, Identity, and Self-Determination*, ed. Hent De Vries and Samuel Weber (Stanford: Stanford University Press, 1997), 85–87.

9. Substantial portions of "Thoughts for the Times on War and Death" contrast civilized and "primitive" societies. See my book *Gone Primitive: Savage Intellects, Modern Lives* (Chicago: University of Chicago Press, 1990), chap. 10.

10. Paul Fussell's classic study *The Great War and Modern Memory* (New York: Oxford University Press, 1975) describes cynicism about official communications as one consequence of the war, as well as various defensive measures such as a stress on British pastoralism. I return to Eliot, Hemingway, and Lawrence in the Conclusion.

11. Edith Wyschogrod makes the point about technological speed in *An Ethics of Remembering: History, Heterology, and the Nameless Others* (Chicago: University of Chicago Press, 1998), xiii, 42. I have added the idea of government auspices and the burning or vaporization of bodies.

12. The series was conceived and written by Janny Scott and ran for well over a year.

13. The "middle distance" can overlap with eyewitness status but usually operates independently of personal connections through family or friends. In this instance, I was close enough to see the buildings burning and to be an eyewitness to what happened in New York, but not close enough to see what was actually happening at the site later called Ground Zero.

14. For objective measurements that confirmed my observations, see Lauren Slater, "Repress Yourself," *New York Times Magazine,* February 23, 2003, 48), which cites reactions in New York, post—September 11 and makes a case that, in some instances, repression can be an effective coping mechanism, one separable from trauma.

15. Compare W. G. Sebald, paraphrasing Stendhal: "even when the images supplied by memory are true to life one can place little confidence in them." For images from paintings, photographs, or (in our time) television, "will displace our memories completely, indeed . . . destroy them" (*Vertigo*, trans. Michael Hulse [1990; New York: New Directions, 2000], 7–8). Perhaps for that reason, I remain unsure, even today, of whether I saw the first Tower collapse as I stood in the street or saw it on TV.

16. While the Prologue as a whole was written subsequent to November 2001, my account of the actual events of 9/11 was left substantially unaltered.

17. Called "Here is New York," after E. B. White's essay, the show galvanized community energy but then, like Ground Zero itself, became a tourist attraction. White's essay, published in 1949, refers to planes bearing the A-bomb but seemed prophetic in 2001.

18. See "Photography, Journalism, and Trauma," *Journalism After September 11,* ed. Barbie Zelizer and Stuart Allan (London and New York: Routledge, 2002).

19. Joan Didion claims that "secular democracy has been up for grabs" in recent events such as the Clinton impeachment and the 2000 election; in observations that tallied with mine, she connects the dots between "political process and what had happened on September 11 . . . between our political life and the shape our reactions would take and was in fact already taking." See "Fixed Opinions, or the Hinge of History," *New York Review of Books,* 50:1 (January 16, 2003): 54; www.nybooks.com/articles/15984, 1 of 7.

20. As elsewhere around the United States and the world, dissent in New York continued up to the invasion of Iraq. One protest drew sidewalk-to-sidewalk crowds from Washington Square Park to Thirty-fourth Street, stopping traffic completely along Fifth Avenue. Although President Bush positioned the invasion as a response to 9/11, New Yorkers expressed great skepticism from the start. See James Barron, "With Tighter Security, New Yorkers Tense Up for Prospect of Life in Wartime," *New York Times,* March 19, 2003, A-21.

21. In the weeks after September 11, CNN lost some of its credibility by sensationalizing the news. The streaming banners it ran, for example, preannounced a war; it both created

and sustained hysteria about anthrax. Many people I know felt that our only power against the media was the power to turn them off.

22. On press reliance on official sources after 9/11, see the following essays in Zelizer and Allan, eds., *Journalism After September 11:* James W. Carey, "American Journalism On, Before, and After September 11"; Robert W. McChesney, "September 11 and the Structural Limitations of U.S. Journalism"; Annabelle Sreberny, "Trauma Talk: Reconfiguring the Inside and Outside"; and Ingrid Volkmer, "Journalism and Political Crises in the Global Network Society."

Some consequences of the reduced discussion seem tragic. Al Gore, for example, made a major speech in September 2002, against the doctrine of preemptive strikes; the media barely covered it and, when they did, dismissed its contents as political jockeying. Gore withdrew as a candidate for 2004 shortly afterwards, perhaps partly because press coverage seemed to auger defeat. Many op-ed columnists and cartoonists were relentless in raising questions, as were men and women I encountered on the street. The disjunction between public sentiment and government action has not been larger in my memory.

23. The quoted part of this definition is Lionel Trilling's in "Manners, Moral, and the Novel," in *The Liberal Imagination*. First published in 1949 and reprinted many times since, the definition seems to me to have aged well. See Raymond Williams, *Keywords: A Vocabulary of Culture and Society*, rev. ed. (New York: Oxford University Press, 1985), 87–93, for a summary of the complications that surround the word *culture*. In addition to classic texts like Michel Foucault's *Discipline and Punish* and *The History of Sexuality*, vol. 1, see also Geoffrey H. Hartman, *The Fateful Question of Culture* (New York: Columbia University Press, 1997), 1–59. Brian Massumi in *Parables for the Virtual: Movement, Affect, Sensation* (Durham, NC: Duke University Press, 2002) describes culture as the bridge between individuals and societies and so a network of emotions that register on bodies. He uses the term *affect* in a way similar to how I use memoir and personal writing in this book.

Introduction

1. F. Scott Fitzgerald, *The Great Gatsby* (1925; New York: Simon and Schuster, 1995), 7. Gatsby presents himself as a former soldier and the winner of multiple medals, and he and Nick bond initially over the war. Priscilla Wald suggested the pertinence of *The Great Gatsby* to my project, for which my thanks.

2. Although I like the directness of the word "wartime" I use "wartime consciousness" to avoid confusion that seems inevitable in English with periods of active combat.

3. In the psychological lexicon, *cognitive dissonance* and *derealization* resemble the phenomenon I am describing. A short essay by Sigmund Freud called "A Disturbance of Memory on the Acropolis: An Open Letter to Romain Rolland on the Occasion of his Seventieth Birthday" (1936) defines *derealization* in this way: assuming "I had (or might have had) a momentary feeling: *'What I see here is not real.'* . . . I made an attempt to ward that feeling off, and I succeeded, at the cost of making a false pronouncement about the past." In context, he treats the phenomenon as individual and as linked to family plots but might have claimed a wider applicability. See *The Standard Edition of the Complete Psychological Works of Sigmund Freud, vol. 22, 1932–36* (London: Hogarth, 1964), 244.

4. Tom Brokaw popularized the phrase used in the title of his book *The Greatest Gener-*

ation (New York: Random House, 1998). The United States dominated the first and major trial at Nuremberg, the International Military Tribunal, and held later trials there on its own. Many scholars agree that, since 1985, the United States has become a primary repository for the collective memory of the Holocaust. See Peter Novick, *The Holocaust in American Life* (Boston: Houghton Mifflin, 1999); Alan Mintz, *Popular Culture and the Shaping of Holocaust Memory in America* (Seattle: University of Washington Press, 2001); Alvin H. Rosenfeld, *The Americanization of the Holocaust* (Ann Arbor: the University of Michigan Press, 1995); and Anson Rabinbach, "From Explosion to Erosion: Holocaust Memorialization in America since Bitburg," in *Passing into History: Nazism and the Holocaust beyond Memory: In Honor of Saul Friedlander on his Sixty-Fifth Birthday,* ed. Gulie Ne'eman Arad (Bloomington: Indiana University Press, 1998), 226.

5. See, for example, Stephen E. Ambrose, *Citizen Soldiers: The U.S. Army from the Normandy Beaches to the Surrender of Germany, June 7, 1944–May 7, 1945* (New York: Simon and Schuster, 1997), and *D-Day, June 6, 1944: The Climactic Battle of World War II* (New York: Simon and Schuster, 1994).

6. Gray writes: "Millions of men in our day—like millions before us—have learned to live in war's strange element and have discovered in it a powerful fascination. . . . the delight in seeing, the delight in comradeship, the delight in destruction," in which, "absorbed into what he sees," a soldier enjoys "the feelings of superiority of the secure." See *The Warriors: Reflections on Men in Battle* (New York: Harcourt, Brace and Company, 1959), 28–29, 33–34. See also Craig Hedges, *War Is a Force That Gives Us Meaning* (New York: Public Affairs, 2002). The military historians named are cited later in this book.

7. James Bradley's *Flags of Our Fathers* (New York: Bantam, 2000), a memoir by one of the soldier's sons, disclosed that the raising of the flag was a faked shot—although still one much memorialized and recalled without irony. The facts may not matter, for the image has become a fixed spot in national memory. For example, although Peter Jennings reported on ABC that the toppling of Saddam Hussein's statue in Baghdad was accomplished by approximately seven Iraqis, egged on by the U.S. military and accompanied by more reporters than Iraqis, the facts have not affected subsequent references.

8. Maurice Halbwachs, *On Collective Memory,* ed. and trans. Lewis A Coser (Chicago: University of Chicago Press, 1992), all quotations 182–83, except "the group . . . relation," 52. The volume edited by Coser reprints selections from Halbwachs' important books: *Les cadres sociaux de la mémoire* (1925) translated as *The Social Framework of Memory* (1975) and a posthumous book called *La mémoire collective* (1950). Maurice Halbwachs remains the locus classicus for all sociological studies of collective memory; his formulations from the 1920s and 1930s sometimes show their age and can seem overly confident but remain suggestive. One of life's little ironies is that Halbwachs, a German Protestant, died after he was arrested by the Nazis for protesting the arrest of his father-in-law, who was a German Jew. His ideas bear comparison with Émile Durkheim on "the need of social integration." Zygmunt Bauman offers a trenchant critique of the outcome of sociology's emphasis on social integration in the Nazi state in *Modernity and the Holocaust* (Ithaca, NY: Cornell University Press, 1989). Walter Benjamin makes some interesting observations about shock and its relation to memory in "Some Motifs in Baudelaire," in *Illuminations,* ed. Hannah Arendt (New York: Schocken Books, 1969). Jacques Rancière suggests disagreement as an alterna-

tive model for policy making in *Dis-agreement: Politics and Philosophy*, trans. Julie Rose (Minneapolis: University of Minnesota Press, 1999). In this context, Jürgen Habermas has published other important work, especially *The Theory of Communicative Action*.

In *The War Complex*, I use the term "cultural memory" instead of "collective memory" to underscore my method of cultural analysis rather than the statistical surveys often associated today with the term "collective memory."

9. See Gerhard L. Weinberg, *A World at Arms: A Global History of World War II* (Cambridge: Cambridge University Press, 1994), 894, and, for even more recent developments, Benjamin Schwarz, "A Job for Rewrite: Stalin's War," *New York Times*, 21 February 21, 2004, A-17, 19. Exhibits at the Imperial War Museum in London stress Soviet losses in ways that most American sources do not.

10. Jeanne Wakatsuki Houston and James D. Houston's *Farewell to Manzanar: A True Story of Japanese American Experience during and after the World War II Internment* (Boston: Houghton Mifflin, 1973) greatly publicized this history. Until recently, the Japanese internment camps were remembered more on the West than East Coast; a public memorial in Washington D.C. was long delayed.

11. Initial British decisions to bomb only industrial sites in Germany blurred over time because of poor visibility, proximity to neighborhoods, and similar conditions, leading to acceptance of the principle of area bombing of cities. U.S. policies, while for a time more resistant to such erosions in Germany, followed Britain's example in Japan where prevailing conditions made accuracy "impossible." See Weinberg, *World at Arms*, 577–80, 870.

12. For a recent version of the debate for mutual deterrence, see Scott D. Sagan and Kenneth N. Waltz, *The Spread of Nuclear Weapons: A Debate* (New York: Norton, 1995). An updated version was published in 2003.

13. Kurt Vonnegut, *Slaughterhouse Five, or The Children's Crusade: A Duty-Dance with Death* (New York: Delacorte Press, 1969), 165.

14. Published in the United States as part of *On the Natural History of Destruction*, trans. Anthea Bell (New York: Random House, 2002).

15. Frederick Taylor, *Dresden: Tuesday 13 February 1945* (London: Bloomsbury, 2004). Gabriel Schoenfeld's review in the *New York Times* focused on the apologia to the extent of seeming to blame the victims; see "Firebombing: A New Look at the Destruction of Dresden," *New York Times Book Review* (May 2, 2004): 20.

16. Christopher Hitchens notes that the allegation that Churchill knew in advance about Coventry and used it for political purposes "has now been in print for fifteen years, and I have never seen it addressed by the Great Man's defenders, let alone rebutted" ("The Medals of His Defeats," *Atlantic Monthly*, April 2002, 13 of 24), available online at www.theatlantic.com / issues / 2002 / 04 / hitchens.htm.

17. The kamikaze attacks followed a certain logic: since an extremely high percentage of pilots and planes were shot down on their first mission, the idea was to make the losses count as much as possible. See Weinberg, *World at Arms*, 847–48. The battle for Okinawa lasted three months until well into June 1945; the United States suffered 75,000 casualties (see Weinberg, 827 and 881–82).

18. See John Keegan, *The Second World War* (New York: Penguin, 1989), chap. 22, for an excellent history of the policy of "strategic bombings."

19. See Lawrence Lifschultz and Kai Bird, "The Legend of Hiroshima," xlvii–xlviii,

and Barton Bernstein, "Seizing the Contested Terrain of Early Nuclear History," in *Hiroshima's Shadow,* ed. Kai Bird and Lawrence Lifschultz (Stony Creek, CT: Pamphleteer's Press, 1998), 163–97.

20. The first two, gateway, charges at IMT were conspiracy to wage aggressive war and the waging of such war or crimes against peace. The United States and the Soviets (whom the defendants also accused of war crimes) had been attacked.

21. See Elizabeth Olson, "Enola Gay Reassembled for Revised Museum Show," *New York Times,* August 19, 2003, A-16.

22. For an excellent selection of debate in 1946–47, reprinted from many sources, see *Hiroshima's Shadow,* ed. Bird and Lifschultz, 237–316. I provide more detail about these subjects in chapter 4.

23. Some books: Hersey's anecdotal and journalistic book (1946); *Megamurder* by E. L. M. Burns (New York: Pantheon, 1967); Jonathan Schell's *The Fate of the Earth* (New York: Knopf, 1982); Richard Rhodes's *The Making of the Atomic Bomb* (1986; New York: Touchstone, 1988); Robert Jay Lifton's *Death in Life: Survivors of Hiroshima* (1967; repr., Chapel Hill, NC: University of North Carolina Press, 1991); Lifton and Greg Mitchell's *Hiroshima in America: A Half Century of Denial* (New York: Putnam's Sons, 1995); John Whittier Treat's *Writing Ground Zero: Japanese Literature and the Atomic Bomb* (Chicago: University of Chicago Press, 1995); and the edited volumes *Hiroshima in History and in Memory,* ed. Michael S. Hogan (New York: Columbia University Press, 1996); *Living with the Bomb: American and Japanese Cultural Conflicts in the Nuclear Age,* ed. Laura Hein and Mark Selden (Armonk, NY: M.E. Sharpe, 1997); and Bird and Lifschultz, eds., *Hiroshima's Shadow*—with scant others.

Rhodes's book won a Pulitzer Prize, the National Book Award, and the National Book Critics Circle Award. But Lifton's books have received the most sustained attention, with *Death in Life* winning a National Book Award. Schell's book, a best seller and hence widely read, is a plea for nuclear disarmament. *Hiroshima's Shadow* was published by a very small press and is not even shelved in many libraries. In addition, there are some, but not a very large number, of memoirs and several books specifically on the 1995 debacle at the Smithsonian.

24. After summarizing in some detail what actually happened in Hiroshima, Schell repeats the exercise to describe what would happen if a more powerful bomb were dropped on Manhattan—a place and a population, after all, closer to "us." While the size of weapons had grown, the effect of the repetition is to diminish the historical material in favor of a future doomsday scenario. Rhodes's book strikingly recounts the flight of the Enola Gay from the crew's point of view, then switches to the point of view of those on the ground.

25. Compare Lifton and Mitchell, *Hiroshima in America,* quoting from an unnamed source: "the 'usual place' for Hiroshima in Western literature is 'the unconscious'" (374).

26. The prevailing commonsense attitude resembles Tull's in Faulkner's *As I Lay Dying:* "Now and then a fellow gets to thinking about it. Not often, though. Which is a good thing . . . that's ever living thing the matter with Darl: he just thinks by himself too much" (1930; New York: Vintage, 1957), 67.

27. The military occupation actively prohibited the printing of such photographs, perhaps because of their resemblance to images flowing from Europe. In fairness, one must

note that Nazi propagandists exploited the bombing of Dresden, exaggerating what was already a huge number of deaths, and that controversy also existed among the Allies. See Taylor, *Dresden*, 361–71.

28. See Hannah Arendt, *Eichmann in Jerusalem* (New York: Penguin, 1963) and Giorgio Agamben, *Homo-Sacer: Sovereign Power and Bare Life*, trans. Daniel Heller-Roazen (Stanford: Stanford University Press, 1998).

29. Those released from Guantánamo, including five Britons, have been the beneficiaries of state action. See Alan Cowell, "Five Britons Released from Guantánamo Return Home," *New York Times*, March 10, 2004, A-12.

30. R. J. Rummel, *Death by Government* (New Brunswick, NJ: Transaction Press, 1987). See also Gil Elliot, *Twentieth Century Book of the Dead* (New York: Scribner's, 1992). See also the final section of chapter 1.

31. The idea of family and personal love may be the greatest and most deceptive of fictions—part of our cultural wiring. But, if so, I am not prepared to say so, being wired that way too. I note for the record that the 1950s featured the idealization of family life at all levels of culture, including the celebrated exhibition and book of photographs by Edward Steichen called *The Family of Man* (New York: published for the Museum of Modern Art by Simon and Schuster, 1955).

32. In *Beyond the Pleasure Principle,* Freud describes how a child throws a toy out of his crib to simulate his mother's departure and return and to achieve some sense of mastery over his anxiety. He calls the simulation *Fort/Da*. In an analogous way, apprehension and the "othering" I describe in the next paragraph are key psychological phenomena within the war complex.

33. Among the many theorists of "othering," I would cite as a special source Martin Buber, *I and Thou* (New York: Scribner's, 1958) whose work has in turn influenced that of Emmanuel Levinas; I would also point to M. M. Bakhtin, and to Romain Rolland. See also Edith Wyschogrod, *An Ethics of Remembering: History, Heterology, and the Nameless Others* (Chicago: University of Chicago Press, 1998). Additional important thinkers, including Edward Said and Jacques Derrida, have written about the phenomenon of "othering," sometimes in connection with imperialism and sometimes with modern war, but rarely linking the two. One could, of course, go on to add Sartre, de Beauvoir, Fanon, and others. The chapters that follow cite individual texts. In addition, I use as a source and say more below about Alain Badiou.

34. See Gray, *Warriors,* 153–58.

35. In "Thoughts for the Times on War and Death," Freud read world war in the context of imperialism. So did Arendt, quite brilliantly and in ways to which I am indebted, in *Origins of Totalitarianism* (New York: Harcourt, Brace, 1951), first edition; an expanded second edition appeared in 1958 and a third edition with new prefaces followed. See Elisabeth Young-Bruehl, *Hannah Arendt: For Love of the World* (New Haven: Yale University Press, 1982), 535–36. Many important works on ethics surround both World War I and II (see below).

36. Emmanuel Levinas's *Totality and Infinity: An Essay on Exteriority,* trans. Alphonso Lingis (Pittsburgh: Duquesne University Press, 1969) considers war consciousness as a heightened form of "totality" thinking, which is systemic, political, and always suspect, in

contrast to an ethics based on recognition of the face of the other, which for Levinas is a sign of infinity. See especially the opening sections.

37. Many of my terms are taken from or based upon Alain Badiou, *Ethics: An Essay on the Understanding of Evil*, trans. Peter Hallward (1998; London: Verso, 2001). Badiou and his commentators tend to position his work in opposition to that of Levinas and other ethical theories based on "othering." It seems more precise to see dialogue and differences around these points to which Badiou also brings his earlier Sartrean orientations, an interest in Deleuze, and a secularized but religious sensibility evident in his writings about St. Paul. For more about Badiou and possibilities for meaningful action (including situations where an emotion or an utterance are in themselves meaningful actions) see also and especially chapter 3 and the conclusion. Recognition of what I call the middle distance—a feeling of emotional, spatial, or temporal connection available to many people, but not always chosen—is a necessary stage in the processes I describe.

38. Some critics (Homi Bhabha, Michael Hardt, and Antonio Negri) have declared the death of the nation-state as the primary mover in history. Others, for example, Benedict Anderson, have proclaimed the end of transnational social organization by religion. Both kinds of proclamations seem, at the very least, premature. Since 9/11, we have become aware of new and potent forms of transnationalism, a phrase that includes not just corporate structures but fundamentalist Islamisms; we have also been reminded of how national governments, including that of the United States, can work in tandem with corporations, but also through other nations or unilaterally. History makes long-term pronouncements on such matters quite risky.

39. See Freud, "Thoughts for the Times on War and Death," 273. The issue of "heroic" death and the need to individualize the dead by name recur pressingly in war monuments and memorials; I return to the subjects in chapter 1 and in the Conclusion. See Robert Pogue Harrison, who says that "the grave domesticates the inhuman transcendence of space and marks humans off from the timelessness of the gods and the eternal returns of nature" so that the burial of bodies satisfies a profound need in human nature ("Hic Jacet," *Critical Inquiry* 27 [Spring 2001]: 398). See also the book form of Harrison's argument, *The Dominion of the Dead* (Chicago: University of Chicago Press, 2003) and one of Harrison's sources, Giambattista Vico, *The New Science*, trans. Thomas Goddard Bergin and Max Harold Fisch (Ithaca, NY: Cornell University Press, 1958). On the issue of war and, specifically, of Holocaust memorials, see James E. Young, *The Texture of Memory: Holocaust Memorials and Meaning* (New Haven: Yale University Press, 1993). I use Edith Wyschogrod's definition of the uniqueness of the Holocaust in this sentence, particularly the use of technology and speed (*Ethics of Remembering*, xiii, 42).

40. Peter Novick, *The Holocaust in American Life* (Boston: Houghton Mifflin, 1999), 7. In a longer discussion of Novick's book, I would note that secular forms of Judaism have coexisted with religious forms for a long time. I would also note that tradition and cultural identification form strong bonds and give more immediate coherence to contemporary Judaism than the factors Novick stresses. The modification I propose in the next sentence removes some of the provocation from Novick's thesis; it also modifies Novick's absolute distinction between Jews and gentiles (his word) on the basis of identification with the Holocaust.

41. The 1993 opening of the Holocaust Memorial Museum and films like *Schindler's List* (1993) marked and accelerated but certainly did not initiate American identification with the Holocaust. Popular work such as *The Diary of Anne Frank* and *Judgment at Nuremberg* (a television drama before it was a celebrated 1961 film) come much earlier, during the 1950s. The form of identification Novick describes clearly includes the feeling of emotional connection I call "the middle distance," although it is more strongly based on self-interest.

42. See D. D. Guttenplan, *The Holocaust on Trial* (New York: Norton, 2000), 71. By 1978 and the television series *Holocaust,* these facts could be mentioned as a matter of course. They appear also in later cultural representations such as Art Spiegelman's *Maus: A Survivor's Tale I, My Father Bleeds History* (1986) and Roman Polanski's *The Pianist* (2003).

43. Part Two of Arendt's *Origins of Totalitarianism,* "Anti-Semitism," offers a magisterial and weighty history that clearly rebuts the accusation that Arendt was an amateur. I see it also as rebutting the charge that Arendt was an anti-Semite, although her relationship to Judaism was vexed and unclear, even, I would say, to herself. Part of a three-part work in 1951, it has been published under separate cover by Harcourt Brace Jovanovich since 1968. Arendt was, of course, a German Jew who fled to France and then the United States in World War II. Early essays like "We Refugees" (reprinted in *The Jew as Pariah,* see below) acknowledge her status; in most of her prose, including (as I discuss in chapter 2) *Eichmann in Jerusalem,* she rejects the introduction of life history and affect. Ironically, her affair with Martin Heidegger has become a central item in her memory.

On the lasting impact of the dispute over *Eichmann in Jerusalem* as "a modern form of excommunication," see Hannah Arendt, *The Jew as Pariah: Jewish Identity and Politics in the Modern Age,* ed. Ron H. Feldman (New York: Grove Press, 1978), 17. Arendt often did not handle herself wisely or well during the controversy, seeming arrogant and cold in her responses or going over the top in attacking others: see her exchanges (reprinted in *Pariah*) with Gershom Scholem and Walter Z. Laqueur as examples. On the Arendt controversy, see also Elizabeth Young-Breuhl, *For Love of the World* (New Haven: Yale University Press, 1982), chap. 8; Novick, *Holocaust in American Life,* 135–41; and chapter 2 of this book.

44. Christopher Browning, *Ordinary Men: Reserve Police Battalion 101 and the Final Solution in Poland* (New York: HarperCollins, 1992).

45. Goldhagen's book, subtitled *Ordinary Germans and the Holocaust* (New York: Knopf, 1996) was accused of inadequately acknowledging earlier historians, like Browning. His thesis—that anti-Semitism pervaded German society and had caused the Holocaust as the end point of a continuum ranging from casual prejudice through actual murder—was both obvious and hard-hitting in the context of prevailing historical debates about details rather than the whole. Goldhagen also focused on the death marches at the end of the war, which, like the *Einsatzgruppen,* tend to be both well documented and repeatedly forgotten.

46. One political reason for the effacement: the pragmatic postwar need for the Allies to work with former members of the *Wehrmacht* in postwar Germany.

47. In Hamburg (1994) and Munich (1998–99), the Institute for Social Research mounted a controversial exhibition of photographs that showed how the *Wehrmacht* supported, and sometimes even worked with, the killing squads. It excited protests and even a

bombing, although Arendt and Hilberg had already discussed these facts in print, decades earlier. The German Right saw a conspiracy to revive the idea of universal German guilt. The *Wehrmacht* felt moved to honor a new role model, Anton Schmid, who had aided Jews during the war and whom the Nazis had executed as a traitor. (See Roger Cohen, "The German Army Hero, Updated," *Sunday New York Times*, May 12, 2000, section 4, 14. We will meet Sergeant Schmid again in chapter 2.) After closing and the removal of some questionable photographs, the exhibition, "Crimes of the Wehrmacht: The Dimensions of the War of Extermination, 1941–44," reopened. Although it was scheduled for 1999 in New York, the exhibition had to be postponed; a symposium planned at the New School in conjunction with the exhibit became instead a symposium on the postponement, marked by some contentious exchanges. At one session, a noted scholar said that the material was difficult for "some persons present, for reasons I won't say." It provoked a reaction from the audience: "Let's hear!" A noted scholar, who had stated the obvious—how could the *Einsatzgruppen* have done their work without at least the tacit support of the *Wehrmacht?*—shouted at one point to his colleagues: "If we were honest, we would say what we know. I could say things." But, as can be all too typical of how even scholars handle such topics, he did not say them.

48. See, for example, Cathy Caruth's extremely useful anthology, *Trauma: Explorations in Memory* (Baltimore: Johns Hopkins University Press, 1995) and her book *Unclaimed Experience: Trauma, Narrative and History* (Baltimore: Johns Hopkins University Press, 1996). In her work, the Holocaust remains the figure in the carpet and the Ur modern trauma—though it is not (she would say, hence it is not) even named in fidelity to the principle that trauma can be transmitted, but not stated. In *Testimony: Crises of Witnessing in Literature, Psychoanalysis, and History* (New York: Routledge, 1992) Shoshana Felman, who has worked with Dori Laub and the Yale Project on Holocaust testimony, quotes from survivor testimonies but also validates silence. I would note that, in the 1940s and 1950s, when the term "the Holocaust" was not yet in general use, the term "the Catastrophe" was often used instead, forming a linguistic as well as conceptual link to trauma.

49. Andreas Huyssen, *Twilight Memories: Marking Time in a Culture of Amnesia* (New York: Routledge, 1995). For Novick and Guttenplan, see 153n4 and 158n42.

50. Raul Hilberg describes two waves of Holocaust testimony: one in the 1940s, when the survivors were still in Europe, and the second in the 1980s and 1990s, under the impetus of the survivors' aging. See *Sources of Holocaust Research: An Analysis* (Chicago: Ivan R. Dee, 2001), 47. Yad Vashem in Jerusalem continued collecting testimonies after survivors left Europe. Dori Laub, working with Geoffrey Hartman and Shoshana Felman among others, has collected testimony at Yale. Since 1993, the United States Holocaust Memorial Museum has included archival and research wings. And the Shoah Project, funded by Steven Spielberg, has interviewed some 50,000 survivors since the late 1990s.

51. Ruth Leys, *Trauma: A Genealogy* (Chicago: University of Chicago Press, 2000) gives a compact and informative history of *trauma* and trauma theory up to the present, noting that the terms have physiological as well as psychological reference. Freud's writing on trauma remains too extensive and diffuse to cite, even in an omnibus footnote. Relevant texts include: *Introductory Lectures to Psychoanalysis, The Interpretation of Dreams, Beyond the Pleasure Principle,* and the very late *Moses and Monotheism.* The most pertinent texts for me are *Beyond the Pleasure Principle* (1922) and *Civilization and Its Discontents* (1930) and

also less well-known but, for my purposes, important texts like "Thoughts for the Times on War and Death" (1915) and "Why War?" (1932).

52. *Diagnostic and Statistical Manual of Mental Disorders: DSM-IV-TR,* fourth edition (Washington, D.C.: American Psychiatric Association, 2000), 471–72, 467–68. Even as I want to use this document as ballast, I am given pause by the echo between "DSM-IV-TR" and the terminology of the S.S., in which Adolf Eichmann occupied Bureau IV-B-4. In the interest of space, I elide in this paragraph distinctions between "trauma" and "posttraumatic stress disorder" determined by the timing and duration of symptoms.

53. Ley, *Trauma: A Genealogy,* 2

54. My interest in individual and group psychologies—looking-away or derealization, the variable effects of group identification and othering, reactions to mass death including apprehension, and so forth—assumes that such effects can be influenced by the media and manipulated for political purposes, although they do not, in the end, remain predictable or completely under media or political control. In short, I combine psychological and political or cultural approaches, as trauma theory usually does not.

55. Adorno's comments are repeated both ways in part because he wrote different statements about "poetry after Auschwitz." The original and clearest source was a 1949 essay called "Cultural Criticism and Society," reprinted in Theodor Adorno, *Prisms,* trans. Samuel and Shierry Weber (Cambridge: MIT Press, 1986); the relevant sentence appears on page 34, at the end of a complex essay. In *The Fateful Question of Culture,* Geoffrey Hartman quotes a more trenchant remark from Adorno: "All culture after Auschwitz, including the most penetrating criticism of it, is garbage" (New York: Columbia University Press, 1997), 107, and sees Adorno as indicating a more general crisis in writing (quoted from Theodor Adorno, *Negative Dialectics,* trans E. B. Ashton [New York: Continuum, 1992], 367). Beryl Lang agrees in *Act and Idea in the Nazi Genocide* (Chicago: University of Chicago Press, 1990), 125. Stressing a different essay called "Engagement" in Adorno, *Notes to Literature,* ed. Rolf Tiedemann, trans. Shierry Weber Nicholsen (1962; New York: Columbia University Press, 1991), 76–94, Ernst van Alphen stresses that Adorno objected only to representations that distort history (*Caught by History: Holocaust Effects in Contemporary Art, Literature, and Theory* [Stanford: Stanford University Press, 1997], 18–20). The essay, called "Commitment" in other translations, is also cited by Marianne Hirsch in *Family Frames: Photography, Narrative, and Postmemory* (Cambridge: Harvard University Press, 1997), 274, note 10. Adorno's remark, which drew over 5,000 "hits" when I entered the words "Adorno and After Auschwitz" into a computer search, was written in different ways and has obviously been used in different ways. For my purposes, the salient fact is that the remark remains a consistent point of reference in cultural memory, even though its meaning has become the subject of a mini-industry. For a discussion of postwar poetry, see Susan Gubar, *Poetry after Auschwitz: Remembering What One Never Knew* (Bloomington: Indiana University Press, 2003). For relevant work by Hartman, see also chapter 3. Theorists more broadly associated with language theory, philosophy, and psychology, such as De Man, Derrida, and Lacan have also written texts part of or addressed by trauma theory. See Caruth, *Unclaimed Experience.*

56. Maurice Blanchot, *The Writing of the Disaster,* trans. Ann Smock (Lincoln: University of Nebraska Press, 1986), 21; Cathy Caruth, *Unclaimed Experience,* 4; Shoshana Felman, "Education and Crisis; or the Vicissitudes of Teaching," in Caruth, ed., *Trauma,* 29.

57. In an important essay, Saul Friedlander states that, when the subject is the Nazi era, "the voice of the commentator must be heard" to disrupt formulaic, linear narratives. See "Trauma, Memory, and Transference," in *Holocaust Remembrance: The Shapes of Memory*, ed. Geoffrey H. Hartman (Oxford: Blackwell, 1994), 257–63. I agree with his formulation and would expand its applicability. Friedlander himself published a memoir under separate cover titled *When Memory Comes* about his separation from his Jewish parents when he was hidden and raised among Catholics.

58. Virginia Woolf, *Three Guineas* (New York: Harcourt Brace Jovanovich, 1938), 53. See also Paul Fussell, *Wartime: Understanding and Behavior in the Second World War* (New York: Oxford University Press, 1989), 180–81. Recent historians have now documented that some of Churchill's speeches were delivered by a different voice, possibly because Churchill himself had been tippling. For a review of this scholarship, see Hitchens, "The Medals of His Defeats," and www.theatlantic.com/2002/04/hitchens.htm. Fussell claims that ordinary soldiers hated Churchill's speeches though they have become venerable in the United States (*Wartime*, 182–83).

59. See Susan Sontag, *Regarding the Pain of Others* (New York: Farrar, Straus and Giroux, 2003), 70.

60. See Hein and Selden, eds., *Living with the Bomb*, 25. See also Lifschultz and Bird, "The Legend of Hiroshima," in *Hiroshima's Shadow*, ed. Bird and Lifschultz, xlvii.

61. The phenomenon in which visual images stick in memory, sometimes called "flash-bulb memory," deserves more investigation, especially in degrees of visual memory and in which half of the juxtaposition individuals emphasize: the unusual event and the image itself or banal accompanying details about when and how they perceived the image.

62. Frederick A. Kitler makes this point quite strikingly in *Gramophone, Film, Typewriter*, trans. and Introduction, Geoffrey Winthrop-Young and Michael Wutz (1986, Stanford: Stanford University Press, 1999), 249–63.

63. By "media," I mean print as well as visual or auditory media. See Andre Schiffren, *The Business of Books* (New York: Verso, 1999) for some eye-opening statistics. By 1999, 85 percent of books published came from houses owned by the same six transnational conglomerates. The situation has worsened since. See also Naomi Klein, *No Logo: Taking Aim at the Brand Bullies* (New York: Picador, 2002). The use of the term *transnationals* for business conglomerates has become confusing after 9/11, when we have become acutely aware of organizations like al-Qaeda as transnationals too—and hostile to big business. For precision, I use the term transnational conglomerates in most instances.

Benjamin R. Barber's *Jihad versus McWorld* (New York: Times Books, 1996) claims that neither big business nor religious fundamentalism necessarily fosters democracy. On PBS's *Charlie Rose Show*, Senator Paul Wellstone articulated quite brilliantly the danger to free enterprise and the danger to democracy caused by monopolies, which will inevitably influence and control the press and government, in a July 2001 interview rebroadcast after his death in October 2002. See also Paul Krugman, "For Richer," *New York Times Magazine*, October 20, 2002. The phenomenon of media conglomerates, still largely unrecognized in 1999, had registered for the public by 2002 or 2003, though no clear solutions seem in sight.

64. See George Orwell, *1984* (1949; New York: Signet, 1961).

65. CNN's success spawned many imitators. When the United States invaded Iraq, Fox News, which outdid even CNN's rigid ideas of patriotism, emerged as a new leader. Since

its founding, al-Jazeera has become a significant alternative to CNN in the Muslim world. See the *New York Times Sunday Magazine,* "What the Muslim World is Watching," November 18, 2001. In 2005, it seems unthinkable how little it was known in 2001. PBS showed a documentary called "Exclusive to al-Jazeera," on *Wide Angle,* July 10, 2003. A new documentary, *Control Room* (directed by Jehane Noujaim, 2004) shows the invasion using footage about and shot by al-Jazeera.

66. In spring 2003, the media avidly courted the FCC, a government agency, for the relaxation of monopoly rules—which they received, in a controversial decision, later (at least as of this writing) reversed by Congress.

67. Like other people I know, by spring 2002, I found myself watching the *BBC Nightly News* and even C-Span and C-Span 2 to get more information. The latter, which I would screen at random, showed two important speeches, one in September 2002, by Al Gore (see Prologue, note 22) and the other by Bill Clinton (discussed in chapter 4) outlining a course of action in the Middle East quite different from the Bush administration's. Mainstream media pretty much ignored the speeches.

68. As I worked on this chapter in May of 2002, the news was filled first by criticisms of how the Bush administration had handled reports about al-Qaeda prior to 9/11 and then by a renewed showing of the WTC tapes, statements from Vice President Cheney and Secretary of Defense Rumsfeld that new attacks were "inevitable," and renewed security alerts in New York and around the nation. Was the confluence accidental? Political? An authentic warning of imminent danger? When I first wrote this note, I did not know. The administration policy, which effectively defused criticism in 2002, now seems to have been designed for that purpose. One treads hard to stay away from conspiracy theories in our times. By spring 2004, a Bush political ad that featured shots of the World Trade Center burning was by and large rejected by the public, which defused (in this instance at least) a politics based on fear. The 9/11 Commission hearings that same year consolidated the change. Nonetheless, terrorism as an issue affected the 2004 election.

On the growth of transnational corporations and the avoidance of conspiracy theories, see Michael Hardt and Antonio Negri, *Empire* (Cambridge: Harvard University Press, 2000). Like much Marxist criticism, the book often ignores racial issues and contains a certain vague utopianism. But it remains useful after fall 2001.

69. Criticism of the press for dodging analysis of Bush administration policy in Iraq has to some extent become mainstream. See Michael Massing, "Unfit to Print?" *New York Review of Books* 51:11 (June 24, 2004). In its May 26, 2004 issue, the *New York Times* acknowledged instances in its prewar coverage and that of the "early stages of occupation" that were "insufficiently qualified or allowed to stand unchallenged" (A-10). Many readers were more broadly critical: see "Other Voices: The Times, the War, and the Weapons," Letters to the Public Editor, *New York Times,* June 6, 2004, section 4, 2. The disjunction between public sentiment and government action on Iraq and that between op-ed pages and the regular news has not been larger in my memory.

70. See also Walter Benjamin's "Art in the Age of Mechanical Reproduction" (part of *Illuminations*), which was written in the same milieu.

71. In the United States, the name "The Frankfurt School" and its term to describe media, "the culture industry," are identified especially with Max Horkheimer and Theodor Adorno and the chapter of that name (subtitle: *Enlightenment as Mass Deception,* in *The Di-*

alectic of Enlightenment [1944; New York: Continuum, 1990], 120–67). Adorno was especially prone to attack other intellectuals once associated with the group. Siegfried Kracauer, for example, was soundly criticized once the group had arrived in the United States for selling-out to mass culture. Kracauer is best known as the author of *From Caligari to Hitler*, an important book on film. But his early work includes a sense that media can develop creatively and in unpredictable ways and bears some affinity to the Situationists. See, for example, the essays reprinted in *The Mass Ornament: Weimar Essays*, ed. Thomas Y. Levin (Cambridge: Harvard University Press, 1995).

72. One of the clearest statements of Foucault's beliefs comes in *The History of Sexuality*, vol. 1, chap. 1, "We 'Other Victorians'" (New York: Pantheon, 1978). Also pertinent are *The Archeology of Knowledge* and *Discipline and Punish: The Birth of the Prison*. Barber discusses the fragile and conditional links between democracy and consumerism in *Jihad versus McWorld*, 16.

73. As I neared completion of this book, it had become fashionable for academics to denounce the politics of fear, prompting conservative critics to note that some fears may be justified. I feel no doubt that as a culture we are still seeking but not yet finding the necessary balance between reasonable, *constitutional* precautions and warranted fears. See Edward Rothstein, "Is Fear Itself the Enemy?" *New York Times*, February 14, 2004.

74. For a fuller, more thematic outline of the book's structure, see the Prologue.

75. The term *defamiliarization* comes from the Russian Formalists. See Victor Shklovsky, "Art as Technique," in *Russian Formalist Criticism: Four Essays*, trans. and ed. Lee T. Lemon and Marion J. Reis (Lincoln: University of Nebraska Press, 1965), 12. Shklovsky speaks of the "stoniness of the stone"; the "apple" image is D. H. Lawrence's in "Introduction to These Paintings," an essay that is really a mini-history of Western civilization; reprinted in *Phoenix: the Posthumous Papers of D. H. Lawrence*, ed. Edward D. McDonald (New York: Viking, 1936), 551–84.

Chapter One

1. Reagan's death on June 5, 2004, meant that his celebrated 1984 speech, popularly known as "The Boys of Pointe du Hoc," was repeatedly rebroadcast on the sixtieth anniversary of D-Day, overshadowing President Bush. Reagan's speech bolstered, though it certainly did not originate, the image of citizen soldiers charging totalitarian forces. In 2004, aging survivors of the invasion marched to the strains of the theme from the film *The Longest Day*. Given the age of the former soldiers, the march inevitably had a *triste* air and the addition of the movie theme conflated history and showbiz. In anticipation of such effects, David Greenberg posted "Why World War II Nostalgia Has Gone too Far" on the *Slate* Web site (www.slate.msn.com/id/2101752) on June 4, 2004. The posting provoked fighting words.

2. The D-Day Museum includes the original statement Eisenhower wrote and its Web site reproduces it. See www.ddaymuseum.org.

3. The percentages given come from John Keegan, *The Second World War* (New York: Penguin, 1989), 384–85.

4. While it would certainly be possible to summarize newspaper stories in multiple cities for D-Day and similar topics, such extensive summaries would require separate articles or even books. I have by and large chosen to cite the *New York Times*, *Life*, and other periodi-

cals that have national audiences. The Library of Congress Web site, www.loc.gov, reproduces the *New York Times* front page discussed.

5. *Life* called its story "Beachheads of Normandy," subtitled "The Fateful Battle for
Europe is Joined by Sea and Air," June 19, 1944, 25.

6. Gerhard L. Weinberg covers preparations for D-Day and the invasion itself in two
ten-page sections of a much longer chapter called "The Assault on Germany from all
Sides," which begins with a section called "Preliminaries in the East" and ends with a sec-
tion called "Offensives in the East." The embedded format makes good scholarly sense. See
A World at Arms: A Global History of World War II (Cambridge: Cambridge University
Press, 1994), 676–96.

7. See Keegan, *Second World War*, 419–35, and Weinberg, *World at Arms*, 234; 574–81.

8. As "the arsenal of democracy," the United States supplied vehicles and arms but the
Soviets experienced the heaviest fighting.

9. Stephen E. Ambrose reports the color footage, once stored in the Eisenhower Center
and known to exist in 1964, as lost. See *D-Day June 6, 1944: The Climactic Battle of World
War II* (New York: Simon and Schuster, 1994), 397. Some of Capa's shots for *Life* were
dried too quickly and destroyed. See Ambrose, *D-Day June 6, 1944*, 394–95.

10. Susan Sontag, *Regarding the Pain of Others* (New York: Farrar, Straus and Giroux,
2003), 64.

11. Sometimes also called the *Movietone News* or the *Movietone War News;* the D-Day
footage is available on some VHS editions of *The Longest Day* (1962) or from the University of South Carolina library.

12. When Ted Koppel gave an omnibus reading of names on a segment of *Nightline*
called "The Fallen" (April 30, 2004), some affiliates refused to carry the program.

13. The later figures were reported mid-summer 2003 as those confirmed by two separate newspaper sources. Once again, the actual totals can be expected to be higher and all
figures remain uncertain. In August 2004, the Web site Iraq Body Count listed 13,458 dead
Iraqi civilians. See www.iraqbodycount.net. By fall 2004, some reports said one hundred
thousand.

14. *Saving Private Ryan* was filmed in color, but, like *The Longest Day*, aims at the feeling of documentary. Using special filters, Spielberg drained many of the initial scenes of
color, so that they register almost as black and white in tones that say, "fact, not fiction." To
strengthen the documentary motif, *Saving Private Ryan* identifies date or place in small white
letters (e.g., D-Day plus three). Since virtually all of the characters are fictional, it eschews
the labeling of characters. An interesting convention: "history" as the small white letter.

15. J. Glenn Gray, *The Warriors: Reflections on Men in Battle* (New York: Harcourt,
Brace and Company, 1959), 28–29.

16. Ambrose, *D-Day*, 361.

17. See Martin Meisel, *Realizations: Narrative, Pictorial, and Theatrical Arts in Nineteenth-
Century England* (Princeton: Princeton University Press, 1983).

18. *We Were Soldiers*, for example, shows the flag when the women report men's
deaths—so that the display becomes emotionally dissonant, especially since the deaths
seem unnecessary and a few shots indicate the Vietcong's women too. Near the end of the
movie, the Vietcong leader, who has been rendered sympathetically, ponders (but does not

displace) a tattered-looking toy-sized American flag; the flag's size and condition—and the officer's final indifference—serve as a synecdoche for the eventual U.S. defeat.

19. In the final battle, the German soldier wears no helmet and so is more recognizable for the viewer; he is in turn shot by the cowardly corporal after the battle. This soldier's reappearance is ham-handed—an aspect of the film I cannot defend. It yields no irony and should have been cut.

20. In contrast, *We Were Soldiers* represents a historical incident and the film ends with Colonel Moore visiting the Vietnam Memorial, followed by a list of names of men actually killed; like 9/11, the event memorialized allowed such listing. Although *Black Hawk Down* (directed by Ridley Scott, 2002), similarly records a specific incident in Somalia, the film garbles characters' names, an effect at odds with the motor for all the action: the desire to leave no man behind. The contrast made the film work for me as an antiwar film although most reviewers saw it as a guy-talk action thriller.

On related issues of naming and memorials, see Robert Pogue Harrison, *The Dominion of the Dead* (Chicago: University of Chicago Press, 2003) and Geoff Dyer, *The Missing of the Somme* (London: Phoenix Press, 2001).

21. As *Saving Private Ryan* begins, viewers see an opening shot of a bleached-looking American flag that recurs at the beginning of the epilogue, which returns us to the American cemetery at Colleville. The shot may be intended to capture the actual appearance of the flag in the sun but it also suggests the passage of time and potential alterations in the values the flag represents. While it's possible that a flag is a flag is a flag and that (as in vaudeville) flags always signal national self-congratulation and applause, I believe that context affects the meanings of the flag's image. The flag we see at the end of *Saving Private Ryan* flies over the cemetery at Colleville, which we know by the end contains the bodies of some of the characters we have followed through the film. That knowledge reinforces the audience's doubts about the ethics of expenditure. In fact, I would argue that the final shot of the flag is highly mediated by the emotional dissonance the audience feels when it sees Captain John H. Miller's name on the marker in Normandy, instead of another soldier's—which it still had the right to hope as the war sequence ended and the epilogue began. The reviews I read kept the secret of Miller's death—wisely.

22. In emphasizing movement and tactility, I am following Brian Massumi's use of the term *affect*. See the Prologue, note 23.

23. See the Introduction for a discussion of topics within World War II from which cultural memory has looked away to produce consensus. With regard to D-Day, a quasi spin-off from *Saving Private Ryan*, HBO's *Band of Brothers* (produced by Steven Spielberg and Tom Hanks, 2001) shows GIs looting and getting nastily drunk and violent months after the invasion—two taboos in earlier films about World War II, though not in films about Vietnam. While it shows war and sex as narcotics for soldiers, it mutes truly serious actions like rape and the murder of prisoners or civilians.

24. The camps were not common knowledge before 1945, and most of those with knowledge did not move against Hitler because of his persecution of the Jews. See Hitchens: "The argument about World War II and its worthwhileness is the most apparently settled and decided question in our culture. There may be an occasional flinch. . . . But the evidence adduced at Nuremberg has the effect of retrospectively annulling all such

doubts" ("The Medals of His Defeats," *Atlantic Monthly*, April 2002, 8, available online at www.theatlantic.com/issues/2002/04/hitchens.htm). In *Wartime*, Paul Fussell maintains that ordinary soldiers felt substantial cynicism about the war and bitterness that their doubts were not registered and were even falsified at home (New York: Oxford University Press, 1989).

25. See the *New York Times*, July 17, 2003, 1.

26. Some recent signs in 2004: episodes of shows like *Without a Trace* and *Law and Order* have shown Gulf war veterans in ways reminiscent of Vietnam or include sentiments against the war in Iraq.

27. One Web site that offers figures notes: "Often the least authoritative sources (such as dilettantes like me or partisan propagandists) are the most accessible, while the most authoritative (serious scholars, with no vested interest) are the most obscure." The Web site (www.users.erols.com/mwhite28/warstats.htm) uses a wide range of sources. I will list three other useful Web sites: www.gi.grolier.com/wwii/wwii_16.html, www.infoplease.com/ipa/0/0/0/4/6/1/A0004619.html, and www.ddaymuseum.org.

28. Martin Gilbert, *The Second World War: A Complete History*, rev. ed. (New York: Henry Holt, 1989), 534. Ambrose's *D-Day* also specifies 4,900 Allied casualties though the book's descriptions of Omaha suggest higher losses.

29. *Army Battle Casualties and Nonbattle Deaths in World War II* (Washington, D.C.: Department of the Army, 1953), for example, breaks losses down by month, gender, rank, and theater, but not by day.

30. The National Parks Service provided the figure for Antietam (www.nps.gov/anti); Fussell the figures for the Somme, *Wartime*, 13.

31. Weinberg, *World at Arms*, 769.

32. Our image of D-Day has in some ways become less rather than more accurate. For although a film like Spielberg's conveys carnage with visceral realism, a qualitative triumph in the representation of war, it produces the illusion of more dead and wounded than was in fact the case. To my surprise, *The Longest Day* and the *Movietonenews* prove, after all, in some ways at least, to give the more accurate historical picture.

33. See Benjamin Schwarz, "A Job for Rewrite: Stalin's War," *New York Times*, February 21, 2004.

34. In Ted Widmer, "The Wayward Media," *New York Times Book Review* (March 16, 2003). While normally in favor of colorful writing, I found the phrase quite distasteful.

35. David E. Sanger, "Threats and Responses: News Analysis; A New Doctrine for War," *New York Times*, March 18, 2003.

36. Although available literature at the cemetery clearly states that many of those buried there died later in the European campaign, the visual evidence of 10,000 gleaming graves tends to trump any qualifications.

37. Weinberg, *World at Arms*, 769–70.

Chapter Two

1. *The Trial of Adolf Eichmann* (ABC, 1997) reports the trial as the first to be fully televised. Capitol Cities Broadcasting, an American company, relayed continuous images of Eichmann, the judges, the witnesses, and the audience free of charge to a specially designed media room; see Moshe Pearlman, *The Capture and Trial of Adolf Eichmann* (London: Wei-

denfeld and Nicolson, 1963), 90–91. On Israel's reactions to the trial, see Tom Segev, *The Seventh Million: the Israelis and the Holocaust* (New York: Hill and Wang, 1993), 350–51.

2. Adolf Eichmann, "Adolf Eichmann Tells His Own Damning Story: Eichmann's Story, Part I," *Life*, November 28, 1960.

3. Hannah Arendt, *Eichmann in Jerusalem: A Report on the Banality of Evil* (1963; New York: Penguin, 1994).

4. In several columns, Tom Friedman accepted the analogy, mentioning the discovery of mass graves as reason enough to have invaded Iraq. See "The Meaning of a Skull," *New York Times*, April 27, 2003, 13, and "Two Right Feet," *New York Times*, May 14, 2003, A-25. Philip Gourevitch felt manipulated in "Might and Right," Talk of the Town section of *The New Yorker*, June 16 and 23, 2003, 69–70.

5. See Craig S. Smith, "NATO Agrees to U.S. Proposals to Revamp Alliance," *New York Times*, June 13, 2003, A-3, and Elizabeth Becker, "U.S. Suspends Aid to 35 Countries over New International Court," *New York Times*, July 2, 2003, A-8. *BBC World News* reported the first story on June 12, 2003.

6. Controversies around the torture of prisoners, including secret memoranda and secret detainees, were ongoing as this book went to press. Secretary General of the United Nations, Kofi Annan, strongly criticized the United States for seeking immunity from the International Criminal Court. See Warren Hoge, "Annan Rebukes U.S. for Move to Give Its Troops Immunity," *New York Times*, June 18, 2004, A-13. With the Abu Ghraib scandal ongoing as this book went to press, albeit somewhat muted in summer 2004, the United States withdrew its request on June 23.

7. *The Trial of Adolf Eichmann: Record of the Proceedings of the District Court of Jerusalem*, English edition, 9 vols. (Jerusalem: Trust for the Publication of the Proceedings of the Eichmann Trial, in Co-operation with the Israel State Archives and Yad Vashem, the Holocaust Martyrs' and Heroes' Remembrance Authority, 1992). Later referred to as *Transcripts*.

8. I admire Arendt's book and use it extensively below. But in a longer piece exclusively on Arendt, I would spin out some disagreements. I return to her views on survivor testimony, for example, later in this chapter and in Chapter Three.

9. The films and videos listed here constitute only a partial archive of readily available materials. For the documentary with the most extensive footage of survivor testimony, which occupied almost half the trial, see *Witnesses to the Holocaust* (directed by Leo Hurwitz, 1987). Hurwitz was the cameraman at the trial; his film was made in conjunction with a 1987 traveling exhibition. Eyal Sivan's *The Specialist* was made entirely from footage Hurwitz shot in court (much of it believed at first to have been lost), recut and rearranged. Together, the films provide excellent records. Sivan's film acknowledges Hannah Arendt's influence.

10. In this chapter, I try to address both people my own age or older, who sometimes know quite a lot about Eichmann, and younger readers, like graduate students, who (I have learned by asking), know just a little and most of that either inaccurate or wrong.

11. My description of Eichmann is consistent with more general patterns described by Claudia Koonz in *The Nazi Conscience* (Cambridge: Harvard University Press, 2003).

12. My summary of Eichmann's career relies on three sources: the *Transcripts*, Arendt's *Eichmann in Jerusalem*, and the *Life* interviews. When sources conflict, I indicate particulars.

13. The judges rewrote most charges dating to actions before 1941, essentially sidestepping the bone of contention between "intentionalist" and "functionalist" historians of the Holocaust about when Nazi intentions became genocidal.

14. A history of the IMT and of the subsequent Nuremberg trials (run solely by the United States in the late 1940s) that takes into account media representations needs to be written since we have lost almost entirely the sense of how controversial, and even unpopular, the trials were in 1946, not just in Germany but also among British and American observers and politicians. On the IMT, see G. M. Gilbert, *Nuremberg Diary* (New York: Farrar, Straus and Company, 1947), Werner Maser, *Nuremberg: A Nation on Trial* (New York: Scribner's, 1979), and Raul Hilberg, *The Destruction of the European Jews* (Chicago: Quadrangle Books, 1961).

15. Claude Lanzmann's classic film *Shoah* (1985) directly tackles the image Eichmann raised by interviewing just such an engineer.

16. One should add that Eichmann was both a notorious tippler and a womanizer. Israeli agents used his former mistresses to help trace his path in Europe.

17. Many books tell the story of Eichmann's capture, sometimes varying on the details. See Pearlman, *Capture and Trial of Adolf Eichmann*. See also Towiah Friedman, *The Hunter: The First Full Account of the Capture of Adolf Eichmann* (Garden City, NY: Doubleday, 1961); Isser Harel, *The House on Garibaldi Street* (New York: Viking, 1975); Peter Z. Malkin and Harry Stein, *Eichmann in My Hands* (New York: Warner Books, 1990); and Zvi Aharoni and Wilhelm Diehl, *Operation Eichmann: The Truth about the Pursuit, the Capture, and the Trial*, trans. Helmut Bögler (New York: John Wiley, 1997). Television broadcasts include a dramatization called *The House on Garibaldi Street* (directed by Peter Collinson, 1979) and *The Man Who Captured Eichmann* (directed by William A. Graham, 1996).

18. The IMT sentenced twelve of the defendants to hanging, imprisoned seven, and released three. (Robert Ley had committed suicide before the trial; Gustav Krupp was considered too frail to stand trial.) In 1946–49, the United States ran the so-called Subsequent Trials in Nuremberg for Nazi doctors, judges, lawyers, and others. Poland, Hungary, and Czechoslovakia held the so-called Successor or national trials for Nazis like Rudolf Höss (commander of Auschwitz) and Dieter Wisliceny (Eichmann's henchman), who were tried and hung in Poland and in Czechoslovakia, respectively. Years later, in 1958, Germany initiated the National Socialist trials, indicting some 816 former Nazis, though often giving lighter sentences than some had hoped. Later still, laws in France would change, making possible the explosive trial of Klaus Barbie. See Hilberg, *Destruction*, and Maser, *Nuremberg*.

19. The term *the Holocaust* was not generally in use at the time of Eichmann's trial, nor was the term *genocide*. In this chapter, I use, as the court did, the words "Final Solution," though I would otherwise avoid that term because, like "extermination," it encodes Nazi points of view. Before the 1970s, the Nazi murder of European Jews was usually called "the Shoah," "the catastrophe," "the Final Solution," or the "extermination" of the Jews.

20. On Hitler's retirement plans, see Brigitte Hamann, *Hitler's Vienna: A Dictator's Apprenticeship* (New York: Oxford University Press, 1999), 5.

21. Hamann, *Hitler's Vienna*, 166.

22. Adolf Eichmann, "Eichmann's Own Story: Part II," *Life*, December 5, 1960, 161.

23. The defendants consistently claimed not to have known about the murder of Jews

and blamed dead or absent Nazis. See Michael Musmanno's chapter in *The Verdicts Were Just: Eight Lawyers Present Their Most Memorable Cases*, ed. Albert Averbach and Charles Price (New York. David McKay, 1966), 91–98.

24. Gitta Sereny, *Albert Speer: His Battle with Truth* (New York: Knopf, 1995), 544. Sereny disagrees with Speer's assessment of the moment's meaning, though not of its importance, noting that Speer had a long series of dreams about Hitler afterward.

25. The Speer *Playboy* interview, by Eric Norden, appeared in June 1971.

26. Sereny, *Albert Speer*, 712–17; on Margret Speer's fidelity, 640.

27. On Speer's relations with the women, see also Sereny, *Albert Speer*, 336 and 532. The quotations in the preceding sentence come from Albert Speer, *Inside the Third Reich: Memoirs*, trans. Richard and Clara Winston (New York: Macmillan, 1970), 93.

28. Sereny, *Albert Speer*, quotes Galbraith, 551.

29. Gilbert, *Nuremberg Diary*, 31.

30. Sereny, *Albert Speer*, quotes Ball, 550.

31. See Maser, *Nuremberg*, 186–89, for a critical view of Speer's strategy. Galbraith agrees with Maser on the essential facts (see Sereny, *Albert Speer*, 552) but nonetheless admires Speer. Sereny sees Speer's conduct as an inevitable effect of his complex personality.

32. The actual phrase (quoted in Sereny, 335) belongs to Dutch theologian W. A. Visser 't Hooft. Speer claimed that he followed Hitler's order: "Think of nothing except your own sphere of activity" (Sereny, 364).

33. Quoted in Sereny, 103.

34. *Inside the Third Reich* (1970), published as *Erinnerungun* in Germany (1969), and six years later, *The Secret Diaries*.

35. Decades later, Israel released the memoir for the Irving-Lipstadt trial. It quickly appeared on Web sites.

36. Because Hungary was Eichmann's full-fledged command away from Berlin, his actions there were especially important at the trial.

37. The friend was Karl Hanke and the camp was Auschwitz (Sereny, *Albert Speer*, 463). In *Inside the Third Reich*, Speer says that this conversation with Hanke made him "inescapably contaminated morally" and led to his acceptance of moral guilt at Nuremberg (Speer, *Inside*, 376). Hanke had been Magda Goebbels's lover; we may recall that Speer disliked Hitler when he broke up the affair.

38. My description of Göring draws upon Sereny, Speer, Gilbert, and Maser who all agree in substance.

39. He was already on record as saying, "Good, we have destroyed an enemy." *Life*, November 28, 1960, Part II, 160.

40. The event, usually referred to as the "Jews for Goods" deal, shadowed a larger deal Himmler's agent (and Eichmann's rival) Kurt Becher had made that aborted when Joel Brand, sent abroad to gather money to save Hungary's Jews, was detained by the British. A broken man, Brand testified at Eichmann's trial. See Hilberg, *Destruction*, 847 and Segev, *Seventh Million*, 265.

41. See "Right to Try Nazi in Israel Queried," *New York Times*, May 26, 1960, 18, for misidentification of Eichmann's rank. On the same page, "Killer of 6,000,000" reports on Eichmann's "effeminate" "baby face." Most sources explain Eichmann's long period of freedom as the result of Israel's facing too many security threats close to home prior to 1960

to pursue Nazis abroad. Segev reports that Israel ignored earlier reports from a German official that Eichmann was alive in Argentina and living under the name Ricardo Klement (325).

42. Each of these events formed a controversy within a controversy. In appointing the judges, Prime Minister Ben-Gurion succeeded in changing Israeli law to prevent Benjamin Halevi (President of the Court of Jerusalem), a maverick judge who had thwarted him in other cases, from appointing himself as the presiding judge at Eichmann's trial. He failed to change the law enough to prevent Halevi's appointment altogether. See Segev, *Seventh Million*, 343. The U.N. debate featured Henry Cabot Lodge, Golda Meir, and other famous figures and ended with a formal apology from Israel to Argentina and a tacit consensus that Israel could hold its trial since neither Germany nor Argentina wished to extradite Eichmann.

43. *Transcripts*, IV, 1822.

44. Quoting Eichmann, Dieter Wisliceny used the "5 million" figure in a remark at the Nuremberg trials. In *Life*, Eichmann substantially admits Wisliceny's testimony was accurate, revising only to the extent of claiming that he had indicated joy at the death of 5 million "enemies of the Reich," not Jews. But Nazi code often referred to Jews as "enemies of the Reich" or as "partisans," so that the revision hardly helped his case. Eichmann's estimate helped establish the figure of 6 million, which has become standard (see Hilberg, *Destruction*, 987–88).

45. David Ben-Gurion, "The Eichmann Case as Seen by Ben-Gurion," *New York Times Sunday Magazine*, December 18, 1960, 7, 62. His pronouncements, which appalled Arendt, were nonetheless quite forthright. In rebuttal, Telford Taylor, who had been a judge at the so-called subsequent Nuremberg trials, claimed that Israel's trial endangered valuable international precedents; see the *New York Times Magazine*, January 22, 1961, 11–22.

46. Prosecutor Gideon Hausner was new in office at the time Eichmann was captured and responsive to Ben-Gurion. With a research team, he assembled documents not at the time generally available to show the scope and effect of Nazi actions. In his memoir, he describes the difference between his appeal to the emotions and the fact-based approach at the Nuremberg trials. See Gideon Hausner, *Justice in Jerusalem* (New York: Harper and Row, 1966). Arendt vividly objected to the prosecution strategy and the judges tried to rein it in, using the survivor testimony as background only. Nonetheless, the testimony did strongly color the trial and has remained one of its most notable features.

47. See Joel Greenberg, "Eichmann Memoirs Released to Assist a Libel Defendant," *New York Times*, March 1, 2000, A-6. See also D. D. Guttenplan, *The Holocaust on Trial* (New York: Norton, 2000), 424–43, and Adolf Eichmann, *Ich, Adolf Eichmann* (Leoni am Starnberger See, Germany: Druffel-Verlag, 1980), part of the memoir, leaked earlier. The entire manuscript is now posted on the Web. A sample page can be found in Peter Edidin, "Eichmann's House: the Bureaucracy of Murder," *Sunday New York Times*, March 5, 2000, The News of the Week in Review, 3.

48. For a host of reasons toward which I can only gesture here, Arendt found the violation of the private / public boundary intolerable both personally and intellectually. Immediately before the sentence I have just quoted, Arendt atypically groups herself with the audience in the court in the first person. But she usually resisted the personal voice. Elsewhere in *Eichmann in Jerusalem*, she refers to Gurs (a camp where she was imprisoned and from which others were later deported to Auschwitz); the experience was a personal motive for

wishing to report on Eichmann's trial, although she does not indicate in the text her personal connection. See *Hannah Arendt/Karl Jaspers Correspondence, 1926–1969,* ed. Lotte Kohler and Hans Saner, trans. Robert and Rita Kimber (New York: Harcourt Brace Jovanovich, 1992), 409.

49. As a result of her position, Arendt names only a handful of the witnesses and criticizes all but a few. Measured against the transcripts and available videos, she seems to me to exaggerate substantially the witnesses' self-display.

50. On Novick, see Introduction, note 40. For a more volatile treatment of ethnic identity through the Holocaust, see Walter Benn Michaels, *Our America: Nativism, Modernism, and Pluralism* (Durham, NC: Duke University Press, 1995).

On media representations of the Holocaust prior to Eichmann's trial, including *The Diary of Anne Frank* and television versions of the film *Judgment at Nuremberg* (directed by Stanley Kramer, 1961) see Alan Mintz, *Popular Culture and the Shaping of Holocaust Memory in America* (Seattle: University of Washington Press, 2001), 93. Such representations help to set the trial in its proper perspective. Mintz notes, correctly, the absence of references to Jews in Kramer's film; but it counts a great deal that he, his family, and virtually everyone else in the audience identified the subject of the film as Nazi persecution of Jews (see Mintz, *Popular Culture,* 103–4).

51. *Life,* April 21, 1961. Golden was author of an advice book called *For Two Cents Plain.* In the same article, a caption notes the theatrical setting.

52. See American Jewish Committee, *The Eichmann Case in the American Press* (New York: Institute of Human Relations, 1962). This pro-trial source notes nonetheless that differences of opinion quickly merged into a consensus.

53. In this televised special, Eichmann, and not Heydrich, presides at Wannsee and invents the idea of the Final Solution; he is fluent in Hebrew and Yiddish, although the real Eichmann knew those languages only slightly.

54. See American Jewish Committee, *Eichmann Case in the American Press.*

55. The June 30, 1961, issue reports that "Eichmann, mouth shrunken by the removal of his teeth, sat in bulletproof glass," but, in the same article ("An arrogant Eichmann finally gets on the stand"), includes some photographs that clearly show teeth.

56. Eyal Sivan's *The Specialist* (1999; 2000) makes Eichmann's mouth a leitmotif and can help us gauge the effect that multiple images of Adolf Eichmann had in 1961 when they formed part of public culture. Several reviewers mentioned that Eichmann's facial tic suggests guilt or suppressed rage.

57. An editorial published along with Part II of *Life*'s Eichmann interview noted that "The depressing fact is that Eichmann is basically a rather un-extraordinary man. . . . Apart from an excessive 'German patriotism,' his personality had no sharp edges" ("Eichmann and the Duty of Man," December 5, 1960, 46). In this editorial, *Life* justifies having published the interview; the editorial may indicate an untold story about negative reactions to Part I. Perhaps as a result, Part II was buried in the back of the magazine; its accompanying pictures stress the victims and not Eichmann or his family.

58. Judge Halevi's cross-examination of Eichmann included a brilliant exchange on the question of "civil courage"; see *Transcripts,* IV, 1812–22.

59. Zygmunt Bauman, *Modernity and the Holocaust* (Ithaca, NY: Cornell University Press, 1989), 177.

60. Yehiel Dinur is the spelling used in the *Transcripts;* the name is also spelled De-Nur (on the title page of his book *Shivitti*) and Dinoor (by Arendt). He was to be the prosecution's keystone witness, linking Eichmann to Auschwitz, but he fainted after a few minutes of testimony in a moment that Hannah Arendt considered melodramatic but has become a symbol at Israel's Holocaust Memorial Day and for writers like Shoshana Felman. See Shoshana Felman, "Theatres of Justice: Arendt in Jerusalem, the Eichmann Trial, and the Redefinition of Legal Meaning in the Wake of the Holocaust," *Critical Inquiry* 27:2 (Winter 2001), and my response, published in 28:3 (Spring 2002). The remarks quoted come from "The Devil Is a Gentleman," *Sixty Minutes* (CBS, 1983; interviewer, Mike Wallace). Wallace repeats the words, "Eichmann is in all of us" several times, sometimes attributing the words to Dinur and sometimes pressing other interviewees to utter them.

61. I completed this book in Summer 2004, at the time of the scandal about U.S. abuse of prisoners in Iraq. But I am willing to bet that war crimes will still be relevant when it appears.

62. See Roger Cohen, "The German Army Hero, Updated," *Sunday New York Times*, May 12, 2000, section 4, 2. Arendt reports that when a witness recounted Schmid's (she misspells the name as Schmidt) story at Eichmann's trial, the court seemed to maintain two minutes of respectful silence (231). The German government honored Schmid's memory by renaming a barracks after him.

63. On the possibility of transferring out of the *Einsatzgruppen,* see Arendt, *Eichmann in Jerusalem,* 91, and, more extensively, Christopher Browning, *Ordinary Men: Reserve Police Battalion 101 and the Final Solution in Poland* (New York: HarperCollins, 1992).

64. The law under which Eichmann was indicted excludes those who acted under threat of death in order to save their own lives. Eichmann's gestures toward the need for suicide may have been designed to fit him through this loophole, designed to protect survivors who had worked as Nazi officials or in the gas chambers.

65. Some reports say that Eichmann provided his wife with food and poison as the war came to an end: food were she to find herself in territory occupied by Americans or British; poison should the Russians come instead. The episode represents a curious kind of "care" consistent with Eichmann's own melodramatic gestures toward suicide.

66. In Dickens's *Hard Times,* only shallow and unfeeling characters "look out for number one." The idiom, used as a tag-phrase in that novel, has traveled in our culture.

67. In one recent television ad, a woman sits at an airport as the gate attendant makes an annoying announcement: her flight has been cancelled, but another flight, leaving in half an hour from a different gate, still has five seats. The camera shows distressed passengers, including a group of nuns wearing full habits. The woman at the gate, dressed in a business suit, has been using her computer. As the attendant speaks, she points, clicks, and books a ticket on the flight. "Correction," the attendant announces, "make that four tickets." The people at the gate dash off hurriedly while the woman closes her notebook and smirks.

In a second ad, passengers are standing on a crowded commuter train. The train stalls. The conductor announces a delay. Every passenger, including one woman who is our focus, reaches for a portable phone. Suddenly, the train jerks forward. Hands on phones, everyone falls to the floor—except the woman, who has just bought and now enjoys a new phone, one that requires just one hand to hold and dial. She snaps her phone shut, places it back on her belt, and steps—smiling, and without a moment's concern beyond her desire to get off the train—over the many people scattered on the floor around her. After 9 / 11 and the 2004 train attacks in Spain, such images of looking out for Number One with regard to airplanes or trains may seem less acceptable.

68. See Introduction; see also Bauman, *Modernity and the Holocaust*. In recent developments whose practical efficacy remains unclear, U.S. courts have agreed to allow those who are not U.S. citizens to file for violations of human rights committed outside the United States and not by U.S. citizens. Nonetheless, enforcement of the usual rights can be suspended in the United States—as for Haitian refugees, for some Cubans from the Mariel boatlift, and for some of those arrested after 9/11. Some of these instances are still being tested in the courts.

69. When Ben-Gurion's Mapai party forced Kastner, a party minister, to sue for libel a journalist who accused him of collaborating with the Nazis when he was a member of Budapest's Jewish Council, Halevi ruled against Kastner, commenting that he "had sold his soul to the Devil," arguably Eichmann himself. Mapai appealed Halevi's ruling; it was reversed by the Supreme Court but not before Kastner was assassinated by vigilantes. On the Kastner case, see Segev, *Seventh Million*, 268–74, 278–89.

In the Kafir Kassem case, Halevi convicted Israeli soldiers of wrongfully shooting unarmed Arabs; the verdict was allowed to stand, but the soldiers' sentences were later commuted. See Segev, *Seventh Million*, 301.

70. The final outcome and practical effect of recent developments (see note 6) remained unclear as this book went to press.

71. On decisions made by the Allies, see Michael J. Neufeld and Michael Berenbaum, eds., *The Bombing of Auschwitz: Should the Allies Have Attempted It?* (New York: St. Martin's Press, 2000). On the history of genocide, see Samantha Power, *"A Problem from Hell":* *America and the Age of Genocide* (New York: Basic Books, 2002). Early U.S. support for Bin Laden and Hussein are well-documented facts in the public record.

72. Flaubert compiled a dictionary throughout his life of *sottises* (idiocies) usually published as an appendix to his last novel *Bouvard et Péchuchet* (1881) or printed under separate cover as *The Dictionary of Received Ideas.* Comparable concepts include George Orwell's Doublespeak in *1984* (1949) and the patterns of euphemism Orwell describes in "The Politics of the English Language" (1950, reprinted in many places). Comparisons also include what Victor Klemperer calls LTI (the Language of the Third Reich) in *I Will Bear Witness: A Diary of the Nazi Years, 1933–1941,* and its second volume, *1942–1945* (New York: Random House, 1998,1999).

Chapter Three

1. See Alon Confino, "Collective Memory and Cultural History: Problems of Method," *American Historical Review* (December 1997): 1386–1403, and Roy Baumeister and Stephen Hastings, "Distortions of Cultural Memory," in *Collective Memory of Political Events*, ed. James W. Pennebaker and others (Mahwah, NJ: Lawrence Erlbaum, 1997), 279–87.

2. Inga Clendinnen, *Reading the Holocaust* (New York: Cambridge University Press, 1999), 183.

3. A member of a lecture audience at Emory University informed me that a film I re-

called about the Resistance in Norway was called *Snow Treasure*. My feelings about World War II are connected to my essay "Slasher Stories," in *Crossing Ocean Parkway* (Chicago: University of Chicago Press, 1994).

4. Judaism traces identity through the maternal line. Although she would need to convert under religious law, the Nazis would have considered my younger daughter Jewish by virtue of my husband's four Jewish grandparents and my own mixed marriage. Raul Hilberg reproduces the text of the laws in *Sources of Holocaust Study: An Analysis* (Chicago: Ivan R. Dee, 2001), 87–88. They make informative reading and include substantial jargon that became life and death matters under the Nazis. *Mischlinges* I were, in practice, treated as Jews; my younger daughter's precise status (I or II) might have depended on factors such as her own marriage (if any), how she described herself (Jewish or Catholic), or on how she was described by others. On the revisions the text underwent, see especially Ian Kershaw, *Hitler, 1889–1936 Hubris* (New York: Norton, 1998), 568–73; see also Martin Gilbert, *A History of the Twentieth Century, vol. 2, 1933–1951* (New York: Morrow, 1998), 79–82.

5. See the Introduction, note 40, and Chapter Two for additional comments on Novick's book.

6. Alongside Novick's and Guttenplan's very good books, which made me reconsider some familiar ideas, some fairly bad books on the Holocaust in contemporary culture appeared around 2000. Tim Cole makes insensitive use of cultural studies methodologies in *Selling the Holocaust* (New York: Routledge, 2000), seeing *Schindler's List* as Disneyesque fantasy and using the term "the Holocaust myth" to refer to the 1970s origins of the term "Holocaust" rather than (as is more usually the case) with regard to those who deny the factuality of Nazi genocide or aspects of it. In the best parts of his book, Cole describes the mishandling of museum structures at Auschwitz by the Polish government, which inadvertently fueled Holocaust denial. Norman Finkelstein, who was severely attacked after he attacked Goldhagen's *Hitler's Willing Executioners* retaliated in an ill-considered book called *The Holocaust Industry* (New York: Verso, 2001). The book provides excellent documentation of debacles that all sides acknowledge about the payment of Holocaust reparations, too little of which has gone to actual survivors, but it uses a conspiracy rhetoric that makes the book offensive.

7. Primo Levi's *If This Is a Man* (*Si questo è un uomo*) was published in 1958. But the immediate quotation is from *The Drowned and the Saved*, trans. Raymond Rosenthal (New York: Summit Books, 1986), 78, 79; see also 82.

8. Levi's family has never accepted the idea that Levi's death was suicide and accidental death remains a possibility. See Carole Angier, *The Double Bond: Primo Levi, A Biography* (New York: Farrar, Straus and Giroux, 2002).

9. Alan Mintz, *Popular Culture and the Shaping of Holocaust Memory in America* (Seattle: University of Washington Press, 2001), 3–4. See also Hilberg, *Sources of Holocaust Research* and the Introduction to this book for additional information.

10. Bauman offers a critique of "how the memory of the Holocaust had been appropriated and deployed. It had been all-too-often sedimented in the public mind as a tragedy that occurred to the Jews and the Jews alone. . . . narrated by Jews and non-Jews alike as a collective (and sole) property of the Jews, as something to be left to, or jealously guarded by, those who had escaped the shooting and the gassing, and by the descendants of the shot

and the gassed (*Modernity and the Holocaust* [Ithaca, NY: Cornell University Press, 1989], viii–ix).

11. Binjamin Wilkomirski's *Fragments* (1995; New York: Schocken Books, 1996) was at first received with rapturous praise directed, I believe, not just at the book but also at the lost milieu of *Yiddishkeit*. After a report commissioned by Wilkomirski's agent confirmed that the author of *Fragments* had been born Bruno Grossjean, adopted as Bruno Dossekker, and spent the war years entirely in Switzerland, the book was roundly condemned. Publishers pulled it from bookstores; it now appears in print only as the discredited appendix to Stefan Maechler, *The Wilkomirski Affair: A Study in Biographical Truth*, trans. John E. Woods (New York: Schocken Books, 2001), the book form of the publisher's report; it also appears on Web sites issued by Holocaust deniers. For excellent articles on the controversy as it evolved, see Philip Gourevitch, "The Memory Thief," *The New Yorker*, June 19, 1999, and Elena Lappin, "The Man with Two Heads," *Granta: The Magazine of New Writing* 66 (Summer 1999). For books on the topic, see Blake Eskin, *A Life in Pieces: The Making and Unmaking of Binjamin Wilkomirski* (New York: Norton, 2003), and Maechler, *Wilkomirski Affair*.

Recent critics, including Jacques Derrida and Cathy Caruth, stress ethical identification as a way out of trauma. My reading of the Wilkomirski case suggests that it challenged in multiple ways the idea of identification as well as the idea of testimony. See Michael Bernard-Donais, "Beyond the Question of Authenticity: Witness and Testimony in the *Fragments* Controversy," *PMLA* 116:5 (October 2001): 1302–16. See also the introduction.

Geoffrey Hartman's excellent Introduction to *Holocaust Remembrance* (Oxford: Blackwell, 1994) calls for evaluation of Holocaust testimony but then ends with a lyrical passage suggesting its impossibility.

12. See Hilberg, *Sources*, 47–48. In terms of age, for example, those neither too young nor too old at the time they entered the concentration camps were the most likely to survive. Tenacity, knowledge of German, and other special skills also increased the chance for survival.

13. See *Generations of the Holocaust*, ed. Martin S. Bergmann and Milton E. Jucovy (1982; New York: Columbia University Press, 1990) and Helen Epstein, *Children of the Holocaust: Conversations with Sons and Daughters of Survivors* (New York: Putnam, 1979). On how the Holocaust haunts later generations, see also James E. Young, *The Texture of Memory: Holocaust Memorials and Meaning* (New Haven: Yale University Press, 1993), Marianne Hirsch, *Family Frames: Photography, Narrative, and Postmemory* (Cambridge: Harvard University Press, 1997), and (on "post memory"), Susan Rubin Suleiman, "Reflections on Memory at the Millennium," *ACLA Bulletin* 53:3 (Summer 1999): xi.

14. On *trauma*, see the Introduction.

15. On the conference held by the Holocaust Memorial Museum, see Joseph Berger, "The Second Generation Reflects on the Holocaust," *New York Times*, January 17, 2000, A-11.

16. See Priscilla Wald, *Constituting Americans: Cultural Anxiety and Narrative Form* (Durham, NC: Duke University Press, 1995).

17. In *Eichmann in Jerusalem*, Hannah Arendt stressed that the Nazis removed German citizenship from Jews with the Nuremberg Laws before escalating action and, across Europe, targeted noncitizen Jews before others for deportation. It was one way to ease the cooperation of occupied nations, only a few of which, notably Denmark, resisted the strategy (1963; New York: Penguin, 1994).

18. Most of my respondents replied in writing. Reiko and Chris supplied their information orally.

19. The first person quoted is Simon During, the second remains unnamed, the third is James Kincaid, and the fourth Alex Zwerdling. I note the limitation of my having had so many respondents who are experts on literature, but I also cannot help but be grateful for how well these people and those I identify and quote here, with their generous permission, express themselves.

20. Many reviewers and critics noted flaws in the 1994 survey released under the popular title *Sex in America:* for example, it interviewed only people at home during the day and omitted homosexuals as too small a part of its sample; and it produced answers that seemed designed to support its initial purpose, AIDS prevention, by demonstrating that the United States is a serially monogamous country in which people sleep with people like themselves in terms of race and socioeconomic class. In using a survey that does not pretend to be social scientific, I am closer to what is said "around the water cooler," which seems to me to have value too.

21. The pattern of chance encounters in specific places informs, in different ways, Sebald's narratives and Badiou's ethics. I want to flag the connection without claiming equivalent stature.

22. These communications were oral and may not have been covered in a subsequent written statement and permission I received. I have, therefore, omitted my informant's name and changed some details in his identity.

23. Noting the polished, literary quality of some of the responses I received, I considered the possibility of distortion. But *all* oral histories include some element of distortion, just as stylization occurs in any representation. My respondents had absolutely nothing to gain by distorting memory knowingly and are, in many instances, known to me as trustworthy people. It seems churlish to question their responses. I would note, in addition, published statements that tally with those I gathered; two examples: Susan Sontag reports the shock of learning about the Holocaust by seeing photographs as a preteen (see Novick, *The Holocaust in American Life* [Boston: Houghton Mifflin, 1999], 64); in *French Lessons* (Chicago: University of Chicago Press, 1993), Alice Kaplan records discovering photographs from the camps in her father's desk, gathered as part of his work as a prosecutor in postwar Germany.

24. My respondents were not selected on this basis nor had I tried to identify ethnic or religious background beforehand.

25. Hana Wirth-Nesher, "A Dual Legacy: How Is the Child of Holocaust Survivors Different from Other Children?" *Moment* 6:3 / 4 (March / April 1981): 26–28.

26. On the single-child phenomenon, see Sara Bershtel and Allen Graubard, *Saving Remnants: Feeling Jewish in America* (New York: Free Press, 1992).

27. Since I gathered these memories, Rosa has joined a group of survivors' children but has still not wanted to read these books. Another, more casual friend has "come out" as a Holocaust survivors' child after years of not mentioning it. Both developments testify to rapid changes I mentioned earlier.

28. Germany executed many Polish leaders, professionals, and intellectuals soon after occupying the country. Their standard reprisal for every German killed was the mass execution of civilians, chosen at random. Hannah Arendt and others have speculated that

Hitler planned further genocide had he won the war (see Gerhard L. Weinberg, *A World at Arms: A Global History of World War II* [Cambridge: Cambridge University Press, 1994], 59). In 1944, an uprising of the Warsaw Resistance failed after the Soviets halted their advance and refused to allow the United States to supply badly needed arms and supplies. Many Poles died; the city was razed. See Norman Davies, *Rising '44* (New York: Viking, 2004), also the subject of a June 2004 documentary on CNN.

29. On Goldhagen's reception in Germany, see *Unwilling Germans?: The Goldhagen Debate*, ed. Robert R. Shandley, with essays translated by Jeremiah Riemer (Minneapolis: University of Minnesota Press, 1998). Along with many articles, a spate of books includes *The "Goldhagen Effect": History, Memory, Nazism—Facing the German Past*, ed. Geoff Eley (Ann Arbor: University of Michigan Press, 2000), and Frank Wesley, *The Holocaust and Anti-Semitism: The Goldhagen Argument and Its Effects* (San Francisco: International Scholars Publications, 1999). The phrases I include are quoted by Wolfgang Wipperman in "The Jewish Hanging Judge? Goldhagen and the 'Self-Confident Nation,'" in *Unwilling Germans?*, ed. Shandley. Comments about Goldhagen's origins, one should add, arose without Goldhagen's stressing his origins.

30. See Volker Ullrich, "A Triumphal Procession: Goldhagen and the Germans," in *Unwilling Germans?*, ed. Shandley, 197.

31. Frederick Kempe sees Goldhagen as appealing to younger Germans by positing that anti-Semitism has disappeared in democratic postwar Germany. See *Father/Land* (New York: Putnam, 1999), 134–41.

32. The terms "intentionalist" and "functionalist" have become standard in histories of the Holocaust. For an excellent discussion of these terms and the "buffering" effects of functionalism, see Saul Friedlander, "Trauma, Memory, and Transference," in *Holocaust Remembrance*, ed. Hartman, 257–63. See also Omer Bartov, *Holocaust: Origins, Implementation, Aftermath* (New York: Routledge, 2000).

33. Norman G. Finkelstein and Ruth Bettina Birn, *A Nation on Trial: The Goldhagen Thesis and Historical Truth* (New York: Henry Holt, 1998). D. D. Guttenplan describes the negative reaction against the book and attempts to block its publication (*The Holocaust on Trial* [New York: Norton, 2000], 294–95). Clearly angered, Finkelstein replied with his ill-conceived book called *The Holocaust Industry* (see chapter 3, note 6).

34. Robert R. Shandley, "Introduction," in *Unwilling Germans?*, ed. Shandley, 10.

35. Quoted in Ullrich, "Triumphal Procession," in *Unwilling Germans?*, ed. Shandley, 199.

36. The Goldhagen controversy was only one of several other notable controversies within postwar Germany that reveal strong sensitivities. On the *Historikerstreit*, the historians' conflict, see Charles S. Maier, *The Unmasterable Past: History, Holocaust, and German Identity* (Cambridge: Harvard University Press, 1988). See also Andrei S. Markovits and Simon Reich, *The German Predicament: Memory and Power in the New Europe* (Ithaca, NY: Cornell University Press, 1997); and Kempe, *Father/Land*. On ongoing sensitivities, see also Bjorn Krondorfer, *Remembrance and Reconciliation: Encounters between Young Jews and Germans* (New Haven: Yale University Press, 1995). The Introduction, note 47, cites a controversial photo exhibition on the Wehrmacht. Summer 2003 saw two scandals when the Italian prime minister accused a German diplomat of acting like a perfect concentration camp guard and another official criticized the Germans for hogging Italian beaches.

37. I share this view with Giorgio Agamben and Zygmunt Bauman, among other authors I have cited.

38. In his otherwise very good book, Kempe sniffs around his origins until he finds out that an uncle he has never met had been a concentration camp guard; on the basis of just that slender information, in a long and disturbing sequence, he imagines vividly his uncle abusing Jews.

39. A salamandra is a Greek mythological figure, similar to a phoenix, who lives in fire for seven years and then rises from the flames. As his name suggests, Dinur identified himself with his fictions and, although they are written in the third person and use fictional names, critics usually and too facilely identify the books as semi-autobiographical. Arendt dismisses the books as "human interest stories"; Tom Segev claims that Israeli youth originally read them in the 1950s for information about the Holocaust but kept reading for pornography (*Seventh Million*, 5–8). Expecting trash, I found *House of Dolls* (the only one of the novels available in English) a page-turner, a compelling fiction. Although no one could mistake it for a masterpiece and the book is prurient at times, it comes from the heart and did not strike me at all as a contemptible piece of work. What's more, and quite surprising, the novel includes aspects of the Holocaust relatively unfamiliar in 1955, aspects Arendt herself would later be pilloried for airing, including a condemnation of the prominent role played by the Judenrate in policing ghettos and in making selections for deportation.

For admiring views of Dinur, see Shoshana Felman, "Theatres of Justice: Arendt in Jerusalem, the Eichmann Trial, and the Redefinition of Legal Meaning in the Wake of the Holocaust," *Critical Inquiry* 27:2 (Winter 2001), and Chapter Two, note 60; see also Omer Bartov, *Mirrors of Destruction* (Oxford: Oxford University Press, 2000), 188–212. Bartov's interpretation is the most complete, although I find some of his points based on a misunderstanding of literary techniques. Arendt depicts Dinur as a voluble clown and uses him to accuse most of the other ninety prosecution witnesses of lacking "the rare capacity for distinguishing between things that had happened to the storyteller more than sixteen, and sometimes, twenty, years ago, and what he had read and heard and imagined in the meantime" (Arendt, *Eichmann in Jerusalem*, 224). Contra Arendt, the transcripts and videos from the trial show that Dinur spoke very, very briefly—for less than one page of volume III—a length unusually short for any witness and far shorter than Arendt's description suggests (see *Transcripts*, III, 1237). The films also show that, rather than enjoying the display of testifying, Dinur seemed from the very start pained and uncomfortable, as did most of the witnesses. Ironically, a kernel of truth beneath Arendt's misleading portrait emerges in later images of the man, as in the interview I cited in Chapter Two and as in *Shivitti*.

40. See Ka-Tzetnik 135633 [Yehiel Dinur], *Shivitti: A Vision*, trans. Eliyah Nike De-Nur and Lisa Herman (1987; San Francisco: Harper and Row, 1989), 110.

41. For the passages described or quoted, see especially 96–104.

42. Dinur makes the character usually identified as his persona in the novels work in a camp hospital; his memoir suggests that Dinur may have worked, at least for a time, in or around the gas chambers. Israeli law, including the law that would indict Eichmann, took the Judenrate and *sondercommandos* (Jews who worked in the gas chambers) into account by exempting from war crimes those who had committed their actions under the threat of imminent death. The legal exemption clearly did not prevent strong and (in Dinur's case) perhaps displaced feelings of guilt. All quotations come from *Shivitti*, 47–51.

43. The Dutchman's ethical action aids ethnic others but, as Badiou might say, otherness (alterity), being all we have, it is all we have to work with: "There are as many differences, say, between a Chinese peasant and a young Norwegian professional as between myself and anybody at all, including myself. As many, but also, then, *neither more nor less*" (*Ethics: An Essay on the Understanding of Evil*, trans. Peter Hallward [1998; London: Verso, 2001], 26). The ethnic identity of those in the pit is thus not insignificant but also, in this instance, not necessarily decisive. Badiou might be distinguished on this basis from Buber and Levinas, but, as I suggest, the difference rests on a more inclusive definition of otherness not ultimately incompatible with Buber or Levinas.

44. In theoretical terms, the utterance is a performative (a statement that has the force of an action), producing the desired result (the Dutch Jew's refusal to kill), albeit not the ideal goal of saving the gypsies.

45. Primo Levi, *If This Is a Man* (*Si questo è un uomo*), trans. Stuart Woolf (1958; London: Orion, 1959), 205, 190, 204.

46. Dinur tells us, "Since his 'No' to the S.S. man and his flight into the fire, I have not been able to get *'Kan niet lopen,'* syllable for syllable, out of my mind." Walking through Noordwijk, the Dutch site of his therapy, Dinur stops a random stranger to utter the words "Kan niet lopen." Modestly, the woman he stops asks him whether she should call an ambulance. He then continues "marching on from street to street, longing to embrace every passerby, murmuring 'Kan niet lopen,' weeping in the arms of a stranger, and saying only, 'Kan niet lopen,' not another word, for I did not have another word, nor would another word ever come to me. I am mute, deprived of the word" (*Shivitti*, 48, 50–51). The book then continues for another seventy pages.

In the original incident, walking (a physical action)—something of which the Dutch Jew felt incapable but Dinur was fully capable in the camp—stands in for the refusal ("No! no!") of which the Dutch Jew was capable but Dinur was not. One might see a Freudian aha; Dinur might too, though that's unclear. Amid a plethora of written and spoken testimonies, Dinur's very public avowal of "muteness" and the symbolic status of his fainting remain equivocal.

47. Badiou capitalizes concepts such as Truth and Goodness, including the Immortal. Writing in a less Platonic idiom, I do not.

48. Two examples: Hitler was democratically elected in 1933, albeit under dubious circumstances; the reception of Wilkomirski's tale revealed a whole class of people who similarly suffer from a kind of Holocaust Münchhausen syndrome.

49. Instead of "secular grace," the phrase Badiou uses is "laicized grace."

50. Peter Hallward, "Appendix, Politics and Philosophy: An Interview with Alain Badiou," in Badiou, *Ethics*, 123.

Chapter Four

1. The term "motivate" comes from the Russian Formalists. See Victor Shklovsky, "Sterne's *Tristram Shandy:* Stylistic Commentary," in *Russian Formalist Criticism: Four Essays*, trans. and ed. Lee T. Lemon and Marion J. Reis (Lincoln: University of Nebraska Press, 1965), 27–29.

2. Important, postwar, in English: my qualifying terms may need some explanation. Using 1945 as a historical boundary, I exclude important novels like Virginia Woolf's *Be-*

tween the Acts (1941)—in which combat remains ambiance rather than full subject—and Ernest Hemingway's *For Whom the Bell Tolls* (1940), set during the Spanish Civil War. I also omit novels of which I am quite fond but that never found audiences in the United States like Anthony Powell's multivolume *A Dance to the Music of Time* (1957) and Graham Greene's psychological drama *The Tenth Man* (1948), which are more about the cultural ambiance war generates (with a panoramic view in Powell; a view focused on a single French prison in Greene) rather than combat or the war per se. Finally, I exclude quality popular fiction like Alan Furst's novels, whose plots often focus on little-known aspects of the war but operate in a mode reminiscent of James Bond novels. When one lists the number of important novels about the Holocaust, the received idea that the Holocaust produced no writing begins to pale. While a full survey exceeds my scope in this chapter, books written about World War II in Russian and other European languages (including, with certain secrets and hesitations of their own, those in French and German) have been more abundant.

3. For fiction in English, Vietnam may have had the same effect I described for film in Chapter One: by creating a strong antiwar tone in the culture, it may have displaced attention. Unlike World War II, Vietnam has produced a robust number of novels, many antiwar in tone.

4. See Paul Fussell, *Wartime: Understanding and Behavior in the Second World War* (New York: Oxford University Press, 1989), 31.

5. Quoted in Fussell, *Wartime*, 134. Fussell sees the literary temperament, already disillusioned by the carnage of World War I, as quickly repulsed by World War II as "indescribably cruel and insane." He essentially describes a general population unsure of why we were fighting the war apart from the need to revenge Pearl Harbor and impacted by the drain of men and rationing. As he describes it, the troops felt quite cynical and a veneer of enthusiasm for World War II was sustained only by the media and by mass propaganda. During the war years in England, James, Trollope, and the Victorians underwent a revival (see 228–29).

6. Although it's about World War I, a more frequent subject than World War II in our time, the combat segments of Pat Barker's *The Ghost Road* (the third volume in her *Regeneration* series), illustrate well how the double time frame and dual settings work. The second half of the novel alternates radically between Billy Prior in the ditches of France and Sir William Pitt Rivers in his British hospital, thinking about his experiences as an ethnographer in Melanesia.

7. Georg Lukács, *The Historical Novel*, trans. Hannah and Stanley Mitchell (New York: Humanities Press, 1965), 53. Ian McEwan's award-winning *Atonement* (New York: Doubleday, 2001) includes a long sequence set at Dunkirk. But the novel takes back or withdraws the sequence by the end, since we learn that the events it records never happened in "reality" or, what counts as "reality" within fiction, in the novel's narrative time. All along, Robbie's actions and feelings at Dunkirk have been a fiction within a fiction, written by the character called Briony as her atonement for having ruined the other characters' lives.

8. Linkages between imperialism and world war are not new—some of Freud's work and, more extensively, Arendt's come to mind—but they are relatively few and underemphasized in theories of culture. (See the Introduction, note 35.) Much of the ethical theory I have cited in this book (Buber, Levinas, Derrida, and others) arose in reaction to

world war, though the theorists tend to position the topic as universal. Wilhelm Reich's theories in *The Mass Psychology of Fascism* (New York: Orgone Press, 1946 [reprinted by Farrar, Straus and Giroux, 1970]) and Klaus Theweleit's in *Male Fantasies*, 2 vols., trans. Stephan Conway (Minneapolis: University of Minnesota Press, 1987–89) are also important. I first encountered the links between spiritual hungers and World War II in my work on primitivism, *Gone Primitive* (Chicago: University of Chicago Press, 1990) and *Primitive Passions* (New York: Alfred A. Knopf, 1997). While I do not adopt his terminology at every turn, as in earlier chapters, Badiou's *Ethics* is for me a pertinent text; he also uses analogies from World War II, although I have chosen different instances and apply his ideas differently from how he himself might do.

9. Rob Nixon first pointed out to me the significance of 1956, which I explore further.

10. In the episode, the character Elaine finds the movie's romanticism sickening and becomes a social pariah as a result.

11. See, for example, page 133: "There is, after Herodotus, little interest by the Western world toward the desert for hundreds of years. From 425 BC to the beginning of the twentieth century, there is an averting of eyes. Silence." I quote from the 1992 Knopf edition of *The English Patient*, published in New York.

12. The back-story of events in Egypt occupies roughly 30 percent of the novel's pages but roughly 60 percent of the film. The change alters the emphasis substantially because, although the war influences the Egyptian plot, mythic parallels prevail: Dido and Aeneas, Candaules and Gyges (as told in Herodotus and again by Katherine), Tristan and Isolde, even the Ingrid Bergman and Humphrey Bogart characters in *Casablanca* (1942).

13. Instead of a father killed in the war, the film more conventionally gives Hana a lost fiancé. Although I cannot pursue the idea in this context, Caravaggio serves almost a psychiatrist's role in the novel for Almasy—he is like a narrative voice, teasing out Katherine's story from the English patient.

14. I am dealing with three entitles: *The English Patient*, the novel (New York: Knopf, 1992); *The English Patient*, the movie (directed by Anthony Minghella, 1996); and The English Patient as a generalized image. I thought about using different typeface for each but, aside from omitting the italics from the image, decided not to do so. When novel and film differ, I indicate the differences verbally. When I refer to *The English Patient* without specifying novel or film, as in this sentence, I mean both.

15. Anthony Minghella, *The English Patient: A Screenplay* (New York: Hyperion, 1996), xi–xii.

16. On Hersey, see Paul Boyer, "'Victory for What?'" in Kai Bird and Lawrence Lifschultz, eds., *Hiroshima's Shadows* (Stony Creek, CT: The Pamphleteer's Press, 1998), 250.

17. For an excellent selection of the essays mentioned in this paragraph, reprinted from many sources, see *Hiroshima's Shadow*, ed. Bird and Lifschultz, 237–316.

18. See Michael Yavenditti, "John Hersey and the American Conscience," in *Hiroshima's Shadow*, ed. Bird and Lifschultz, 288–302, on government supported publicity, including: Karl T. Compton's "If the Atomic Bomb Had Not Been Used," *Atlantic Monthly*, December 1946; Henry L. Stimson's "The Decision to Use the Atomic Bomb," *Harper's*, February 1947; and a film called *The Beginning or The End* (MGM, 1947).

19. See Introduction, note 23.

20. Carla Comellini's "Why a Patient and a Nurse?" points to a scene in the novel in

which's Kip's medical training is registered and then ignored, probably because of the belief that "white" troops would not accept as physician a dark-skinned Indian like Kip (in *Re-Constructing the Fragments of Michael Ondaatje's Work*, ed. Jean-Michel La Croix [Presses de la Sorbonne Nouvelle, n.d.], 159–60.) The film actively obscures the subject by omitting Kip's medical training and by repeating several times that Kip is a Lieutenant while his Anglo partner is lower in rank—no racism at all, thank you very much. Additional perspectives on the medical theme that it would be interesting to develop but cannot be developed here might be drawn from important work like Klaus Theweleit's *Male Fantasies*, which talks about eroticism and violence in the fascist imagination around the image of the nurse.

21. Until quite recently, a white, European and American "us" functioned as the unmarked (the assumed, the "natural") audience of fiction. See Toni Morrison, *Playing in the Dark: Whiteness and the Literary Imagination* (Cambridge: Harvard University Press, 1992). Like Morrison, Ondaatje makes different assumptions and is willing to have some, even most, readers miss certain details. See below for Sikh history.

22. The Sikh religion has some elements of Hinduism and some of the Muslim faith but remains distinct. Its holy book is the Dasam Granth. Relations with larger groups in both India and Pakistan have sometimes been uneasy. See *Selections from the Sacred Writing of the Sikhs*, trans. Trilochan Singh and others, revised by George S. Fraser (1960; London: Allen and Unwin, 1965), and W. Owen Cole and Piara Singh Sambhi, *The Sikhs: Their Religious Beliefs and Practices* (London: Routledge, 1978). For Sikh history, see J. S. Grewel, *Historical Perspectives on Sikh Identity* (Patiala, India: Punjabi University, 1997), and *Sikh History and Religion in the Twentieth Century*, ed. Joseph T. O'Connell, Milton Israel, and others (Toronto: University of Toronto, Centre for South Asian Studies, 1988).

23. See Don Van Natta Jr., "A World Made More Dangerous as Terrorism Spreads," *New York Times*, April 18, 2004, section 4, 1. He reports that Islamic militants "stage attacks weekly in the Indian-controlled part of Kashmir." Bin Laden's group is part of much wider movements for Dar-al-Islam, a transnational Islamic entity that would be ruled by God and the Qur'ân. Like Israel's claim to Palestine, both Indian and Sikh claims to the Punjab form an obstacle to Dar-al-Islam.

24. Later events have included, as of this writing: new signs of cooperation between India and Pakistan; the defeat of the Indian government that had promoted that cooperation; repeated terrorist incidents in Pakistan. News coverage has been spotty and outcomes remain uncertain.

25. The speech, before the Council on Foreign Relations at the Yale Club, aired late at night on C-Span but received scanty coverage in newspapers. In its July 1, 2002 issue, *The New Yorker* profiled it in "Homeland Truths," 33–34, describing it as "a dazzling performance, one which left the members of the audience a little stunned." A transcript of the talk was later available at www.cfr.org. It remains true, of course, that Clinton did not accomplish all the goals he mentions during his presidency, when the United States exported many low-paying jobs abroad.

Apropos of Clinton's talk, Arundhati Roy has pointed out links between world history and the date September 11 before 2001: on September 11, 1990, the first President Bush announced to Congress his decision to go to war on Iraq; the British issued a mandate in Palestine, a follow-up to the Balfour Declaration on September 11, 1922, despite "Arab outrage";

on September 11, 1973, a CIA-backed coup in Chile overthrew Salvador Allende. One might note that any date involves a string of coincidences, but I found her statement interesting. See *War Talk* (Cambridge, MA: South End Press, 2003), 57–64.

26. Some have criticized how Ondaatje makes Kip leap to pan-Asian sympathy when he hears about Hiroshima and Nagasaki, especially since the Japanese had murdered Sikhs. Nonetheless, as someone who knows bombs and has defused them for the British, he would have found the events quite devastating.

27. The passage (301) picks up a fine detail in the novel, recalling a moment when Hana perceives Kip's arm in terms of the arms into which she has injected a fatal dose of morphine (125). The tiny detail functions as one of the "unexploded bombs all over the place" to which the novel alludes (32), but not in any literal sense. For Hana has been injecting morphine into Almasy's arm (42) for quite some time, suggesting a slippage between her devotion to her patient and her more erotic connection to Kip.

28. The bombing of Hiroshima of course preceded Nagasaki; the novel treats them as one event. It is unclear whether Ondaatje collapses the distinction (which would be a bad idea) or whether news has been slower to travel to the front. Hiroshima has come to stand for Hiroshima and Nagasaki, just as Auschwitz has come to stand for all the death camps. I try to make specific references whenever possible but note the synecdoche as typical of cultural memory.

29. Minghella, *The English Patient: A Screenplay*, 4. Capital letters appear in the original to indicate action.

30. If I had the space to develop this interpretation of the film, I would note two things: first, that Katherine gives another meaning to the white flash when she utters, after reckless sex with Almasy: "It's hot. . . . I'm just too hot," making "in flames" a conventional metaphor for passion; second, that the film ends with a shot of Almasy's plane gliding across the desert, moments before the flames (the explosion), which we do not see this time. Because both the novel and the film use light dramatically—the torch light by which Kip displays the ceiling of an Italian church; Caravaggio's body, outlined in the film by a car's headlight; campfires, candles, and so forth—it's hard to insist on a visual reference to Hiroshima in this use of light. Still, in his preface to the screenplay, Ondaatje describes Kip's story and Hiroshima as "the original country of the book" (in Minghella, xvii). And though Ondaatje accepts the changes made for the film, one suspects that Hiroshima formed one of the heated arguments to which Minghella refers in his preface, page xi.

31. In the film, Caravaggio makes no such statement and remains a committed Allied partisan rather than an uncommitted drifter. The film even alludes to Caravaggio, a morphine addict, heading to the postwar trials to translate for the Allies—and the mind boggles at the master-thief-cum-drug-addict in Nuremberg! Characters in the film register sporadic protests against nationalism, mostly in the context of how terrible it is that Almasy's international expedition has to end.

32. I owe the term *warspace* to an unpublished seminar paper by Alex Ruch, which influenced this and the next two paragraphs.

33. Heather Pilatic pointed out the "shedding skins" passage. Because I am talking about cooperative ventures, Pilatic's and Ruch's roles in the final version of this chapter please me.

34. In this sentence and at the very end of the paragraph, the phrases quoted come from

Alex Ruch's unpublished paper, which also brought to my attention the reference to Gilles Deleuze, *Cinema 2*, trans. Hugh Tomlinson and Robert Galeta (Minneapolis: University of Minnesota Press, 1989), xi.

35. The phrase quoted comes from Ruch's unpublished paper. Compare similar statements by Hulme and Marcuse, cited at the beginning of the Conclusion.

36. Libraries often classify novels as World War II novels on the basis of temporal setting. *The English Patient* is so classified; *The Remains of the Day* (1988; New York: Vintage, 1993) and W. G. Sebald's books are not.

37. The Merchant-Ivory film of *The Remains of the Day* (directed by James Ivory, 1994) aims at a pristine fidelity, often achieved, despite some melodramatic touches. The kind of strong distinctions between novel and film I made when discussing *The English Patient* will not be necessary in this instance.

38. Lord Darlington's sympathy for the Germans arose from an old friend's despair after Germany's defeat and its humiliation in the Treaty of Versailles. Such bonding over Germany's fate could forge some strange friendships, as for example, that of Romain Rolland and Sigmund Freud. See my book *Primitive Passions*, Chapter One. In a dramatic instance of Nazism's effect, Darlington directs Stevens to dismiss two Jewish maids, which he does, over Miss Kenton's vehement objections. The film makes the maids refugees, endangering their right to stay in England; in the novel, they are British, a better decision. There is a notable mix of historical and nonhistorical characters and events in these portions of the novel. Sir Oswald Mosley, of course, is historical; Stevens and the two maids are not. Compare Pat Barker's *Regeneration* trilogy.

39. Eichmann's utterance climaxes his statement before sentencing (*Transcripts*, V, 2216). See chapter 2 note 7 for more on *Transcripts*.

40. When Nasser came to power, the British agreed to end their military presence in the Canal zone (a site of previous controversy) unless the area were threatened by an outside invader—hence the use of Israel.

41. On Suez, see Kyle Keith, *Suez: Britain's End of Empire in the Middle East* (London: I. B. Tauris, 2003), and Diane B. Kunz, *The Economic Diplomacy of the Suez Canal* (Chapel Hill: University of North Carolina Press, 1991). Proof of the generalization exceeds my topic, but it seems to me that the Suez crisis, given its past and current salience, is underrepresented in print. The U.S. position—first allied with Britain and France and then opposed to military action—is only one of many complicated histories.

Nasser himself was a secularist who provoked an Islamist reaction in Egypt; others configured in Pakistan and Malaysia. Even after 9/11, clear histories of the rise of militant Islamism are hard to find. Three now available: Samia Serageldin, Introduction to Roland Jacquard's *In the Name of Osama Bin Laden*, trans. George Holoch (Durham, NC: Duke University Press, 2002); Bernard Lewis, *The Crisis of Islam: Holy War and Unholy Terror* (New York: Modern Library, 2003); Salwa Ismail, *Re-Thinking Islamist Politics: Culture, the State, and Islamism* (New York: Random House, 2003).

42. Cited in Paul Fussell, *The Great War and Modern Memory* (New York: Oxford University Press, 1975), 175.

43. In the Boer War, Britain consolidated its hold over South Africa, a source of great mineral wealth. The war included the use of machine guns against "natives" and of con-

centration camps for Boers (Dutch settlers) and was a full-blown imperial adventure. Stevens's father later served, without comment, the general who caused his son's death.

44. Symbolically, in the novel, he apes upper-class speech and wears cast-off clothes. In an important scene, Miss Kenton tries to wrest a book from Stevens. He shrinks and resists, twisting backward in a classically feminine pose. The book turns out to be a society romance, from which Stevens has taught himself upper-class diction; the genre is, of course, usually read by women and not by men (166–68).

45. Ishiguro's next two novels—*The Unconsoled* and *When We Were Orphans*—both feature celebrated figures (a pianist and a detective, respectively) solving mysteries about their pasts amid a substantial temporal confusion or confusion about the facts. Despite some links between the entire canon, these last two novels seem linked, much as Ishiguro's first three novels did.

46. For a fuller discussion of topics elided from cultural memory, see the Introduction to this book. Bauman, Novick, Guttenplan, Huyssen, and Wyschogrod are among the few critics to raise the issue of Holocaust "uniqueness" as a problem. Books and articles that assume the Holocaust's uniqueness are too numerous to cite here.

47. Some of Ishiguro's critics object to bringing his Japanese origins to bear on his work, but, given the subject matter of his first two books, that seems inappropriate and even foolish. See Cynthia Wong, *Kasuo Ishiguro* (Devon, England: Northcote Horse, 2000). Ondaatje's playful autobiography is called *Running in the Family*.

48. I am, of course, speculating in this paragraph. Still, too much attention to Hiroshima by a Japanese-British novelist—especially after two "Japanese" novels—might have seemed inappropriate, even (given Stevens's blind spots about Nazi persecution), disrespectful to the Holocaust. Similarly, as a long-term resident of Toronto, Ondaatje would know that attention to Hiroshima instead of, or even alongside, the Holocaust might seem insensitive or even offensive. As suggested earlier, the issue may even have come up as the novel was transformed into a film.

49. The quotation in this sentence comes from Edith Wyschogrod, *An Ethics of Remembering: History, Heterology, and the Nameless Others* (Chicago: University of Chicago Press, 1998), xiii.

50. Barbie Zelizer suggests in *Remembering to Forget: Holocaust Memory through the Camera's Eye* (Chicago: University of Chicago Press, 1998), that the over-display of Holocaust images has resulted in both effects. Geoffrey Hartman discusses what he calls "antimemory" in *Holocaust Remembrance* (Oxford: Blackwell, 1994).

Chapter Five

1. With the exception of linking words and phrases, almost all the words in this paragraph come from W. G. Sebald, "Air War and Literature: Zurich Lectures," in *On the Natural History of Destruction*, trans. Anthea Bell (1999; New York: Random House, 2003), ix, 23. I give page references but omit the quotation marks in some instances for reasons that should become clear by the end of this chapter.

2. I am using Sebald's statistics in this sentence ("Air War," 3). If Sebald's estimates seem high, as they may, they are nonetheless confirmed by scholarly sources. Keegan reports "altogether some 600,000 German civilians died under bombing attack and 800,000

were seriously injured" (John Keegan, *The Second World War* [New York: Penguin, 1989], 433). With the intention of stressing Soviet losses, Taylor notes that "almost exactly the same number of Soviet citizens died as a result of bombing during the Second World War as Germans: around half a million" (Frederick Taylor, *Dresden: Tuesday 13 February 1945* [London: Bloomsbury, 2004], 411). And we should add to mortality and casualty figures Germany's staggering postwar refugee crisis, when as many as 10 million Germans were on the move.

3. Because Sebald's narrators share many aspects of Sebald's personal history, many commentators identity the author with the narrator—a conflation that narrative theory always cautions against. In this chapter, I note inconsistencies that suggest narrative distance between Sebald, the author, and his narrators. Nonetheless, some references in the narrator's voice may correspond to events in Sebald's life. See, for example, *Austerlitz*, trans. Anthea Bell (New York: Random House, 2001), 23. For additional references to family background in the fiction, see *Vertigo*, trans. Michael Hulse (1990; New York: New Directions, 2000), 243, and other parts of the "Il ritorno in patria" section; page 243 enacts a miniature Freudian drama about the return of the narrator's father from the war and the son's fear-inducing visit to a barber wielding scissors. Although some, even many, details given in the fictions seem factual, only a full-scale biography could determine that. Outside the fiction, see *Natural History*, 70–74 and (perhaps) 78, and "Dark Night Sallies Forth," in *After Nature*, trans. Michael Hamburger (New York: Random House, 2002). On German anti-Semitism and insights into social class similar to Hannah Arendt's, see "Air War and Literature," in *Natural History*, 98–103.

4. See, for example, page 38 of *The Rings of Saturn*, trans. Michael Hulse (New York: New Directions, 1998).

5. The phrases here ("unbelonging" and "expanded geographical space and time") echo those introduced in Chapter Four, and quite deliberately so.

6. Stendhal's image of a mirror traveling down the road in a pack is often cited as an image of realism although many novelists (Brontë, Stendhal himself, Dickens, Nabokov) and narrative theory also explore the mirror as an image of artifice and stylization. Sebald devotes several pages to Stendhal in *Vertigo*.

7. Caleb Smith taught me much during a 2003 course on contemporary fiction in which he was my teaching assistant. In this sentence and in the last sentence of this paragraph, I paraphrase a lecture he gave on selections from *Austerlitz*.

8. *The Emigrants*, trans. Michael Hulse (1992; New York: New Directions, 1996), 21.

9. Some additional details about the first story can help typify the whole. Born in Lithuania and Jewish, Hersh Seweryn came to England only by mistake when the ship carrying him and his family deposited them in London rather than, as they had expected, in New York. Having changed his name to Henry Selwyn and married a Swiss woman, Selwyn "concealed [his] true background for a long time," even from his wife (21). Then, after 1960, Selwyn withdrew from professional life and became the gardener and hermit the authorial narrator and his wife meet in 1971 when they briefly rent an apartment in his house. During their acquaintance, Selwyn tells the narrator about his friend, a famous alpine guide named Johannes Naegeli who disappeared one day shortly after World War I began into (it was assumed) a crevice. Selwyn and the narrator drift apart; Sebald hears that Selwyn has committed suicide. Years later, in 1986, the narrator is taking a train in Switzerland when he

recalls, "or perhaps merely imagine[s], the memory of Dr. Selwyn returned to me for the first time in a long while" (23). Within the hour, his "eye was caught by a [newspaper] report that said the remains of the Bernese alpine guide Johannes Naegeli, missing since summer 1914, had been released by the Oberaar glacier, seventy-two years later." The conclusion flowers out from this quotidian newspaper account: "And so they are ever returning to us, the dead. At times they come back from the ice more than seven decades later and are found at the edge of the moraine, a few polished bones and a pair of hob-nailed boots." No two sentences could be more typical of Sebald in their poetic vivification of the quotidian.

10. *The Rings of Saturn* includes a photograph of the narrator (263), which is a photograph of Sebald himself—linking the author to the narrating "I" with unusual directness.

11. The "self-evidently" marks the kind of connection that some readers may find facile; the ability to test connections nonetheless forms part and parcel of Sebald's powerful imagination.

12. The book's final sequence on silkworms summarizes a German film of the Central Reich Institute of Sericulture, where the killing of the silkworms takes place (294). It is informed by a sense, consonant with Arendt and Agamben, that killing can proceed under medical or "sanitary" auspices in the biopolitical state.

13. The alignment of events by calendar date always gives a sense of portentousness, and some events Sebald lists, like the Nazi retreat, were ongoing rather than confined to a single day. But as reviews of Sebald's work attest, the passage succeeds. The hinted interplay between Sebald's narrator and the wife he calls Clara seems touching and intimate, but Sebald's wife's actual name is Ute. The detail underscores the danger of narrow biographical readings.

14. Bruno Latour uses the vocabulary of networks to describe relations between humans, animals, and things in *We Have Never Been Modern*, trans. Catherine Porter (Cambridge: Harvard University Press, 1993). I adopt that vocabulary here as natural to Sebald's vision.

15. I re-read these words in the spring of 2003, as the United States launched an invasion of Iraq to assure our safety by unclear means. The words took my breath away, auguring as they did the "natural limits" which might produce greater unsafety or one of the shifts in world power that fascinate Sebald.

16. See George Johnson, "What's So New in a Newfangled Science," an article about Stephen Wolfram, *New York Times*, June 16, 2002, section 4, 14.

17. Austerlitz's arrival at Liverpool Street Station (now the site of a memorial to the children of the *Kindertransport*) helps to explain the thematic weight of railway stations in the book.

18. Zoo images recur in *Austerlitz* after the first chapter, where they are introduced. The passage quoted occurs on page 45.

19. The name Austerlitz is, in fact, a name found among Czechoslovakian Jews. It is also, of course, the name of a famous battle during the Napoleonic wars—wars that form one touchstone of Sebald's imagination, quite possibly for the same reason Lukács assigns to the events' importance in *The Historical Novel:* the Napoleonic wars made men conscious of being part of history and was characterized by movement from one end of Europe to the other, and then back (Georg Lukács, *The Historical Novel*, trans. Hannah and Stanley Mitchell [New York: Humanities Press, 1965], 23–25).

20. Although it presides over the book and is used on the dust jacket, this photograph initially looks quite strange. Once the text has identified its subject, it becomes a heart-breaking symbol of time lost and of life's fragility. An image from the Enlightenment, its context may make (more delicately than I can make it here) a criticism of Enlightenment confidence that would be consistent with other aspects of the novel.

21. Sebald's adoption of themes often represents strong recognition of what I call "the middle distance."

22. I also do not like narrowly biographical explanations because Sebald's prose can be quite ambiguous, alluding, for example, in *The Rings of Saturn*, to hospitalization after the narrator found himself "in a state of almost total immobility" (3) and to hospitalization for "surgery," perhaps on an "insensate foot" (17–18). The two references might or might not refer to the same period of hospitalization and hence offer a more pedestrian explanation than extreme depression for the hiker's illness. An additional richness in Sebald's prose: the patient imagines himself as "cocooned" within silent and disorienting space—images evocative, on a second or third reading, of the narrator as silkworm (5).

23. Former colleagues describe Sebald as a private kind of man who generally chose not to engage in departmental politics but as someone who could joke about his serious, even somber, literary persona.

24. Saul Friedlander, "Trauma, Memory, and Transference," in *Holocaust Remembrance: The Shapes of Memory*, ed. Geoffrey H. Hartman (Oxford: Blackwell, 1994), 257–60.

25. Inga Clendinnen's well-received book, *Reading the Holocaust* (New York: Cambridge University Press, 1999), analyses photographs of the Holocaust and makes the claim that we must imagine the Germans sympathetically as well as the Jews because both are in the same picture and the Jews are dead while the Germans may still be living. See Chapter Three. Although I found her book quite interesting, I felt put-off by her point with regard to the photographs. It is, emphatically, not the kind of assertion I see Sebald as making.

26. Geoffrey Hartman discusses the temporal divide between "before and after" in the Introduction to *Holocaust Remembrance* (Oxford: Blackwell, 1994), and again in *The Fateful Question of Culture* (New York: Columbia University Press, 1997).

27. I would note a strong affinity in Sebald's thought to Bauman and Agamben.

28. In Bruno Latour's vocabulary in *We Have Never Been Modern*, Sebald has never been modern and is therefore quintessentially both modern and postmodern.

29. I survey some of the literature on the topic of Nazism and the oceanic in *Primitive Passions* (New York: Alfred A. Knopf, 1997) in the Introduction, the end of Chapter One, and the Conclusion. Relevant theorists include Horkheimer and Adorno, Reich, Theweleit, Latour, and others including (on the oceanic) Freud, Buber, Rolland, and contemporary theories of intersubjectivity. See also Nicholas Goodrick-Clarke, *The Occult Roots of Nazism: Secret Aryan Cults and Their Influence on Nazi Ideology: The Ariosophists of Austria and Germany, 1890–1935* (New York: New York University Press, 1992).

30. Sebald's books seem to me an embodiment of Martin Buber's discovery of I and Thou, of interpenetrating subjectivities through dialogue; they seem to capture the essence behind Levinas's assertion of responsibility for the other through the other's face, even though the description of any character's features within Sebald's work always remains extremely shadowy.

31. Although the overall effect of the narratives is finally quite different (Sebald's more grounded in history and more dependent finally on material such as the accompanying photographs), the use of choral voices which, at certain ecstatic moments, sound together recalls the fiction of Virginia Woolf, especially *The Waves,* a favorite novel on which I have written several times, in *Closure in the Novel* (Princeton: Princeton University Press, 1981), and *The Visual Arts, Pictorialism, and the Novel: James, Lawrence, and Woolf* (Princeton: Princeton University Press, 1985).

32. In *Primitive Passions,* I discuss theories of intersubjectivity as a gateway to the sublime. Sebald's techniques are, I believe, pertinent. Many theorists can be cited in connection with notions of "the historical sublime": Schiller (who originated the term), Nietzsche, Hayden White, and so forth. Other philosophers who should be cited in this regard are Maurice Blanchot in *The Writing of the Disaster* and Emanuel Levinas in *Totality and Infinity.* As will become clear, the sources closest to my heart are Martin Buber, M. M. Bakhtin, and Alain Badiou. See also the introduction.

33. Checking the actual images, I see, in a Sebaldian moment, that I have conflated several photos in my mind: the young, thin Sebald leans against a tree in a photo included in the text of *The Rings of Saturn;* he wears glasses and holds a signature cigarette in the author photograph for *The Rings of Saturn;* an older, visibly thicker Sebald peers out at us without glasses in the author photo on the dust jacket of *Austerlitz.* A favorite image of my father, Salvatore De Marco Sr., shows him as a young man standing in front of a fountain, I believe in Prospect Park.

34. Scanty to date, criticism on Sebald seems destined to grow for, as a 2003 MLA session and my subsequent teaching of his books suggests, he is an author who appeals strongly to the literary imagination. The *New York Review of Books* ran a set of enthusiastic reviews that sound to varying degrees (some far too much) the theme of pessimism: Andre Aciman, *Out of Novemberland* (December 3, 1998; www.nybooks.com/articles/641); Tim Parks, "The Hunter" (June 15, 2000; www.nybooks.com/articles/67), and Gabriele Annan, "Ghost Story" (November 1, 2001; www.nybooks.com/articles/14722). J. M. Coetzee introduces a distinction I share—the difference between characters, narrative personae, and Sebald the author—in "Heir of a Dark History" (October 24, 2002; www.nybooks.com/articles/15756).

35. See introduction and chapter three.

36. I am hovering close to Bakhtin's theory of the novel as dialogic form but not citing it in the text because Sebald's novels do not use dialogic form in the conventional way, i.e., to register different levels of generational, professional, class, and other discourses within a culture. Bakhtin's writings as a whole nonetheless support the idea of connection.

Conclusion

1. Compare T. E. Hulme, "Modern Art and Its Philosophy," in *Selected Writings,* ed. Patrick McGuinness (1914; Manchester: Fyfield Books, 1998): "The fact that . . . change comes first in art, before it comes in thought, is easily understandable" because we are so "soaked in the spirit of the period we live in . . . that we can only escape from it in an unexpected way . . . a side direction like art" (95–96); compare also Herbert Marcuse in *Aesthetic Dimension: Towards a Critique of Marxist Aesthetics,* trans. Herbert Marcuse and Erica Sherover (1977; Boston: Beacon, 1978): "art is also the promise of liberation . . . wrested

from established reality . . . [but] the fulfillment of this promise is not within the domain of art" (46). I am indebted to Caleb Smith for reminding me of these references. See also the discussion of Deleuze and "any space whatever" as a zone stripped of ordinary social constraints in chapter 4 of this book.

2. See the introduction.

3. Sigmund Freud, "Thoughts for the Times on War and Death," reprinted in *On Creativity and the Unconscious: Papers on the Psychology of Art, Literature, Love, Religion*, ed. Benjamin Nelson (1915; New York: Harper, 1958), 207.

4. Qualifications of the word "hero" can be quite controversial, as evidenced by the controversy over William Langewiesche's "American Ground," *Atlantic Monthly*, July / August 2002.

5. My statement refers to the twentieth century. During the Civil War, of course, life in the United States was torn by war, especially in the South.

6. W. G. Sebald, *Austerlitz*, trans. Anthea Bell (New York: Random House, 2001), 14.

7. Susan Sontag correctly notes (*Regarding the Pain of Others* [New York: Farrar, Straus and Giroux, 2003], 30–31) that massive civilian casualties were a fact in colonial encounters but registered on the European imagination only with aerial bombardments of European civilians. In World War I, such bombardments were small and mostly abortive. Bombings during the Spanish Civil War presaged what became business as usual during World War II.

8. Published in 1922, the text has long been seen as a reaction to World War I, though the particular interpretations are my own. See *Beyond the Pleasure Principle*, trans. James Strachey (New York: Norton, 1961), 30–37.

9. Here, as at several points in this Conclusion, I need to move quickly over areas where one might linger for quite a while. *Beyond the Pleasure Principle* forms, for example, a direct antecedent of the much better known *Civilization and its Discontents*, a book written under the shadow of Nazism that revisits many ideas in the 1915 essay. See my book *Gone Primitive: Savage Intellects, Modern Lives* (Chicago: University of Chicago Press, 1990), chap. 10.

10. In this paragraph I am paraphrasing especially pages 33–35 of the Norton paperback edition, 1961.

11. Freud himself vigorously rejected a similar suggestion when it came from his correspondent, the French novelist Romain Rolland who, after writing *The Life of Ramakrishna* (1929), suggested that mystical merging (like a grain of salt "in an ocean, as it were") forms the origin of religious emotions. The opening of *Civilization and its Discontents* (1930) constitutes Freud's rebuttal. See my *Primitive Passions* (New York: Knopf, 1997), 11–12, 40–41, and *Sigmund Freud et Romain Rolland: Correspondance 1923–1936, De la sensation océanique au trouble du souvenir sur l'Acropole*, ed. Henri Vermorel and Madeleine Vermorel (Paris: Presses universitaires de France, 1993).

12. Many materials in common were anthropological. In T. S. Eliot's case, see Robert Crawford, *The Savage and the City in the Work of T. S. Eliot* (New York: Oxford, 1987) for an account of the author's anthropological interests.

13. On the first two parallels, see Paul Fussell, *The Great War and Modern Memory* (New York: Oxford University Press, 1975), 63, 239. On the turn to Eastern religions, see my *Primitive Passions*. Two of only several links between what I call wartime consciousness and an interest in Eastern thought: the spread of spiritualism around World War I and of

Theosophy, with its popularized versions of Buddhism; Romain Rolland's 1929 preface to *The Life of Ramakrishna*, in which he wrote that, in the last war "Europe [like Macbeth] had murdered sleep" and needs to "wet its lips at the artery of immortality," by which he meant mystical thinking.

14. The motif of debased sexuality will be familiar to readers of *The Wasteland* in "A Game of Chess" (with its reference to Eliot's troubled relations with his first wife), Lil and Albert, the young man carbuncular and other instances.

15. The original notes cite Jessie L. Weston's *From Ritual to Romance* as direct source for the wasteland imagery. Published as an abridged volume in 1922 that has been frequently reprinted, Sir James Frazer's *The Golden Bough* first appeared in 1890 in two volumes but was eventually expanded to multiple volumes. An indispensable additional note for Eliot: he labored long and hard on an unfinished play-poem called *Sweeney Agonistes* that reflects a preoccupation with these themes in conjunction with views of tribal ritual common in the West in which "the primitive" tends to be either overly romanticized or regarded as extremely violent.

16. Classic anthropological texts like Bronislaw Malinowski's *Argonauts of the Western Pacific* (1922) and Marcel Mauss's *The Gift: Forms and Function of Exchange in Archaic Societies* (1925) consider economic life alongside kinship and marriage systems. M. M. Bakhtin suggests that concepts circulate for a while in a culture before they receive a name. A great many concepts circulating since the war came together in 1922. See Michael North, *Reading 1922: A Return to the Scene of the Modern* (New York: Oxford, 1999).

17. Rituals can, of course, serve these purposes and others. But ritual forms only part of, rather than a constant state in, non-Western cultures, albeit an important and privileged state. See Victor W. Turner, *The Ritual Process: Structure and Anti-Structure* (Chicago: Aldine, 1969), 130–39.

18. Again, I could (and perhaps should) say more about Lawrence. An indispensable reference is *Lady Chatterley's Lover*, his most famous book, and, I suspect, the only one that casual readers today might still pick up to read—though for all the wrong reasons. It has the reputation of being a paean to sex; but war, death, and sexuality converge in the novel, with Lawrence desperately trying to substitute "life" as the final term. Clifford's paralysis serves as the sign that "ours is essentially a tragic age" when the "great words" ("honor . . . love") are dead; intellectual conversation has replaced physical intimacy as "a strange denial of the pulse of humanity"; and everybody in the novel (including Mellors and Connie) fears sex and finds it a source of trouble. Connie and Mellors's child promises a new birth, but it's still hovering as the novel ends, infinitely deferred, a re-greening of the earth that never happens in narrative time.

19. If one changed "endure" to "live," one would have a more neutral view of a continuum, as in many Buddhist traditions.

20. Dickens always knew that the transition between life and death forms the heart of narrative: witness the death scenes in *Bleak House* and the fabulous scene in *Our Mutual Friend* when Rogue Riderhood, almost drowned, becomes a focus for his community's attention. *ER* regularly suspends narratives of life and death around particular families, a factor to which I will return.

21. The now defunct show *Homicide* formed an intermediate stage, with one character, who worked in the morgue, frequently visited when she discussed autopsies that were not,

on this series, graphically shown. Television series like *Law and Order* (in its various versions) now include stops in the morgue as frequently as they include stops to court psychologists and courtrooms.

22. The quotation comes from "Thoughts for the Times on War and Death," (224). In the same text, Freud notes an element of self-congratulation in how we receive the death of others in all but a few special cases, "a vestige of hostility which can excite an unconscious death-wish" (233). His observation has attracted attention; see, for example, Cathy Caruth, *Unclaimed Experience: Trauma, Narrative and History* (Baltimore: Johns Hopkins University Press, 1996) and Samuel Weber, "Wartime," in *Violence, Identity, and Self-Determination*, ed. Hent De Vries and Samuel Weber (Stanford: Stanford University Press, 1997).

23. John Keegan, for example, gives the German military figure as over 4 million (*The Second World War* [New York: Penguin, 1989], 392); the *Encyclopedia Britannica* and *Encarta* give 3.5 million, the median figure for estimates of German military dead.

24. See www.gi.grolier.com / wwii / wwii_16.html for the complete range of estimates from reliable sources. The site also describes the difficulty of arriving at reliable figures. For the United States, many sources cite no civilian loses; others cite 6,000—a variation that can only involve different definitions. Again for the United States, some tallies do not distinguish between battle and nonbattle deaths and come in closer to 400,000 than to 300,000. See also Keegan, *Second World War*, 591, and Gerhard L. Weinberg, *A World at Arms: A Global History of World War II* (Cambridge: Cambridge University Press, 1994), 894. See also chapter 1, note 27.

25. See Raul Hilberg, *The Destruction of the European Jews* (Chicago: Quadrangle Books, 1961), 987–88.

26. The language used about the atomic bomb by Robert Oppenheimer at Los Alamos included references to passages from the Bhagavad-Gita (11:12) in which Arjuna ("the radiance of a thousand suns") and Krishna ("I am Time grown old to destroy the world") discuss creation and destruction. My colleague Srinivas Aravamudan supplied the reference, which is from a translation by J. A. B. Buitinen (Rockport, MA: Element, 1997).

27. Georges Bataille, "Concerning the Accounts Given by the Residents of Hiroshima," reprinted in Cathy Caruth, *Trauma: Explorations in Memory* (Baltimore: Johns Hopkins University Press, 1995), 221. Caruth's volume marks the first full translation of the essay into English. The delayed translation seems to me one sign of "the war complex"; so does its appearance in the context of trauma theory where it does not, strictly speaking, belong.

28. See also the introduction, note 30.

29. In *Bowling for Columbine* (2002), Michael Moore brilliantly shows how fear forms one of America's dominant emotions; National Public Radio's *Talk of the Nation* for August 11, 2003 featured an instructive conversation about the trend toward gated communities in "fortress America."

30. Mark Slouka, "A Year Later: Notes on America's Intimations of Mortality," *Harper's*, September 2002, 35–43.

31. See Robert Pogue Harrison (*The Dominion of the Dead* [Chicago: University of Chicago Press, 2003]) on burial as a fundamental human need whose denial can be expected to produce consequences.

32. I have used the term "the destructive sublime" in connection with soldiers' experi-

ence of war as described by J. Glenn Gray; it might also be linked to the "fascination" people describe in their first memories of learning about the Holocaust. The term as I am using it here is separate from these usages and closer to the multiple manifestations of the Hindu god Shiva, the destroyer, who exists in conjunction with Brahma, the creator, and Vishnu, the preserver. Bataille arrives at his point via Christian meditations on the cross and Buddhist meditations on the bone heap that transform despair into transcendent joy. He then moves through Nietzsche's sense of "the unrelieved instant."

33. Stalin once said (I paraphrase) that the death of millions is a statistic, while the death of one person can be a tragedy—showing the dictator's uncanny gaze into the heart of his century. See Christopher Hitchens, "Lightness at Midnight," *Atlantic Monthly,* September 2003; www.theatlantic.com/issues/2002/09/hitchens.htm. On families, see also the prologue and introduction.

34. The *Portraits of Grief* series in the *New York Times* often gave cameos of individuals drawn from, and therefore emphasizing, family members. Compare Marianne Hirsch on families as "structurally a last vestige of protection against war, racism, exile, and cultural displacement" and, as such, "particularly vulnerable to these violent ruptures, and so a measure of their devastation" (*Family Frames: Photography, Narrative, and Postmemory* [Cambridge: Harvard University Press, 1997], 13). In narratives about combat, the "unit" functions in much the same way as family, and so what I say here could be expanded. But "the unit" is a temporary formation, while families last a lifetime.

35. I am aware, of course, that I am describing classic views of amelioration and gradual change, which have not transformed human history. But can one say, finally, that—despite reversals and uneven developments, of which World War II would form a spectacular example—the writing of thinkers like Feuerbach, George Eliot, and Martin Buber on these topics has had no effect? To give an instance closer to our time, and perhaps clearer, the revolutionary impulses of the 1960s did not produce revolutionary and irreversible political change, but they did lead to substantial changes in race relations, in women's roles, in sexual mores, and so forth.

36. The first BBC and American news reports on the huge demonstrations in Madrid in March 2004, did not report the outpouring as antiwar, even though the demonstrators' open, white-stained palms and the slogan "No mas" certainly seemed to code that way. Within a week, the result of the 2004 Spanish election was so clearly antiwar as to compel altered readings in the media. The role of the Internet in Howard Dean's campaign was widely noted and may serve as an instance of electronic media altering social and political events.

37. Alain Badiou, *Ethics: An Essay on the Understanding of Evil,* trans. Peter Hallward (1998; London: Verso, 2001), 115.

INDEX

atomic bomb (*continued*)
  Enola Gay, 6, 101, 155n21. *See also* Hiroshima; Nagasaki; nuclear survival; Ondaatje, Michael: *The English Patient;* World War II: statistics
Auden, W. H., 17
Augstein, Rudolf, 89–90
Auschwitz, 46, 48, 49, 50, 61, 91, 92, 142, 160n55, 168n18, 169n37, 170n48, 172n60, 173n71, 183n28. *See also* Dinur, Yehiel; Holocaust
Austria, 51, 72
autobiography. *See* biography

Badiou, Alain, 74, 90, 130, 131, 144, 145, 156n32, 157n37, 176n21, 179n43, 179n47, 179nn49–50, 181n8, 189n32, 193n37. *See also* ethics of identification; Immortal, the
Bakhtin, M. M., 156n33, 189n32, 189n36
Balfour Declaration, 182n25
Ball, George, 55, 169n30
Band of Brothers, 165n23. *See also* Hanks, Tom; Spielberg, Steven
Barber, Benjamin, 161n63
Barbie, Klaus, 74, 168n18
Barker, Pat, 180n6, 184n38
Barron, James, 151n20
Bartov, Omer, 92, 177n32, 178n39
Bataille, Georges, 100, 140–41, 142, 143, 192n27, 193n32
Battle of the Bulge, 22, 41, 43
Bauman, Zygmunt, 65, 76, 153n8, 178n37, 185n46, 188n27
Baumeister, Roy, 173n1
BBC, 28, 90, 162n67, 167n5, 193n36. *See also* television
Beauvoir, Simone de, 156n33
Becker, Elizabeth, 167n5
Becker, Kurt, 169n40
Ben Gurion, David, 59, 61, 69, 170nn45–46, 173n69
Benjamin, Walter, 18, 153n8, 162n70
Berenbaum, Michael, 173n71
Berger, Joseph, 175n15
Bergmann, Martin S., 175n13
Berlin. *See* Germany
Bernard-Donais, Michael, 175n11
Bernstein, Barton, 155n19

Bershtel, Sara, 176n26
Bhabha, Homi, 157n38
Bin Laden, Osama, 69. *See also* al-Qaeda
biography, 53, 55; autobiography/memoir, 19, 56, 61, 91, 111, 113, 152n23, 169n27, 170n46, 170n48 (*see also* Eichmann, Adolf: memoirs of); biographical approaches, 125, 188n22
Bird, Kai, 154n19, 155n22, 181nn16–18
Birn, Ruth Bettina, 88, 177n33
Black Hawk Down, 165n20
Blanchot, Maurice, 14, 160n56, 189n32
Blitz. *See* Great Britain: Blitz; World War II: incendiary bombing
Boer War, 184n41
bombings. *See* atomic bomb; civilian; death: en masse; Germany, Nazi: casualties of; Germany, Nazi: Dresden bombing; Great Britain: and the Blitz; Hiroshima; Japan: casualties; Japan: Tokyo; World War II: incendiary bombing
Borges, Jorge Luis, 119
Bormann, Martin, 49, 52, 59
Bosch, Hieronymous, 29
Bosnia. *See* Yugoslavia
Boyer, Paul, 181n16
Bradley, James, 153n7
Brand, Joel, 169n40
Braun, Eva, 54–55
Brokaw, Tom, 152n4
Browne, Thomas, 119, 120
Browning, Christopher, 12, 158n44, 172n63
Bruehl-Young, Elisabeth, 158n43
Buber, Martin, 10, 48, 93, 130, 156n33, 179n43, 180n8, 188nn29–30, 189n32, 193n35. *See also* ethics of identification; oceanic
Buddhism, 191n13, 191n19
Bulgaria, 47
burial, 43, 157n39, 192n31. *See also* memorials; naming
Burma, 24, 109
Burns, E. L. M., 155n23
Bush administration, ix, xx, 36, 37, 41, 149n1, 152n22, 162nn67–69; Bush, George H. W., 182n25; Bush, George W., ix, x, xviii, 46, 22, 28, 41, 163n1

defamiliarization, xxi, 18–19, 92, 94, 107, 117, 163n75. *See also* cliché

Deleuze, Gilles, 107, 157n37, 190n1

Denmark, 47, 71, 175n17

De-Nur, Yehiel. *See* Dinur, Yehiel

derealization, 2, 4, 8–9, 11, 110, 122, 152n3, 160n54. *See also* Freud; memory; repression; secrets

Derrida, Jacques, 156n33, 160n55, 175n11, 180n8

Der Spiegel, 89

De Vries, Hent, 150n8

Dickens, Charles, 172n66, 186n6, 191n20

Didion, Joan, 151n19

Diehl, Wilhelm, 168n17

Dinur, Yehiel, 66, 90–93, 172n60, 178nn39–42, 179n46

Donitz, Karl, 48

Dossekker, Bruno Grossjean. *See* Wilkomirski, Binjamin

Dresden. *See* Germany; Germany, Nazi; World War II: incendiary bombing

Du Bois, W. E. B., 101

Durkheim, Émile, 153n8

Dyer, Geoff, 165n20

Edinin, Peter, 170n47

Egypt, 105, 109, 181n12, 184nn40–41. *See also* Suez

Eichmann, Adolf, xii, 46–59, 64, 108, 140, 160n52, 167n11, 168n22, 169n36, 169nn39–41, 170n44, 171n52, 171nn55–57, 172nn64–65, 184n39; and "banality of evil," 64, 65, 171n57 (*see also* Arendt, Hannah); Bureau IV-B-4 and, 48, 160n52; documentaries and docudramas about, 46, 63, 64, 65–66, 166n1, 167n9, 168n18, 171n53, 178n39; as family man, 49, 60, 67–68, 171n57, 172n65; Jews, attitudes toward, 47, 49, 170n44; life and career of, 46–48, 49–54, 55, 56–57, 167n12, 168nn16–17, 170n44; memoirs of, 61, 167n21, 168n22, 170nn46–47, 171n57 (see also *Life*); possible identification with, 64, 66–68, 69; as symbol of genocide, 63; trial of, 12, 15, 18, 45–46, 50, 51, 53, 59–60, 61–63, 65–67, 68–69, 116, 166n1, 168n13, 169n40, 170n42, 171n48, 170nn44–46, 171n53, 171n58, 178n39; trial transcripts, 45–46, 60, 167n7, 167n12, 170n43, 171n58, 172n60, 178n39. *See also* Hitler, Adolf; Holocaust; television

Einsatzgruppen, 11, 12, 48, 67, 87, 92, 158n47, 172n63. *See also* Germany, Nazi

Eisenhower, Dwight D. (Ike), 22, 23, 27, 150n3, 163n2

Eley, Geoff, 177n29

Eliot, George, 193n35

Eliot, T. S., xi, 136, 151n10, 190n12, 191nn14–15

Elliott, Gil, 156n30

Enemy at the Gates, 32

England. *See* Great Britain

English (language), 100, 101, 179n2, 180n2, 180n3

English Patient, The. See Minghella, Anthony; Ondaatje, Michael

Epstein, Helen, 175n13

Eskin, Blake, 175n11

ethics of identification (ethical action), 10, 66, 73, 76, 93, 105, 121, 126, 127, 129, 130, 144–45, 175n11, 179n43. *See also* Badiou, Alain; Buber, Martin; "civil courage"; Holland: story of "Dutch Jew"; Levinas, Emmanuel; Schmid, Anton

families, xiv–xv, 7, 9, 10, 98, 106, 119, 121, 123, 143–44, 156nn31–32; 181n13, 193nn33–34; and fathers, 77, 82, 86–87, 89–90, 105, 124, 186n3; and Holocaust, 75, 76, 78, 82–84, 85–86, 89–90, 93; learning about Holocaust in, 80–84; and mothers, 82, 83, 91–92; and secrets, 82, 115. *See also* apprehension; Holocaust: emotional effect of; Holocaust: representations in fiction; novels: Holocaust; war complex

family man, 50, 67–68, 69, 105

Fanon, Franz, 156n33

Faulkner, William, 128, 155n26

Fawlty Towers, 90

fear. *See* apprehension

Felman, Shoshana, 14, 159n48, 159n50, 160n56, 178n39

Feuerbach, Ludwig, 193n35

fiction. *See* narrative; novels

middle distance, xv, 82, 90, 151n13, 157n37, 158n41, 188n21
military-industrial complex, 16
military-industrial-media complex, 16
Milosevic, Slobodan, 46. *See also* Yugoslavia
Minghella, Anthony, 100, 101, 181nn14–15, 183nn29–30. *See also* Ondaatje, Michael, *The English Patient*
Mintz, Alan, 12, 76, 153n4
Mitchell, Greg, 153nn23–24
Mitchum, Robert, 29
modernity, xi, 8, 90, 93, 126, 133, 136–39; post-eighteenth-century (post-Enlightenment), 126, 187n19, 188n29
Mommsen, Hans, 89
Moore, Michael, 192n29
morality. *See* ethics of identification; Holocaust: moral responsibility for
Morrison, Toni, 182n21
Mosley, Oswald, 108, 184n38
Movietonews. *See* Fox *Movietonews*
Moyers, Bill, 16
Müller, Heinrich, 49, 58
Munich. *See* Germany; Germany, Nazi: Munich agreement
Muslim. *See* Islam
Musmanno, Michael, 52, 169n23
mutual deterrance. *See* nuclear survival
myths. *See* narratives

Nabokov, Vladimir, 186n6
Nagasaki, 5, 6, 15, 97, 99, 101, 104, 105, 110–13, 142, 183n26, 183n28. *See also* atomic bomb; Hiroshima; Japan: casualties
naming, 34, 37, 43. *See also* memorials
Napoleon, 31, 119, 187n19
narrative, xiii, xiv, 2, 9, 12, 19, 38, 91, 96, 110, 111, 130, 133, 136–37, 143; *The Aeneid*, xiv, 131; Holocaust, 76–77, 83, 88, 90, 91–93 (*see also* novels: Holocaust); *The Iliad,* xiv, 30, 31; Narratology, 97 (*see also* novels: theory of); *The Odyssey,* xiv, 34; theory of, 96, 110, 180n7, 186n3, 186n6, 188n22, 189n36; war, xiv, 30, 31, 95–96, 97–98. *See also* Ishiguro, Kasuo; Ondaatje, Michael; novels; Sebald, W. G.

narrators. *See* Ishiguro, Kasuo; narrative: narratology; novel: theory of; Sebald, W. G.
Nasser, Gamal Abdel, 109
nations, 8–9, 10, 35, 66, 93, 131, 141, 151n11, 152n22, 157n38, 187n12; nationalism, 131, 183n31. *See also* citizens; statelessness; transnationals
National Socialism. *See* Germany, Nazi
Nato, 46
Nazi. *See* Germany, Nazi
NBC, 46
Negri, Antonio, 162n68
Neufeld, Michael J., 173n71
NewsHour with Jim Lehrer, 28. *See also* PBS
New York, xv–xx, 79, 85, 151n14, 151n19, 155n24, 159n47
New York Daily News, 27
New Yorker, 16, 100
New York Times, 23, 27, 41, 59, 149n1, 149nn3–5, 151n6, 151n20, 162n69, 163n4, 166n25, 169n41, 193n34
Nietzsche, 193n32
9/11, ix, x, xi–xix, xx–xxi, 2, 17, 19, 27, 43, 68, 103–4, 109, 134, 139, 142–45, 150n4, 150nn5–7, 151nn19–21, 152n22, 157n38, 161n63, 173n67, 182n25, 184n41; media and, ix, xiv, xv, xvi, xvii, xix, 151n13, 151n21, 152n22, 162nn67–68, 182n25; photographs of, xvii, 27. *See also* Bush administration; New York; war complex
1960s, 193n35
Nixon, Rob, 181n9
Norden, Eric, 169n25
North, Michael, 191n16
novels, 19, 95, 97, 98, 110, 111, 113, 117–18, 120, 121, 124, 125, 129, 131, 133, 137, 138, 143, 144, 180n1, 180nn2–3, 180n6, 180n7, 184n36, 189n36; Holocaust, 91, 95, 143; theory of, 110, 117, 118, 131, 133. *See also* Ishiguro, Kasuo; Ondaatje, Michael; Sebald; W. G.
Novick, Peter, 11, 12, 62, 75, 81, 130, 153n4, 157n40, 171n50, 174nn5–6, 176n23
nuclear survival, 7, 154n12, 155n23. *See also* atomic bomb
Nuremberg (city), 48, 84–85
Nuremberg laws. *See* Germany, Nazi: law under

Rummel, R. J., 8, 156n30
Rumsfeld, Donald, 162n68
Russia. *See* Soviet Union
Russian (language), 180n2
Rwanda, 8, 17, 142
Ryan, Cornelius, 40

Sagan, Scott D., 154n12
Said, Edward, 156n33
Salisbury, Harrison, 71
SARS, 139
Sartre, Jean-Paul, 156n33, 157n37
Sassen, Wilhelm, 131
Saturday Review, 101
Saving Private Ryan. See Spielberg, Steven
Schell, Jonathan, 7, 155nn23−24
Schiffren, Andre, 161n63
Schindler's List. See Spielberg, Steven
Schmid, Anton, 66−67, 144, 159n47,
    172n61
Schoenfeld, Gabriel, 154n15
Scholem, Gersholm, 48, 158n43
Schwartz, Benjamin, 154n9, 166n33
Scott, Janny, 151n12
Scott, Ridley, 165n20
Scott, Walter, 96
Sebald, W. G. (Max), xii, 5, 84−85, 97, 105,
    107, 113, 115−22, 123−27, 128−31, 144,
    151n15, 154n14, 176n21, 185nn1−4, 186−
    87nn6−14, 187nn19, 188nn21−23, 188−
    89nn30−34, 189n36; "Air War and Lit-
    erature" (in *A Natural History of De-
    struction*), 116−17, 124, 185nn1−2,
    186n3; *Austerlitz*, 117, 121−24, 126−28,
    129, 187nn17−20, 189n33, 190n6; pho-
    tography, and, 117−18, 129, 131, 151n15;
    The Emigrants, 117, 118−19, 121, 126−
    27, 186nn8−9; *The Rings of Saturn*,
    117, 119−21, 125, 130, 186n4, 187nn10−
    13, 188n22, 189n33
Second Front, 24
secrets, 5, 53, 27, 87, 115, 117, 124; family,
    82, 115; and the Holocaust, 74, 76, 78,
    80−82, 83, 115, 117, 124
Segev, Tom, 69, 166n1, 170nn41−42,
    173n69, 178nn39
Selden, Mark, 155n23
September 11, 2001. *See* 9/11
Serageldin, Samia, 184n41

Sereny, Gitta, 54−56, 169n24, 169nn26−
    28, 169nn30−33, 169nn37−38
sexuality, 135, 136−38, 183n30, 190n14,
    190n18. *See also* pornography
Shandley, Robert R., 177nn29−30,
    177nn34−35
Shklovsky, Victor, 18, 163n75, 179n1
Shoah. *See* Holocaust
Shoah (film). *See* Lanzmann, Claude
Sikh. *See* India
Situationists, 163n71
Sivan, Eyal, 46, 66, 167n9, 171n56
Sixty Minutes, 46, 47. *See also* CBS
Slater, Lauren, 151n14
slave labor, 55, 56
Slouka, Mark, 141−42, 192n30
Smith, Caleb, 186n7, 190n1
Smith, Craig S., 167n5
Smithsonian Institution, 6, 101. *See also*
    Enola Gay; Hiroshima
social class, 51, 53, 55, 77, 176n20, 186n3
social science, 73, 79, 176n20. *See also* sta-
    tistics
Socrates, xxi
Somalia, x, 165n20
Somme, 41
Sontag, Susan, 26−27, 161n59, 176n23,
    190n7
Soviet Union (former), 56, 87, 88, 109,
    155n20, 186n2; Stalingrad, 25, 71. *See
    also* World War II: Soviet role in
Spain, 145, 173n67, 193n36
Spandau prison, 56
Spanish Civil War, 180n2, 190n7
spectacle, 138−39. *See also* sublime: the de-
    structive sublime
Speer, Albert, 52, 53−56, 57, 58, 65,
    169nn24−28, 169nn30−34, 169nn37−
    38
Speer, Margret, 169n26
Spiegelman, Art, 77−78, 82, 83, 158n42
Spielberg, Steven, 25, 26, 29, 30, 159n50,
    164n14; *Saving Private Ryan*, 25−26,
    28, 29−35, 36, 42, 165n21, 166n32;
    Schindler's List, 158n41, 174n6
Sreberny, Annabelle, 152n22
Sri Lanka, 113
Stalin, Josef, 193n33
Stalingrad. *See* Soviet Union

stateless people, 8. *See also* nations; refugees

statistics, 39–41, 43, 73, 115, 126, 139–40, 142, 143, 154n8, 164n13, 170n44, 173n1, 185n2, 192nn23–24, 193n33; and Rummel, R. J., 8, 156n30. *See also* civilians; D-Day; Germany, Nazi: casualties; Japan: casualties; World War II: statistics

Steichen, Edward, 156n31

Stein, Harry, 168n17

Stendhal (Henri Beyle), 31, 151n15, 186n6

stereotypes, 28, 73, 80, 87

Stimsson, Henry L., 181n18

St. Louis (ship), 79, 80, 81–82

stories. *See* narrative

Streicher, Julius, 48

Styron, William, 143

sublime, 129, 189n32, 192n32; the destructive sublime, 30, 115. *See also* oceanic

Sudan, 8, 142

Suez, xii, 109, 110, 184nn40–41

Suleiman, Susan Rubin, 175n13

Taipei Rebellion, xi, 119–20. *See also* civilians; China

Taliban. *See* Afghanistan

Tamil, 113

Taylor, Frederick, 5, 154n15, 156n27, 186n2

Taylor, Telford, 170n45

technology, 55, 113, 131, 133, 151n11, 157n39

television, xiv, xv, xix, xx, 15, 16, 18, 27–28, 98, 138–39, 151n15, 161n63, 161n65, 165n23, 172n67, 181n10, 191nn20–21; and Eichmann, 45, 46, 63, 168n17, 171n53, 172n60; history of, 15–18; 9/11, and, xvi, xvii, 151n21. *See also* ABC; al-Jazeera; BBC; CBS; CNN; Fox; HBO; *Holocaust* (NBC, 1978); NBC; PBS

Theresienstadt (Terezin). *See* Holocaust; Sebald, W. G.: *Austerlitz*

Theweleit, Klaus, 181n8, 182n20, 188n29

Third Reich. *See* Germany, Nazi

Thirty Years' War, xi

Tolstoy, Leo, 31

Torgovnick, Marianna, 150n9, 181n8, 184n38, 189nn31–32, 190n9, 190n11, 190n13

totalitarianism, 8, 93

transnationals, 16, 157n38, 161n63, 163n72

trauma, xvii–xviii, 13, 77, 93, 107, 125, 151n14, 159n48, 159n51; definitions of, 13, 77, 160n52; related terms (amnesia, paralysis, repression), 77, 110–11, 115, 151n14; shock as distinct from, xv–xvi, 151n14; trauma-like, 13–14, 77; trauma theory, 12, 77, 159n48

Treat, John Whittier, 155n23

Trilling, Lionel, 152n23

Truman, Harry, 6, 101

Tuchman, Barbara, 109

Turner, J. M. William, 31

Turner, Victor, 191n17

Uganda, 13

Ullrich, Volker, 88, 177n30, 177n35

United Nations, 59, 167n6, 170n42

United States, x, 15, 19, 22, 79, 87, 105, 109, 139, 149n2, 157n38, 164n8, 173n68, 187n15, 192n24; African Americans, 32, 33, 35, 100; casualties in World War II, 28, 29, 39–41, 139–40; Congress, xx; D-Day, participation in, 21, 23, 24, 26, 40–41; Holocaust memory and, 11–12, 153n4, 157n40, 158n42, 159n50; and invasion of Iraq, 27–28, 37, 149n1, 150nn5–6, 151n20; and invasion of Japan, 6, 101; Japanese Americans, internment of, 4, 78, 154n10; and 9/11, ix, x, xx, 17–18, 149n1, 150nn5–7; parochial historical knowledge in, 103–4; reactions to Hiroshima, and, 100–101; and war crimes trials, 2, 6, 48, 55–56, 69, 153n4, 167n6, 168n14; war memory in, x, xi–xiii, 2–3, 4 5, 6–7, 8, 9, 11–12, 14–15, 23–24, 25, 35–37, 39–40, 41–43, 78, 80, 95–96, 100–101, 142, 143 (*see also* memory: collective memory; memory: cultural memory). *See also* Bush administration; D-Day; Iraq; 9/11; Vietnam; World War II: European theatre; World War II: Pacific theatre

University of East Anglia, 130

Uris, Leon, 71

USA Today, 16

U.S. News and World Report, 101

Vanity Fair, 16

Van Natta, Don, Jr., 150n7, 182n23

V-E Day. *See* Ondaatje, Michael: *The English Patient;* World War II: novels about; World War II: Pacific theatre

Vico, Giambattista, 157n39

Vietnam, x, 30, 32, 33, 35, 36, 37, 55, 150n6, 164n18, 165n20, 165n23, 180n3; Vietnam Memorial, Washington, D.C., 165n20. *See also* films; television; post–Vietnam war films

Visser 't Hooft, W. A., 169n32

V-J Day. *See* Ondaatje, Michael: *The English Patient;* World War II: novels about; World War II: Pacific theatre

Volkmer, Ingrid, 152n22

Vonnegut, Kurt, 5, 95, 154n13

voyeurism, 115, 139

Wald, Priscilla, 152n1, 175n16

Wallace, Mike, 172n60

Wallace, Randall, 32; *We Were Soldiers,* 32–34, 164n18, 165n20

Waltz, Kenneth N., 154n12

Wannsee, 52, 63, 171n53. *See also* Eichmann, Adolf

war complex, xi–xii, 7–11, 43, 68, 142, 143–44, 156n32. *See also* apprehension; death: en masse; families; Hiroshima: apprehension and

war crimes, 2, 6, 46, 48–49, 50, 51, 59, 62, 65, 66, 69, 74, 155n20. *See also* International Court; International Military Tribunal; United States: and war crimes trials

war on terrorism, ix, 38. *See also* Bush administration

Warsaw. *See* Poland

warspace, 106–7, 183n32

wartime consciousness, xi–xii, 1–2, 3–4, 119, 137, 150n2, 156n36. *See also* war complex

Weber, Samuel, 150n8

Weinberg, Gerhard L., 3, 41, 154n9, 154n11, 154n17, 164nn6–7, 192n24

Wellstore, Paul, 161n63

Wesley, Frank, 177n29

Weston, Jessie, 190n14

We Were Soldiers. See Wallace, Randall

White, E. B., 151n17

White, Hayden, 189n32

Widmer, Ted, 166n34

Wiesel, Elie, 14, 76, 143

Wilkins, Roy, 101

Wilkomirski, Binjamin, 76, 83, 90, 130, 175n11, 179n48

Williams, Raymond, 152n23

Wipperman, Wolfgang, 177n29

Wirth-Nesher, Hana, 176n25

Wisliceny, Dieter, 52, 53, 168n18, 170n44

Wong, Cynthia, 185n47

Woolf, Virginia, 14, 42, 161n58, 179n2, 189n31

World Court. *See* International Court

World Trade Center. *See* 9/11

world war, theory of, 10, 133, 180n8

World War I, xi–xii, 1–2, 22, 41, 102, 109, 118, 133, 134, 136–37, 151n10, 152n1, 166n30, 180n5, 184n38, 190nn7–9, 190n13

World War II, ix, x, xi–xiii, xv, xx, xxi, 2, 10, 14, 15, 72, 73, 95–98, 99, 102–3, 105, 106, 107–8, 109–10, 111–13, 115, 121, 124, 143, 180nn3–6, 181n8; European theatre, emphasized, 25, 36, 105, 111, 113; incendiary bombing, 4–5, 18, 40, 84–85, 95, 101, 115–17, 154n11, 154n16, 154n18, 185n2, 190n7 (*see also* Great Britain: Blitz; Germany, Nazi: casualties; Japan: Tokyo); and invasion of Iraq, x, 36–37, 42, 150nn4–5 (*see also* Bush administration); missing history of, xii–xiii, 4–11, 14, 26, 41, 43, 86, 100–101, 139–40 (*see also* memory: collective memory; memory: cultural memory; United States: war memory in); novels about, 95–98, 99–100, 102–3, 104–6, 107–8, 110–12, 113, 124–26, 127–30, 131, 133, 143, 179n2, 180n3, 180nn6–7, 184n36 (*see also* Holocaust: representations in fiction; narrative: Holocaust; novels: Holocaust); Pacific theatre, relative neglect of, xii, 4–7, 15, 25, 36, 40, 105–7, 112, 113, 155n22–25; Soviet role in, 4, 24, 25, 32, 41, 48, 71, 88, 121, 139, 155n20, 164n8, 186n2; statistics, 39–43, 115, 126, 139–40, 143, 155n20, 163n3, 166nn27–30, 166n36, 170n44, 185n2, 192nn23–25; vs. Vietnam, 35–37; and World War I, xi–xii,

134. *See also* atomic bomb; Battle of the Bulge; civilians; D-Day; Germany, Nazi; Great Britain; Hiroshima; Holocaust; Iwo Jima; Japan; kamikaze; Nagasaki; Okinawa; Pearl Harbor; United States; United States: war memory in

Wyschogrod, Edith, 151n11, 157n39, 185n46, 185n49

Yad Vashem. *See* Israel

Yavenditti, Michael J., 181n17

Yiddish, 63

Young, James, 157n39, 175n13

Yugoslavia (former), 8; Bosnia, 46, 142; Croatia, 17; Kosovo, 17

Zanuck, Darryl F., 28; *The Longest Day*, 25, 29, 36, 40, 42, 163n1, 164n11, 164n14, 166n32

Zelizer, Barbie, xvii, 151n18, 185n50

Zeller, Tom, 149n1

Zionism, 47